# SOCKS

## Imaginative Mending

**Celia Pym**

Photographs by Michele Panzeri

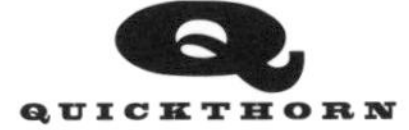

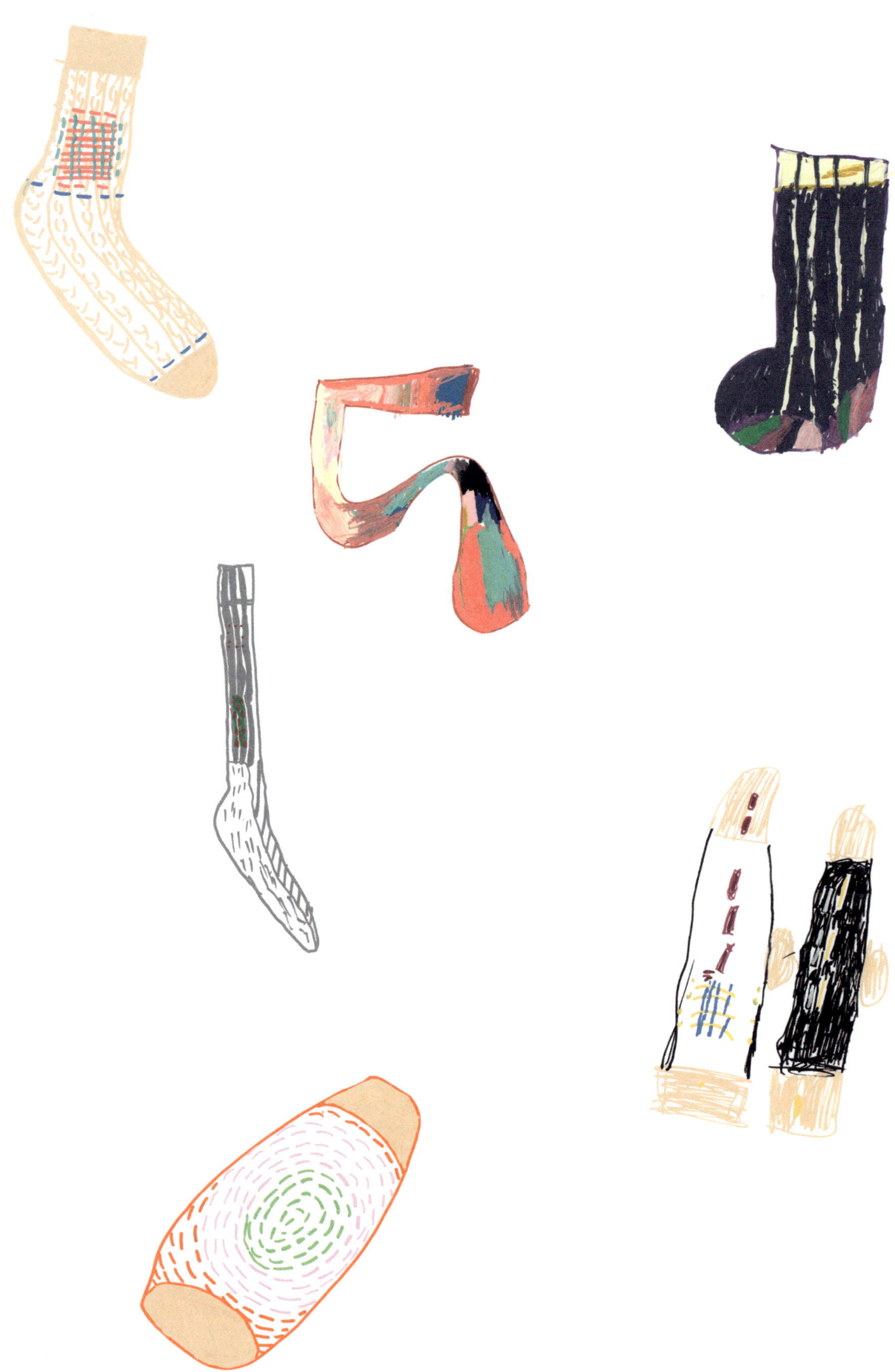

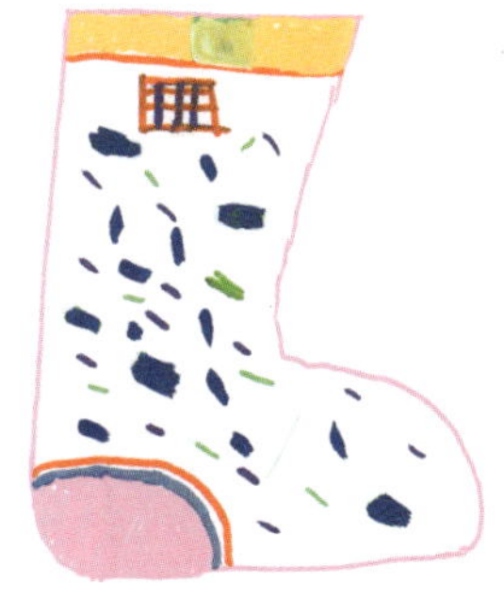

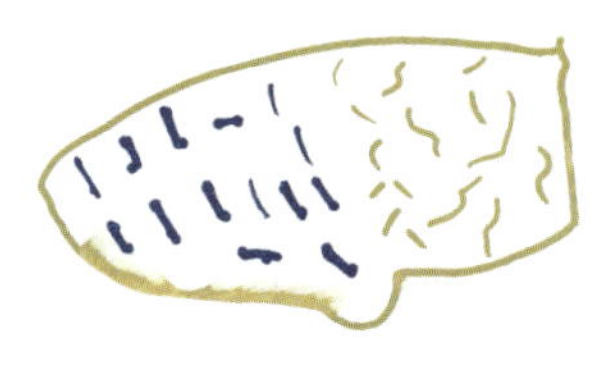

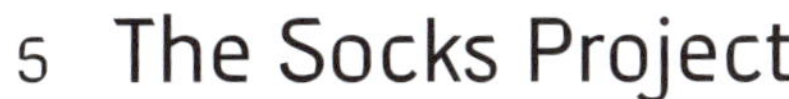



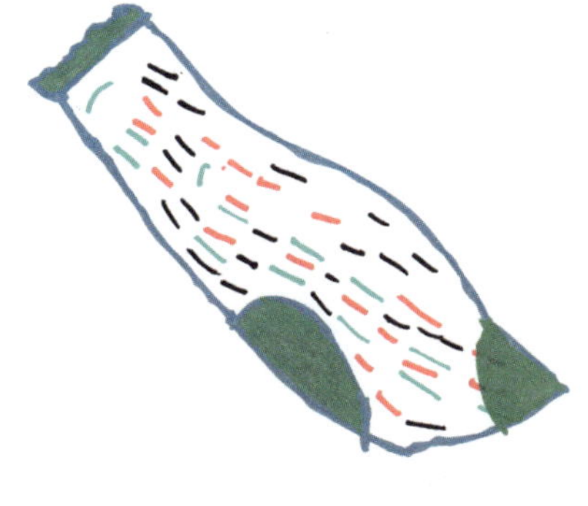

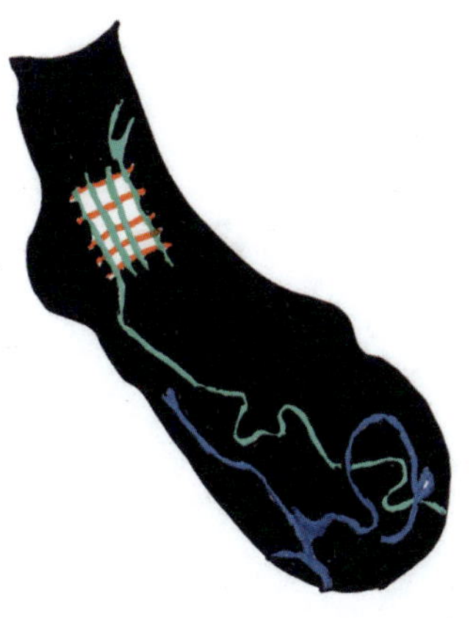

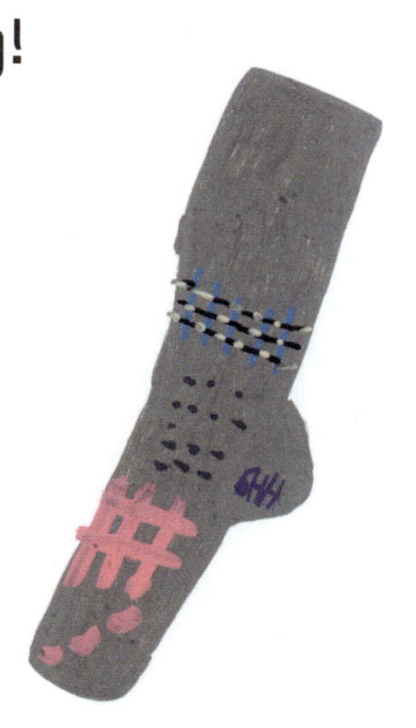

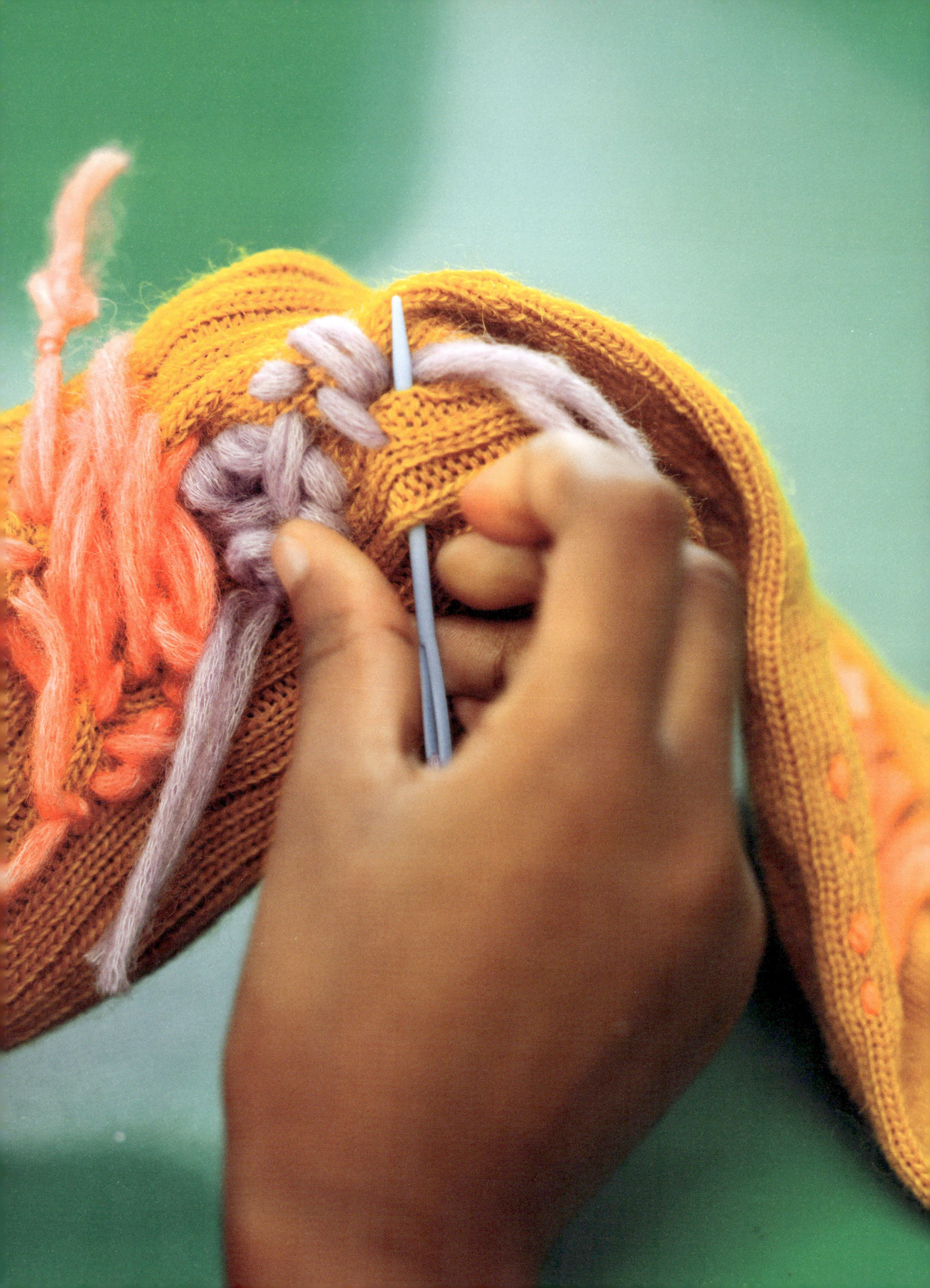

# The Socks Project

In the Summer Term 2024, Hannah Coulson and I delivered twenty-six 'sock mending' workshops at Surrey Square Primary School in Southwark, Central London. We worked with all the children from Nursery Class (the four-year-olds) to Year 6 (the 11-year-olds), as well as their teachers, staff and family members. Together we looked at images of damaged and mended clothes, talked about repair and then practised woven darning and running stitches on 'warehouse waste' socks.

Questioned after the workshops, one child said, 'This is my best day ever. I love sewing.' Another, 'Grandma sews too. I like to do what Grandma does.' And one more, 'It was quite hard and quite easy. The first try I didn't know how to do it that much, but the second and third tries I knew how to do it.'

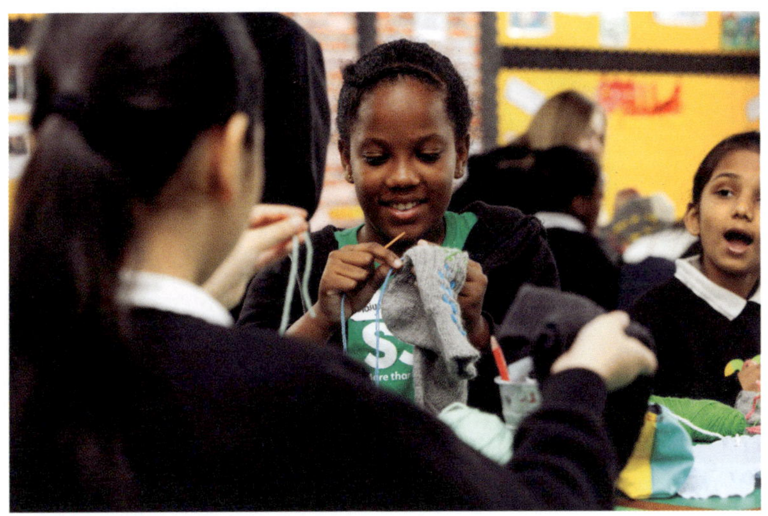

Year 5 practise darning, Surrey Square Primary School

Encounters with craft and 'making' give children a key to opening their creative imagination. It teaches them how to solve problems with their hands. It allows them to experience the joy of exploration through texture, colour and materials. It can connect them to their heritage, and it allows them to see and touch their work in three-dimensions. Craft learning should be embedded into our school curriculums for these practical reasons – but also, *for the sheer joy of it.*

This book describes the Socks Project, why it happened, how it was planned and the impact it had. Perhaps most importantly it celebrates the socks and stitches themselves. This book is for anyone curious about what occurs when you teach a whole community the same thing – and how varied the outcomes can be. It's also, I hope, a reflection of the fun we had.

## 'It was easy because it was fun'

A good place to begin is with Shadave. Here she is with her mended sock. She's in Year 2 and seven years old. Her class was asked to look at a pile of orange, yellow and brown socks and then pick one they liked. Shadave went for orange and chose green and pink yarns for her darning colours. She worked on her stitches for an hour. Darning was not entirely new to her. She'd already done some sewing at home with her Grandma.

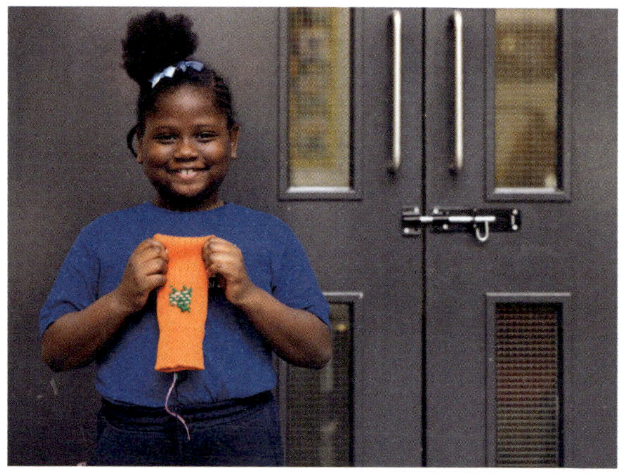

Shadave, Year 2

Shadave began our workshop full of enthusiasm but then in the middle of the session her threads tangled, and the weaving doubled up. She became a little discouraged. It wasn't working out the way she'd hoped. She spoke to Hannah who was teaching with me and together they decided to undo a couple of the threads and rework them. Shadave was patient with herself. She persevered. The knots were challenging. But she figured out how she could make the darn work in the way she wanted. And at the end of the session – as you can see – she was proud of her work.

Earlier I'd glanced across the workshop and noticed Shadave. She was focused on her sewing. Her concentration seemed to have carved out a space around her. It was just her and her work in the corner of our room. Nothing – nothing at all – was distracting her.

## The Project

*Darning is a stitching technique that can be used to mend and repair textiles. A darn is a new woven patch over and across a hole. A darn stops the hole from growing bigger and fills it in – for example, on a sock, to stop your toes poking through.*

The NOW Gallery in Greenwich, South-East London, makes an annual award 'highlighting contemporary stories in fashion' and in 2024 that award went to the 'Socks Project'. This project, which was to conclude with an exhibition at NOW Gallery, was to focus on the idea of sustainability in fashion and our lives more broadly through a celebration of the everyday act of mending through darning.

The aim of the Socks Project was threefold: to teach a whole school community how to make a *woven darn* – a practical skill for mending socks; *to see what different stitches and marks looked like* when produced by children and grown-ups who'd all been given the same task regardless of ability; and *to represent the community* in the collection of socks they stitched and on which they'd practised their darns.

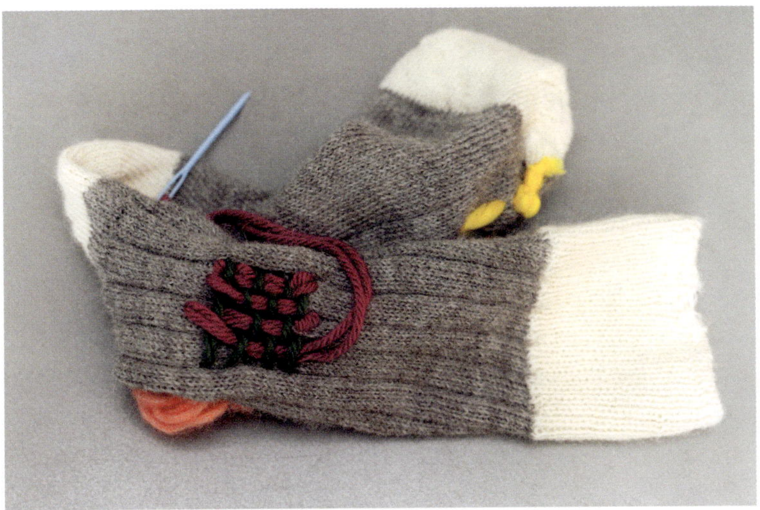

Mended sock, end of workshop, Year 5

I needed a partner for the project, my friend Hannah Coulson, an educator specialising in art and design, was the right person and a natural fit. We discussed how we could work with a whole school – children, teachers, staff, families. Crucially everyone would take part in the same workshop. A sock-mending workshop. We thought a primary school would be good. To show the development of the children's dexterity and imaginative responses. There would be no exceptions, everyone from nursery students to the head teacher would make woven darns and stitches.

The NOW Gallery has a six-metre-high ceiling, with wrap around glass windows and one low curved wall. Thinking large scale about how to create the installation and exhibition was a challenge. The customary scale I'm used to relates to my own body. Clothing scale. What fits in my arms. What I can wear. For this commission I imagined from the start building something large from many small parts.

Individual stitched socks adding to a collective whole. Repetition of a single object, a sock, for instance – each one similar but different – could I thought be visually pleasing. Repetition creates rhythms and patterns. So, with this plan in mind, we were ready for the workshops.

## Imaginative Mending

I've taught art for more than twenty years, working with adults and children in formal settings – schools, universities, art colleges – as well as in less formal spaces such as parks, shops and libraries. But whatever the setting I've observed many times that when individuals 'make and create' together this almost invariably develops into a social activity.

Working with your hands concentrates the mind and creates a space where people can sit sewing together in comfortable silence while engaged in purposeful work. I've also seen the opposite. Working and sitting together, friends or 'stitching strangers' often start to chat, and then – with eyes and fingers on the work – conversation drifts into unexpected places. Permission is granted, unannounced, for serious personal conversation as well as for laughter, jokes and general light-heartedness.

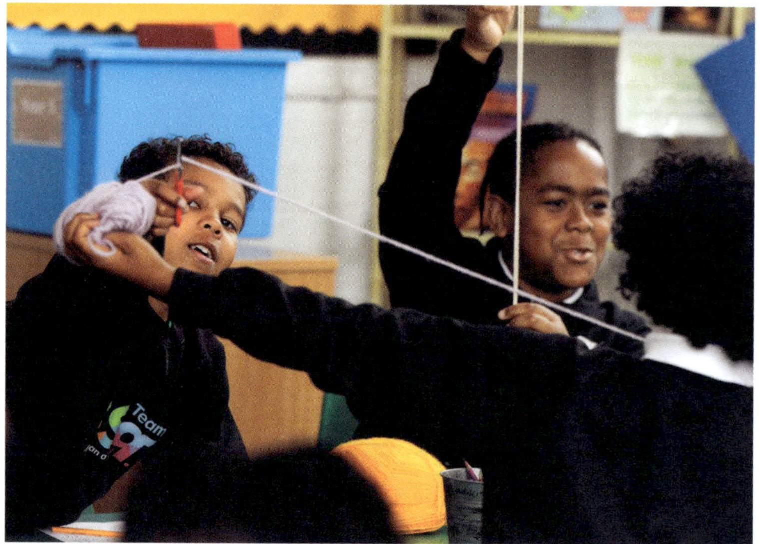

Year 5 measure and cut their yarn

Another side to making in groups or in a classroom is that it lets you see what's going through someone else's mind as reflected in what they're making. In our sock darning sessions everyone was working with the same tools, materials and instructions, yet the outcomes were colourfully and astonishingly different.

# Why Socks?

The choice of 'socks' to learn darning on was not completely random. I love socks. I love their everyday familiarity. You put them on and pull them off morning and evening – and often in between. Your feet experience a sense of relief when released from shoes and socks. Sock elastic sometimes leaves a mark round your ankle, a reminder that you've been busy on your feet all day. It seemed that something practical and familiar – a simple hole in a sock – would be ideal for this project. In addition, mending a sock hole can be achieved in an hour. And an hour is long enough for a child to mend a sock.

My interest in mending and repair began from observing our relationship with our clothes. How clothes carry a trace of our bodies. They remind us of our physical selves. They stretch and wear down to reflect our shape and how we move. Clothing is a second skin, which is why a garment belonging to someone we love can be an emotionally affecting object. Socks have a familiarity that makes them easy to ignore. Who really worries about a lost sock? It will probably turn up. Yet an old worn sock has much to say about its owner.

I've mended many of my own socks and some belonging to others. Unlike sweaters, gloves or jeans which can have more complicated damage, I enjoy the simple practicality of a sock mend. A straightforward repair to the toe or heel. But very often the task doesn't end there. Fresh holes appear unbidden. I mend my socks, they develop new holes, I mend them again. The layering of marks thickens. I can feel them on the soles of my feet.

The V&A Museum in London has a pair of Coptic socks dating from the 4th century CE – they're bright red and were made using a single needle, a technique known as 'naalbinding'. They're toe socks shaped for a sandal. Looking at them, I'm struck by how time collapses. Here is evidence that people 1,700 years ago had the same needs as we do. They wished to keep their feet warm and clean – and to look stylish. The red is a strong bright colour. A contrast to imagining the past in black and white. What would these socks have looked like inside their owner's sandals – what clothes would that person have paired them with?

Another example of historic socks I admire are children's 'sock samplers' from the Netherlands from a hundred years ago. Dutch children practised their darning stitches in red on a white sock which, it seems, they'd sometimes knitted themselves. The sock samplers are beautiful objects, not discardable experiments. I'm moved by imagining children learning and practising their skills. Thinking-through their making. The children who made these socks perhaps held them up with pride – like Shadave, from our project, would hold up her sock in 2024.

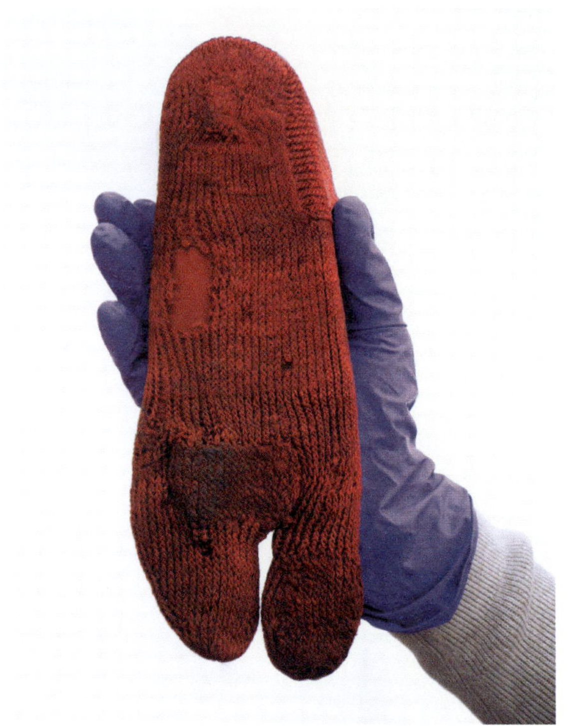
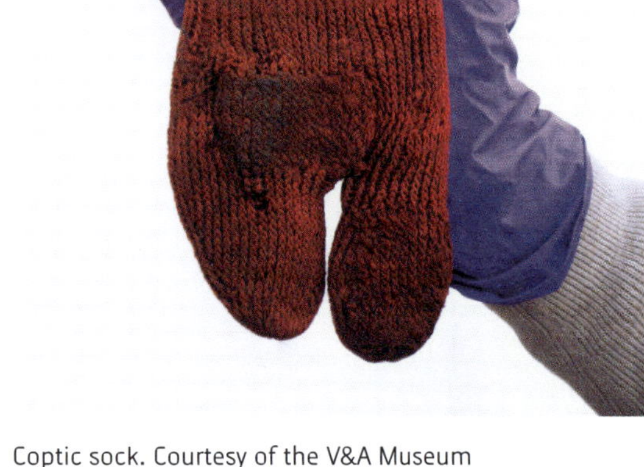

Coptic sock. Courtesy of the V&A Museum

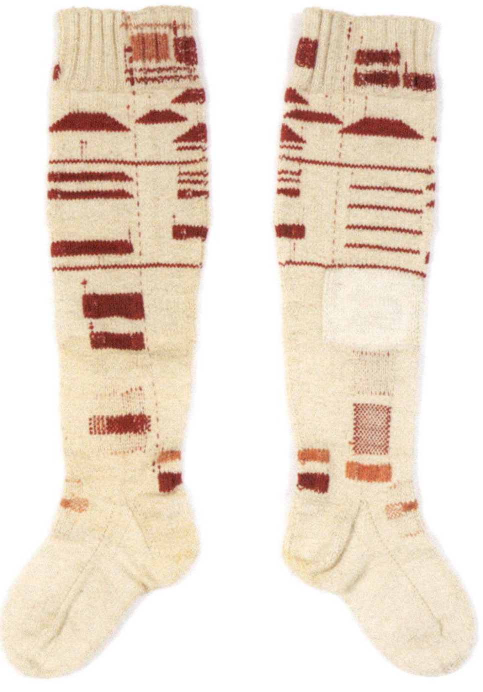

Children's sock samplers. Courtesy of Evelien Verkerk

## Where Our Socks Came From

The initial plan was to ask the children at Surrey Square school to bring any of their own socks which might have holes. To emphasise the usefulness of mending by keeping your own clothes going. But what about the practicalities? There was a chance that not every child would bring in a sock. Or they might not want to practise on their own socks. Most would be small socks, for small feet, which are hard for beginners to work with. My experience of school socks is that they're often finely knit from synthetic and elastic fibres. You'd need a delicate thread and small needle to pull through tight stretchy knitting. Thick thread and large needles were required for this project.

We needed a different supply of socks for the project. I investigated where to find socks in bulk, thinking there might be deadstock or waste from sock factories. Emma Mathews, a friend who runs a company called 'Socko', put me in touch with J. Alex Swift, a family business based in Loughborough in Leicestershire that had been making socks for four generations. The company had two grades of 'warehouse waste', socks that could not be sold because of faults. One grade consisted of socks that looked like long tubes or where the toe of one sock was knitted to another. These were available free. The other grade was of socks with minor flaws. These were sold by weight.

J. Alex Swift factory floor

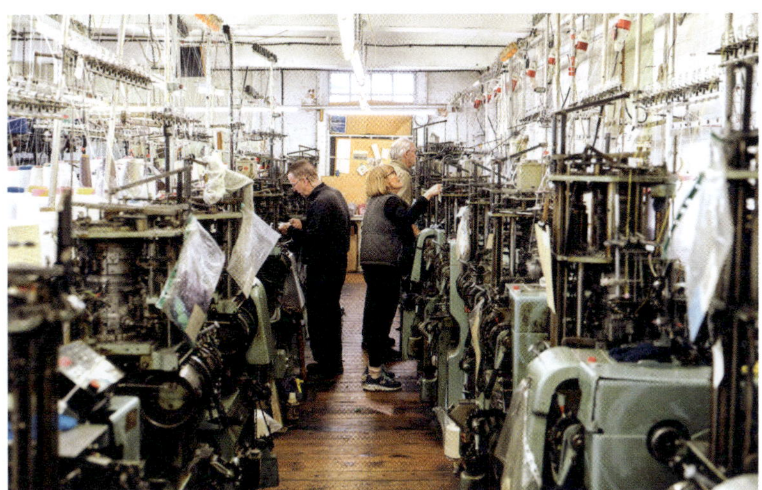

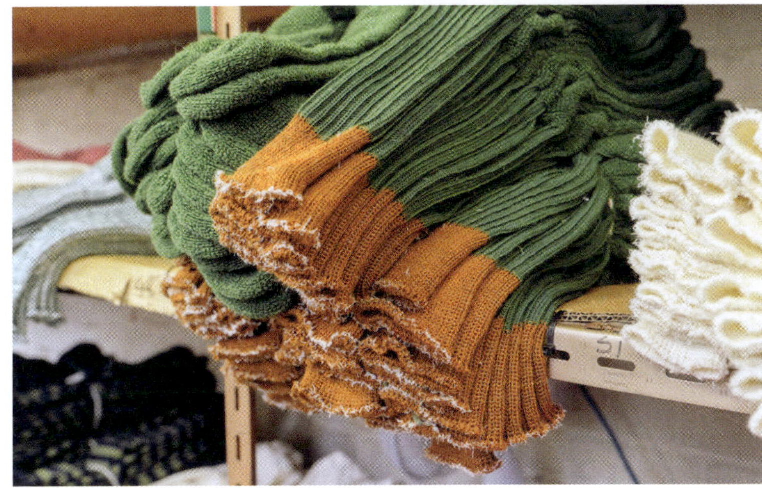

J. Alex Swift socks

The second grade – 'warehouse waste' socks, with minor flaws – was most appealing. Wools and cashmere, ankle socks and over-the-knee kilt socks, all in the most beautiful colours, pinks and yellows, purples and greens. And there were so many of them. I could get thousands of single socks with perhaps a dropped stitch at the cuff, or others that were too tightly knit, or had a twisted thread at the heel that made the foot slightly diagonal. Some had an excessively long foot and a short ankle. They were better than perfect for our project.

These warehouse waste socks would be beautiful and enticing objects to give to the children. One of the surprises in this project has been the feedback from people who can't believe these socks are all *waste*. There's a perception that waste is dirty or simply a by-product of making something. The manufacture of socks, I learned, generates a huge amount of 'waste', even at a factory with small production lines. The waste looks fine but is just slightly imperfect and so must be rejected. The market desires things that are precisely the same. No imperfection allowed.

Avery

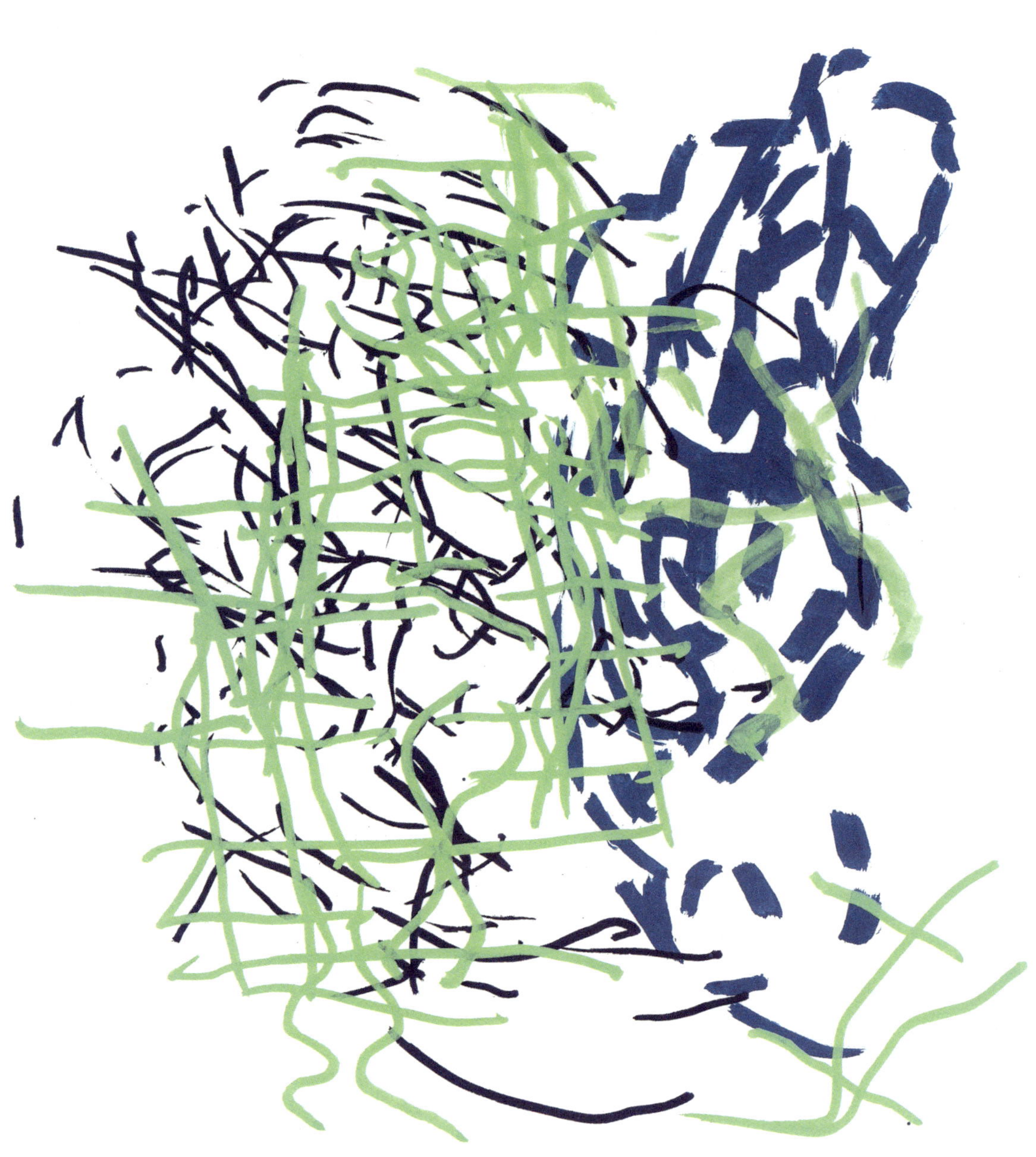

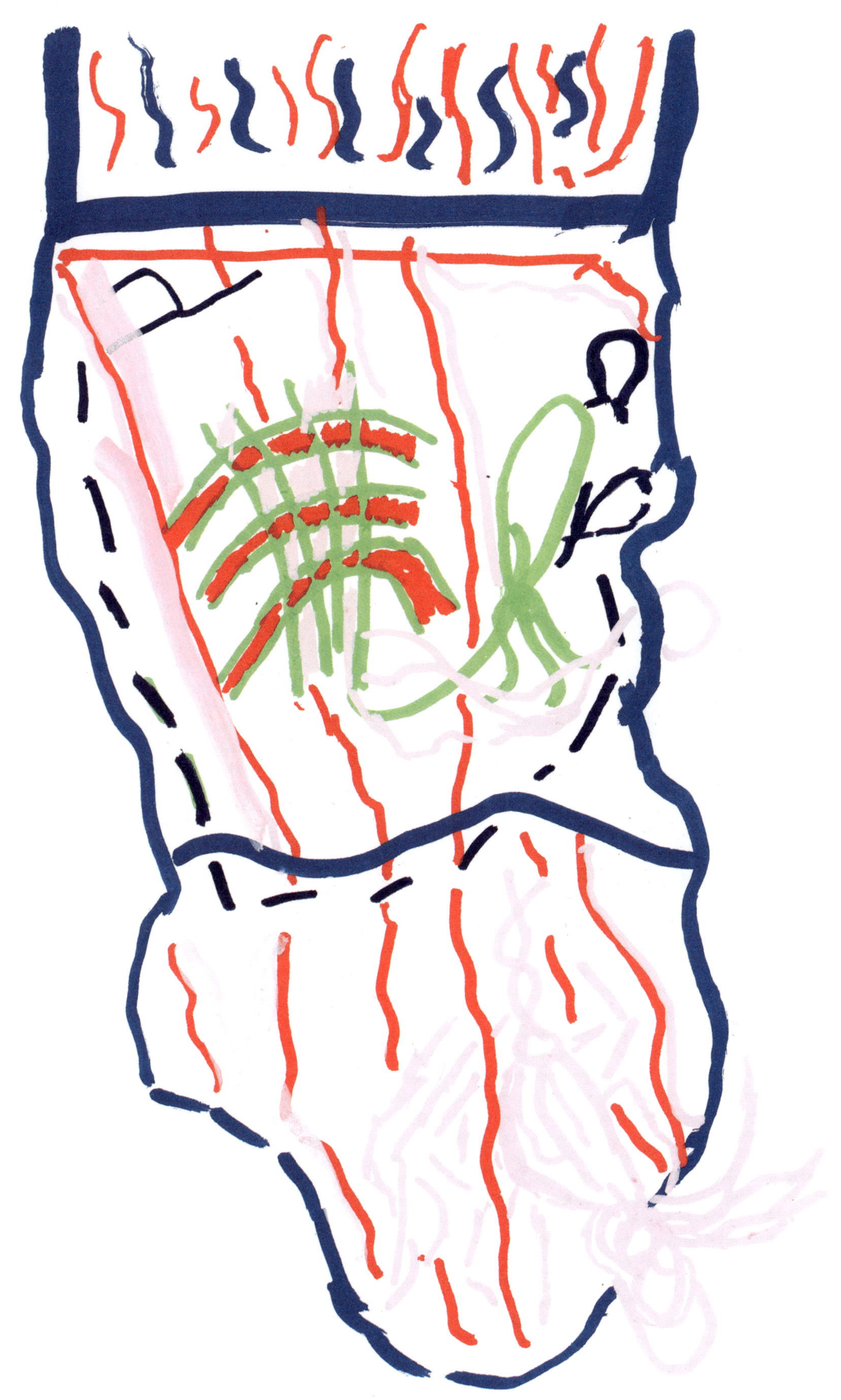

## Surrey Square Primary School

From the start of the Socks Project, Surrey Square Primary School had always been in the front of my mind. I'd partnered with the school's art teacher, Matt Dean, in 2007 for an after-school drawing club. Matt's a great teacher and shares his positive personal feelings about art with his students – he loves making art, looking at it and experiencing it. He wants the children to have the opportunity to do as much art as possible.

Also, and most importantly, Matt made working at Surrey Square very easy. For the Socks Project he said 'Yes' to the idea without hesitation and then we worked backwards to figure how to make the Yes possible – time-tabling, access, coordination with teachers, introductions at assembly, photo permissions. If you ever want to work with a school, a supportive and enthusiastic teacher at your side is essential. We time-tabled twenty-six workshops with each class and year group. Hannah Coulson joined me to deliver the workshops. We could not have done this without Matt's support.

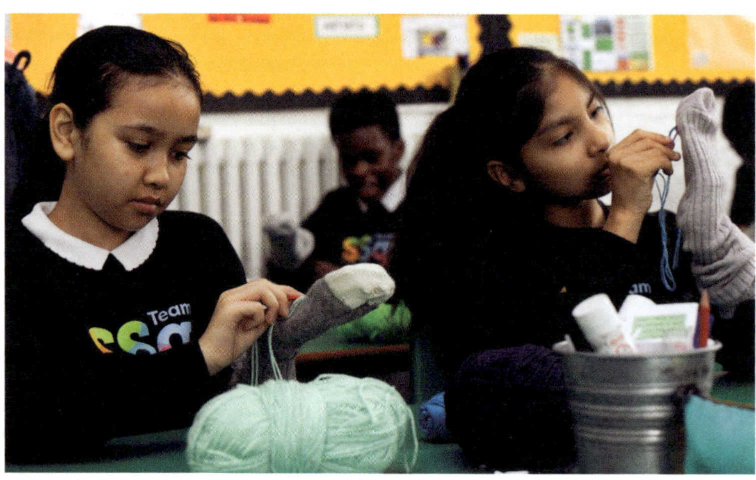

Concentrated stitching, Year 5

Our plan was simple. Every student in the school – and as many teachers and families who were willing and available – would practise a woven darn stitch on a J. Alex Swift waste sock. To prepare for this I made samples of woven darns that the children could feel with their fingers. Then, after showing slides of mended socks and a damaged sweater transformed by visible mending, I demonstrated the woven darn technique.

Our first session was with Matt's Year 4 class. We encouraged the children to cut holes in the socks they'd chosen and attempt to stitch their warp threads across the holes. The classroom had two teachers, thirty students, and Hannah and me.

We gave everyone an orange to slide inside their sock. This we thought would support and stretch the warp across the holes. The room soon smelt like an orange grove – little spritzes of mist shot out as the children scraped and pricked the orange rind. However, cutting the holes and using the oranges was problematic.

The holes made the socks floppy and when you put the firm orange inside the sock the holes grew bigger. The oranges were big – I'd chosen navel oranges – and awkward to hold in small hands. We tried cutting holes in a second session with Year 2 (the seven-year-olds), but then a boy cut a hole in his actual sock – the one which he'd worn to school. His class teacher, Amelia, looked worried. I swiftly mended the hole in break-time. We didn't cut holes in socks after that. From then on, I prepped the socks, so they had prepared warps.

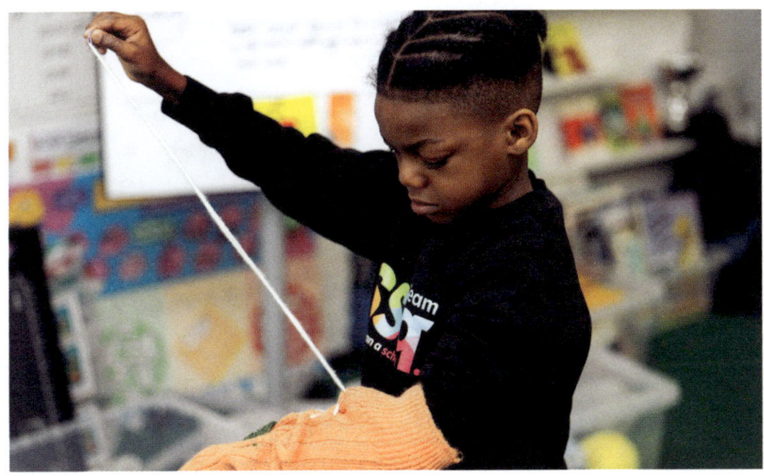

Pulling thread all the way through, Year 2

Each year group and each class responded differently to the session. Some understood the idea immediately. Others really loved it and made multiple socks. Some got speedy and finished quickly. I am always curious about what makes the same session different. Time of day, weather, the way information is shared, the prior knowledge of the students. The through-line, however, was that every child stitched, and in every session, it seemed, there were moments of deep concentration.

The children's stitches were sometimes like mark-making. Long and looping. Moving from one end of the sock to the other. Stitches hung from the shape of the sock giving it 'character'. A thread tugged the toes towards the ankle, giving the sock a jaunty feel. Or perhaps the cuff was stylishly ruched and pleated. Three children plied colours and yarns together to make an extra fat rainbow wool to use as their thread. Some tried to get as much colour into the sock as possible. Others would carefully and methodically weave their warps.

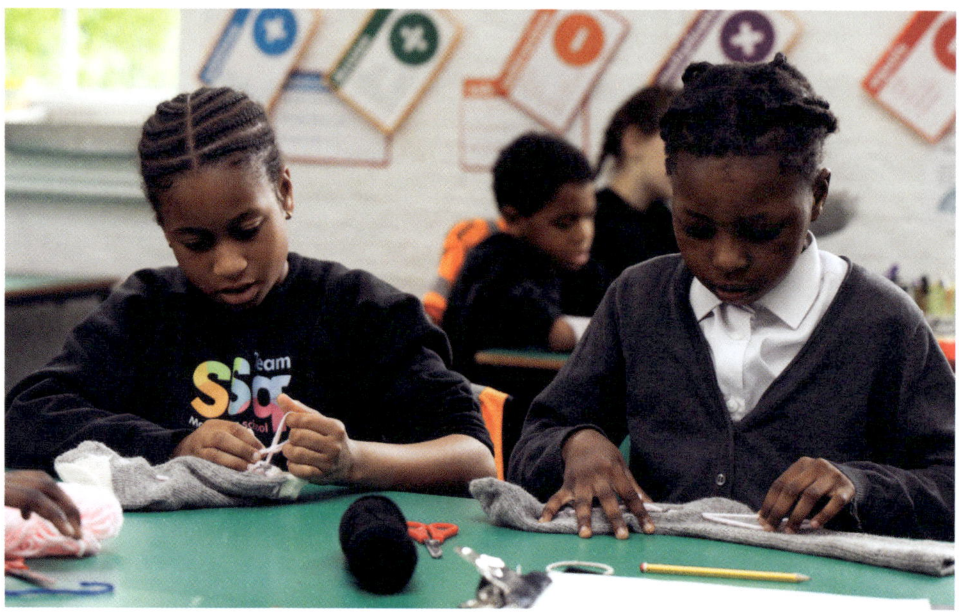

Finishing their darns, Year 5

One child said, 'I love mixing the colours together with the thread.' Another, 'The fun thing I remember was mending and weaving the socks because I liked the way I did different patterns and ranges of blending different coloured yarn.' Everyone had feelings about colour. The colour of the sock they wanted. The colour of the wool they wanted to use. Some children preferred the velvety chenille yarns. Others the thin sock wools. Another child undid and redid their stitches, over and over, until at the end of the session all that remained were cut ends of thread, which reminded me of a tracing of their stitches.

Everyone stitched into a sock. There was concentration and focus. Children in Nursery Class (the four-year-olds) and Reception Class (the five-year-olds) created small 'rocks', pulling their socks together and then adding stitches that bound them into tight bundles. Some of these children stayed for an hour or more patiently turning their stitched sock until it was solidly round.

Here are some observations on the way children sewed. Sometimes they didn't pull their thread all through the material. They'd send the needle through one side of the sock, leaving a long tail hanging from the back. Thinking they'd run out of thread, they asked for a new length. Children often needed encouragement to complete the stitch gesture, stretching their arms high and pulling the thread all the way through. If a child thought the long tail of thread hanging out the back looked great, they might decide they wanted to keep it that way.

Working in three dimensions was difficult. Students would try to work on their sock flat and then sew the sides together. Or they'd make a row of stitches and then pull tightly, gathering the whole sock up into a ball. For children younger than seven or eight years old, it appeared hard to imagine the 'invisible inside' of the sock when working on the outside.

Some students struggled to make knots at the end of their threads. The children who could make knots, I noticed, would often help those who couldn't. Sometimes there was a struggle to thread a needle. An instinct seemed to be to poke the end of the needle into the yarn they were trying to thread, as if the sharp point of the needle would pierce the wool and hold it. These were stitching challenges that Hannah and I would discuss after a workshop trying to figure out a way to solve or look differently at the issue. Often, however, the children in their enthusiasm would just go for it. They wanted to figure out the problem themselves.

Two groups had time to sketch their socks and stitches, warming up with mark-making and 'eyes-closed' drawings, and then representing what they'd just made in two dimensions. The children embraced the project. It combined learning and fun, physical engagement and imagination. They talked about what they already knew about sewing and making either from school or from what they'd learned at home. The marks the children made in their stitching excited me. I wished at times I could sew like that and make marks like theirs. I had a case of stitch envy. Top tip from Lucas, Year 5 at Surrey Square, 'Take your time. Stay relaxed.'

## Staff and Families

Staff and families were important to the project too. Teachers and staff would often join in during the workshops with the children. Stitching alongside them and concentrating as deeply as the children. We also ran a session after school. A group of teachers joined, and we stitched for an hour together, on the small chairs in a Year 4 classroom. The teachers experienced some of the same struggles (and fun) as the children. Moments of doubt about what they were doing, about whether they were doing it 'right', but also like the children becoming absorbed by the moment and having said they might stay for only thirty minutes ended up concentrating on their work and wanting to carry on for longer.

Matt also connected us with the Surrey Square Community Marketplace – a monthly event held at the school that welcomes families and neighbours with a chance to pick up clothes and food parcels, receive an NHS health check, and enjoy activities, drinks, and a hot meal. Hannah and I set up a sock mending table. Some children explained the project to their parents while others simply sat down out of interest or for company. We had a lively table and solid group of stitchers hanging out for a couple of hours sewing and darning.

## An Exhibition

We displayed all 488 socks made at Surrey Square at NOW Gallery, North Greenwich, between December 2024 and March 2025. The socks were arranged by year group and spread over large, elevated display boards. Staff and family socks were distributed around according to their colour. Now you could see waves of stitch marks and darns coming together and the development in the children's work. In addition, we set up a workshop area in the gallery where visitors were invited to have a go at mending a sock – again using the waste socks from J. Alex Swift. All the children and staff came to see the exhibition. One student said after visiting the exhibition 'The most fun thing that I can remember is when I saw the picture of me holding up a sock I made in my class in Year 5. Also, I liked seeing my name on a display board, but it was not as big as my picture display!'

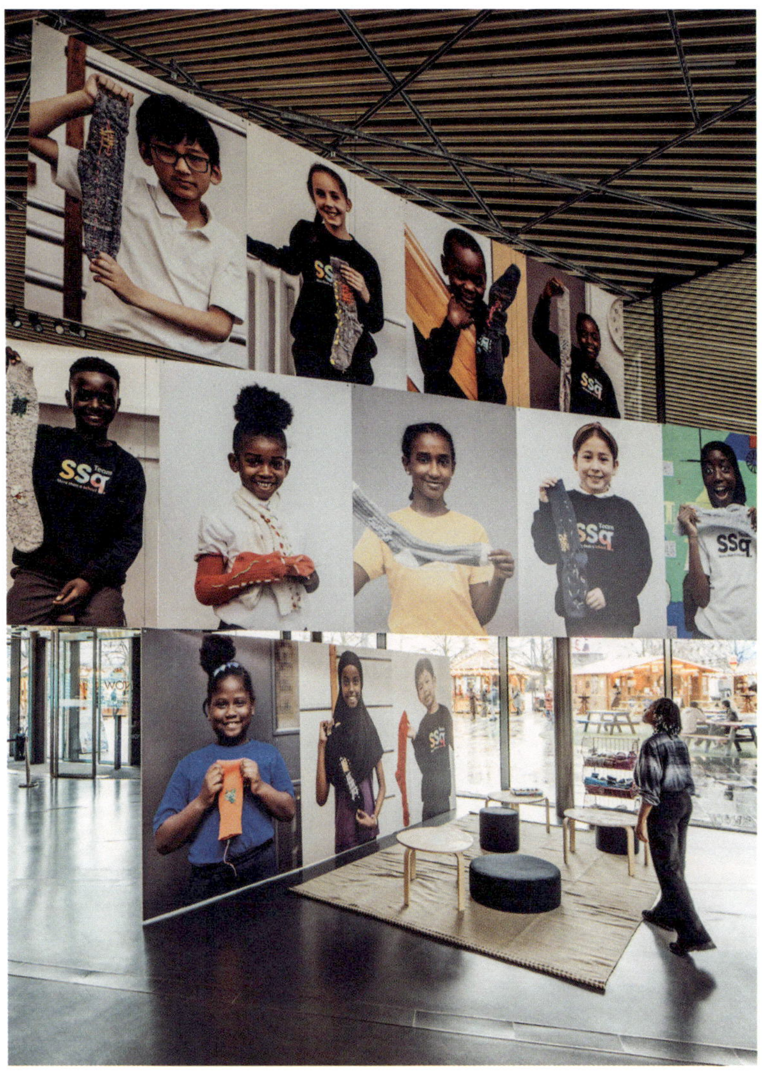

*Socks Project*, NOW Gallery, 2024–25

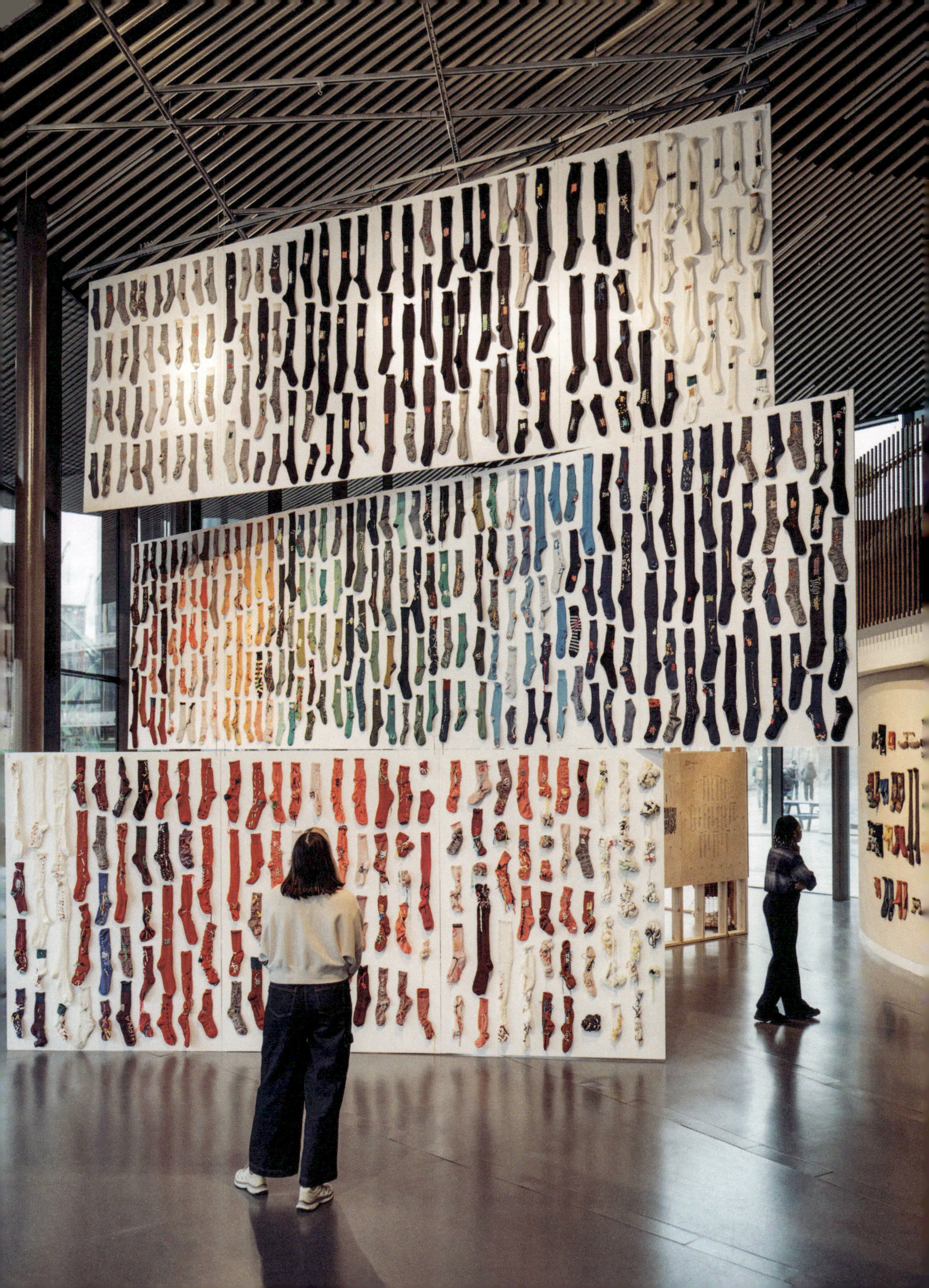

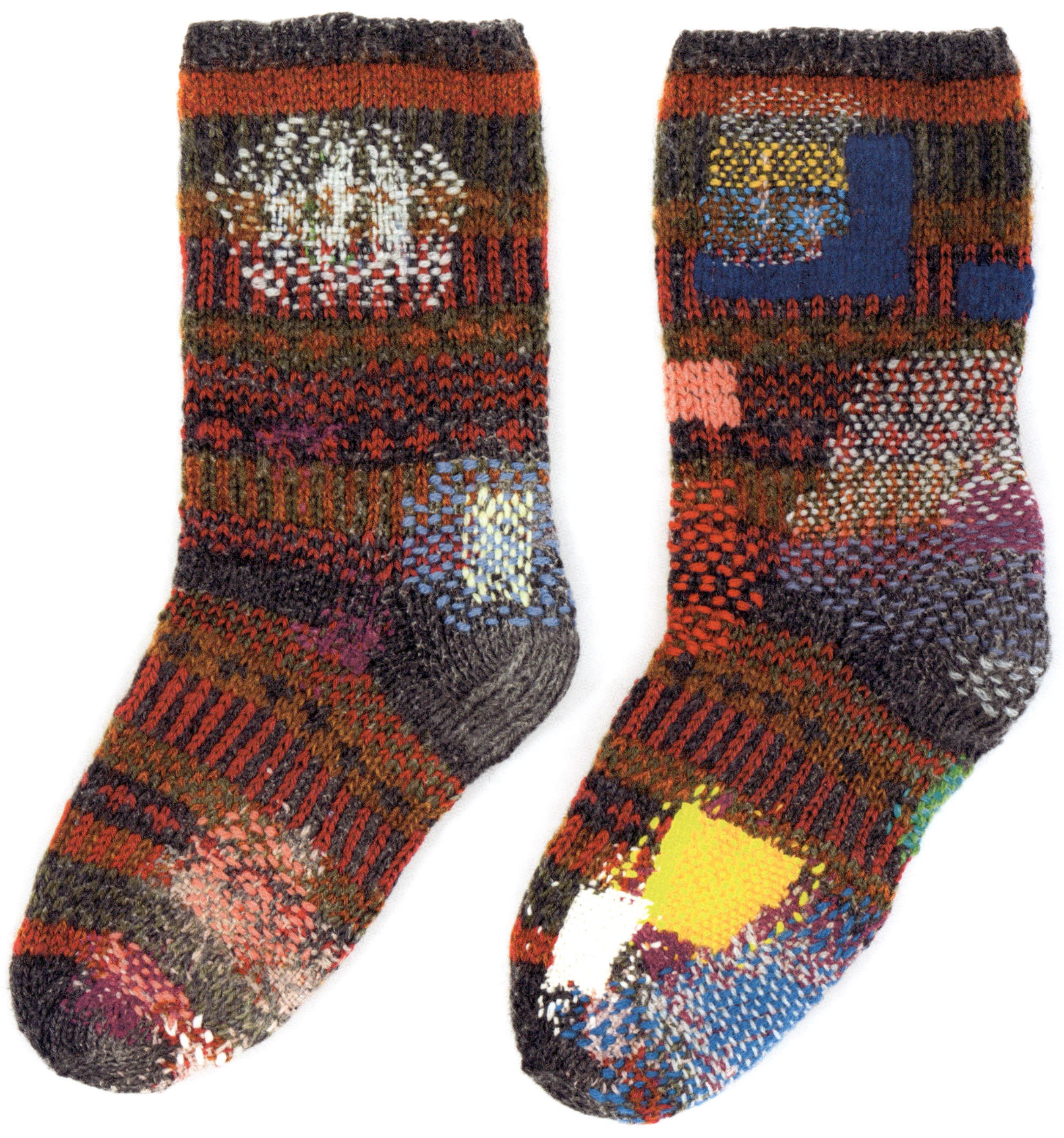

Johnny's socks, mended 2015–24

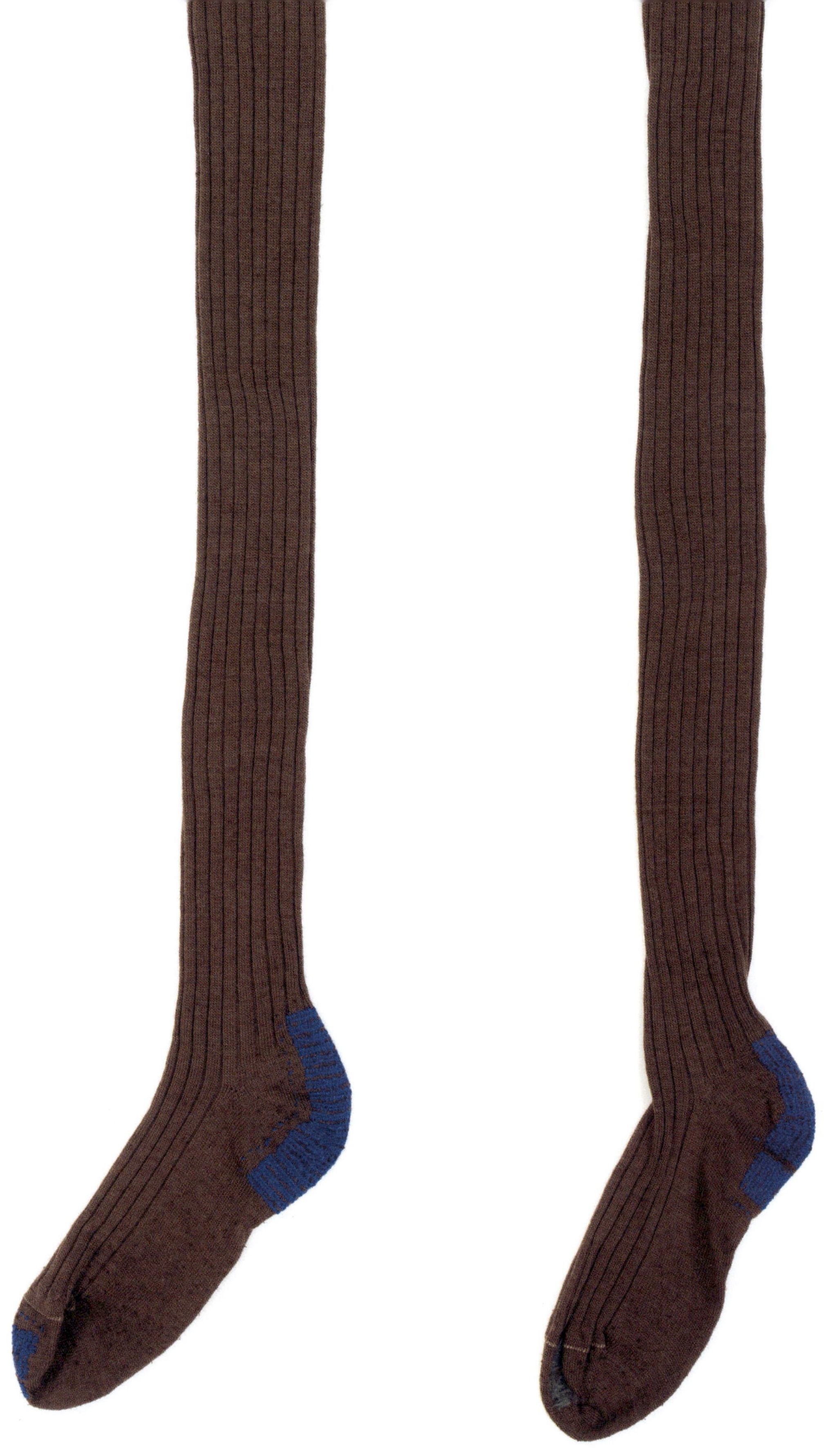

Hope's socks, mended 2024

# Family and Friends Socks

I thought often during the project about my own relationship to mending, community and clothes. My preoccupations have focused for some time around evidence of wear and tear. How the owner's body and habits are written into the damage of their clothing and how, when mended visibly, this highlights something particular about the owners themselves. How mending is a small act of care. And that the slow deliberation of stitching and mending is a thoughtful time spent with the clothes and my thoughts about the people who wear them.

By contrast, the Socks Project was filled with a different kind of excitement. The school, the children and the members of the wider Surrey Square community all embraced the project. And working with that community, I experienced a boundless sense of open-hearted welcome. So much so that Hannah and I were sad when the workshops ended and it was time to leave. I was struck by how significant *care* is to self-expression and the release of imaginative impulses. In this project the children and teachers' care for each other, and Surrey Square's strong sense of community, fostered the imaginative and creative work the children made.

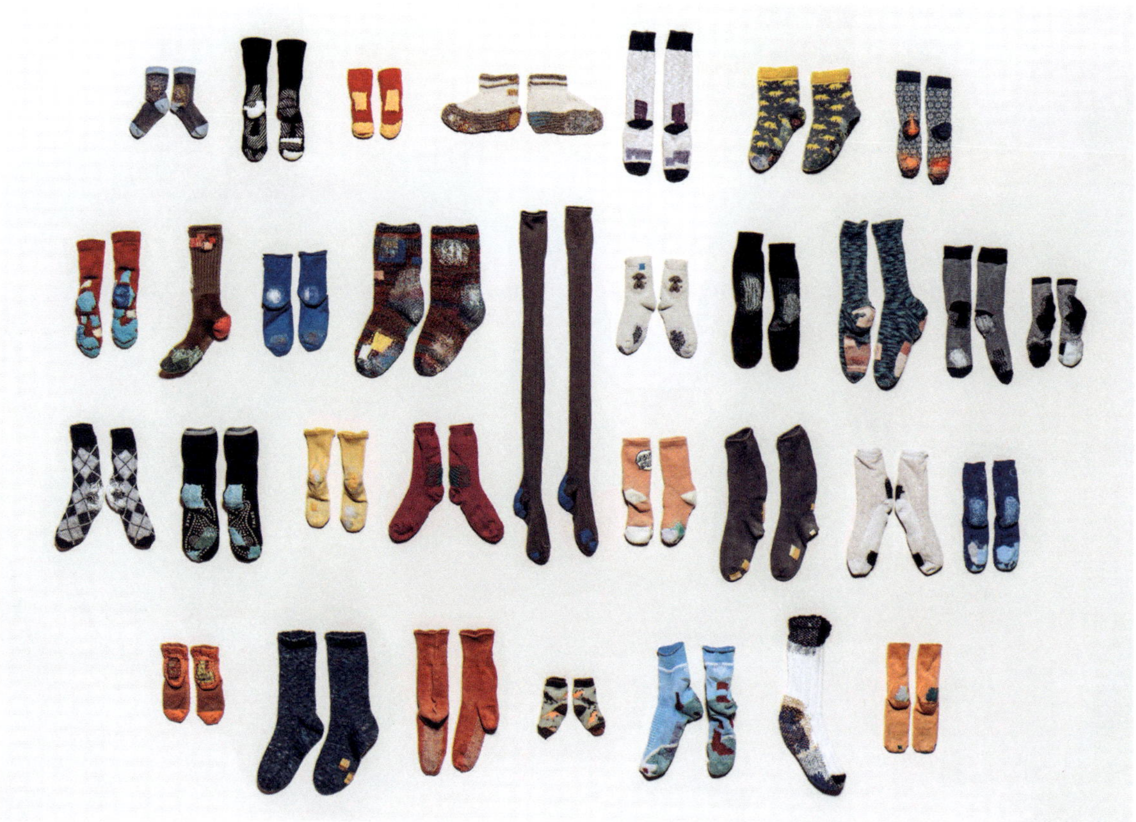

Family and Friends socks, mended on various dates

To accompany the show, I wanted, in addition to the children's work, to make a sock portrait of *my* community, to add examples of genuine worn socks, of real holes that had needed mending. In short, the socks of my family and friends. I sent an email asking if anyone had socks with holes that needed mending. I had many responses. Some socks arrived in the post, two pairs from America, another from Derbyshire. Some socks I went to collect in person. Several people gave two pairs ('in case I didn't have enough') and one pair belonged to a friend's mother who had recently died.

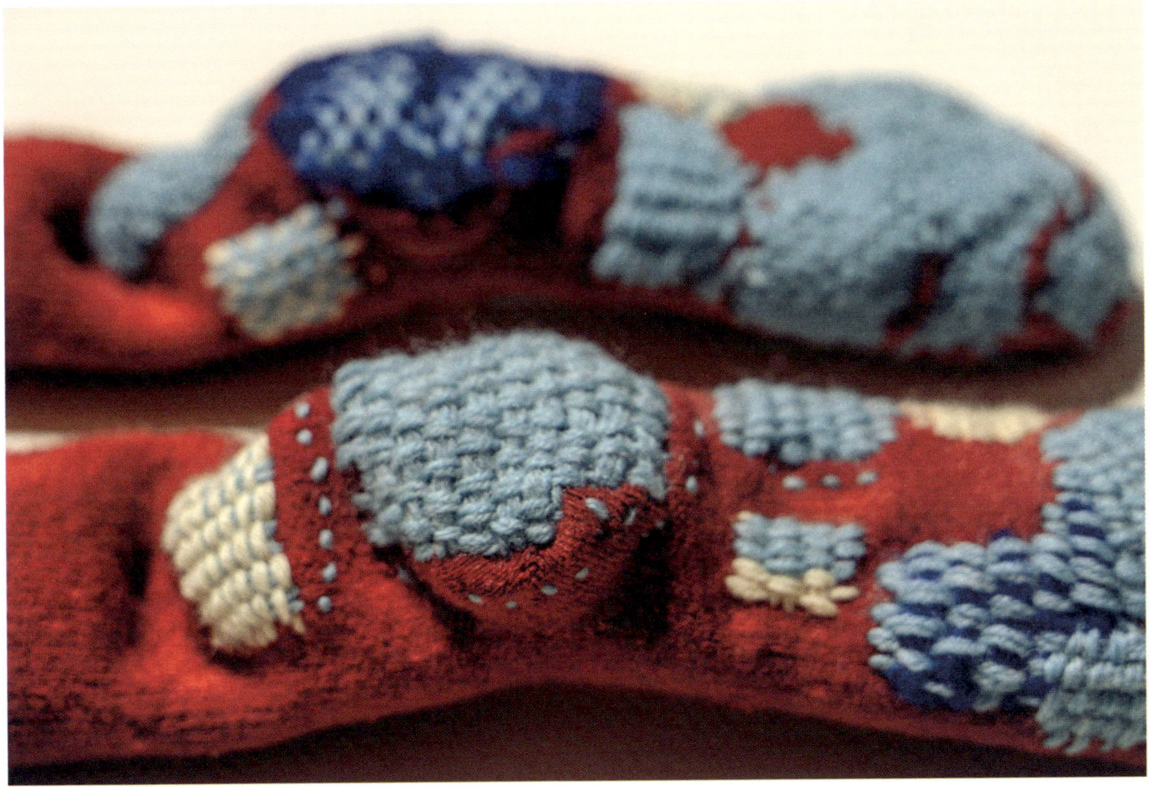

Sei's socks, mended 2024

My 'Family and Friends' sock wall was specific to the people I know and love. With this collection, because I knew each sock-owner well, I was able to imagine what mends would suit them, what colour they'd like for the repair, how it would fit with their style and activities. And I could imagine them wearing their mended socks. The mending was made in contrasting colours. They were all everyday sock holes. My Dad's socks I had mended several times before. I'd bought them for him on a trip to Lithuania in 2007. They became a second pair of socks worn inside his wellington boots and soon developed many holes. The mending marks on his socks were starting to add up to a textured layered surface that could not have happened through careful planning but emerged over time from use and repair.

# Needle and Thread

If you can surprise yourself by putting colours together and seeing them 'zing' and complement each other, or discover that mohair and chenille make a luxuriously soft combination, my hope is it will make you curious – what other combinations of colours, textures and structures could make you feel things that excite you or work in brilliant ways. The motivation for the Socks Project was somewhat similar – a desire to have fun with sewing and to demonstrate to children that learning to hold and use a threaded needle gives you power and agency. And that – with luck and perseverance – you'll find a wide, imaginative and practical world opening before you! And above all perhaps to sow the seed that will grow into *a feeling of care for yourself* – for your clothes and the clothes of other people.

Mending is a constant practice. The wear and tear of clothes is gradual and adds up over time. Nothing is ever mended permanently. A mend holds holes intact for a while until you need to support it again. I've always mended visibly tracing the damage with the new layer of repair. Each bit of damage in a hole, and the moment it arises, presents a particular challenge that requires flexibility and creativity. But first you must have the confidence to pick up a needle and thread and feel that these are somehow the tools of your imagination.

At Surrey Square the emphasis became more about the marks we could make with the stitches than the act of repair. Where previously I've often found myself talking about and studying damage, and in addition thinking about the life of clothing, in this project we were mainly focused on the stitches and the way they looked. As Xyanne, Year 5, said, 'The most fun thing about the project is that we were learning lots of new ways to stitch. I just love sewing in general and I loved working on a real sock.' Perfection was not the aim, encouraging resilience and enthusiasm was. Jaheem, Year 6, put it best, 'Stay focused if you make a mistake, just carry on, once you start to do it, it will only get easier.'

All socks were returned to the children, staff and families at Surrey Square. And my family and friends got their mended socks back too – theirs to keep and wear until they spot another hole.

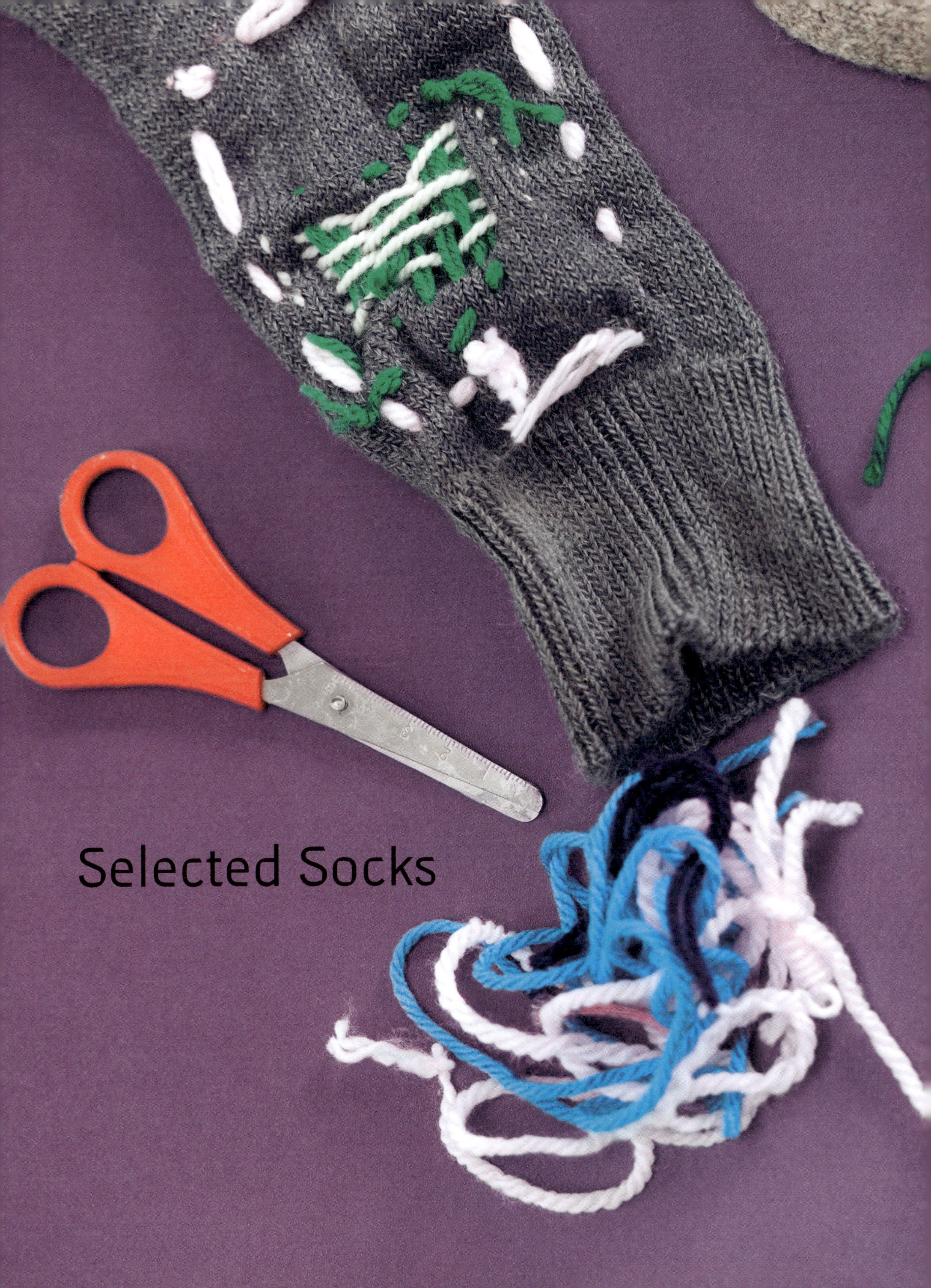

# Selected Socks

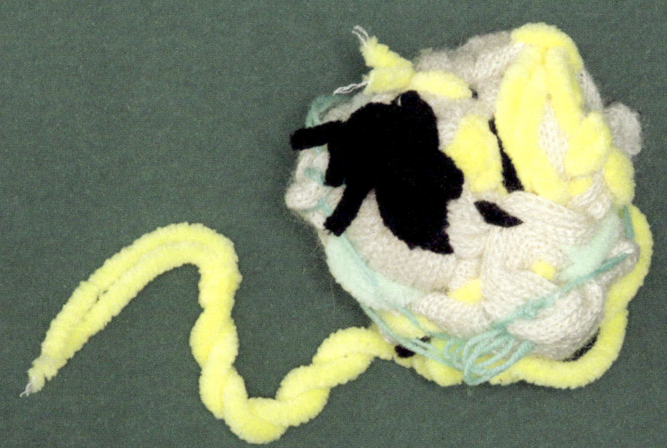

Khadija

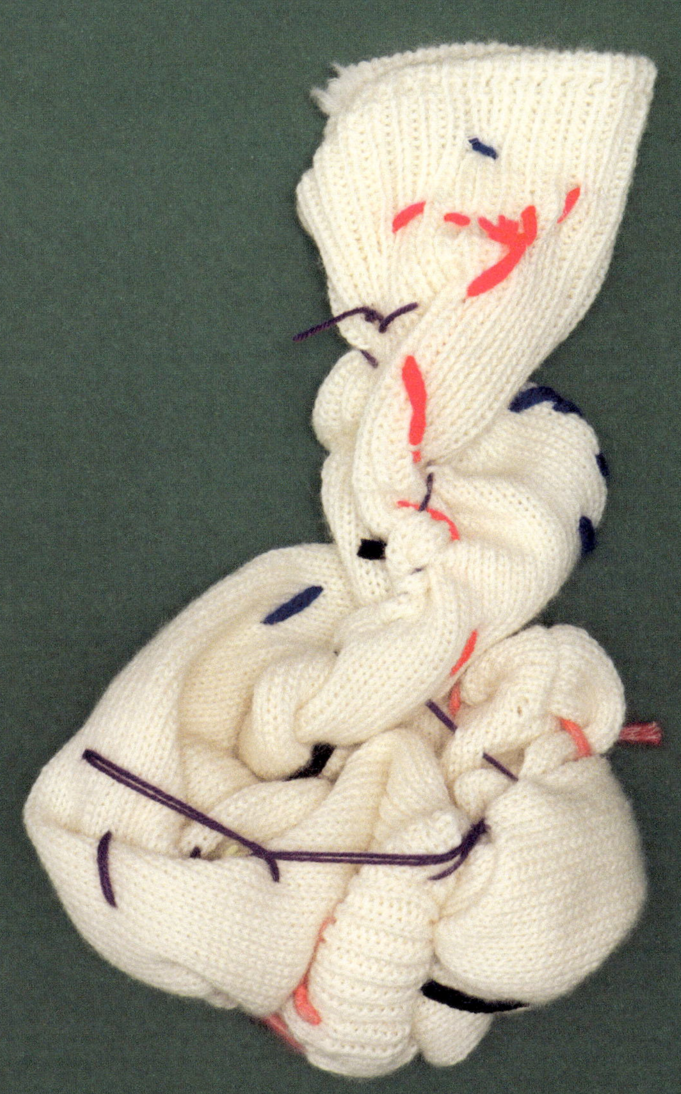

Edom

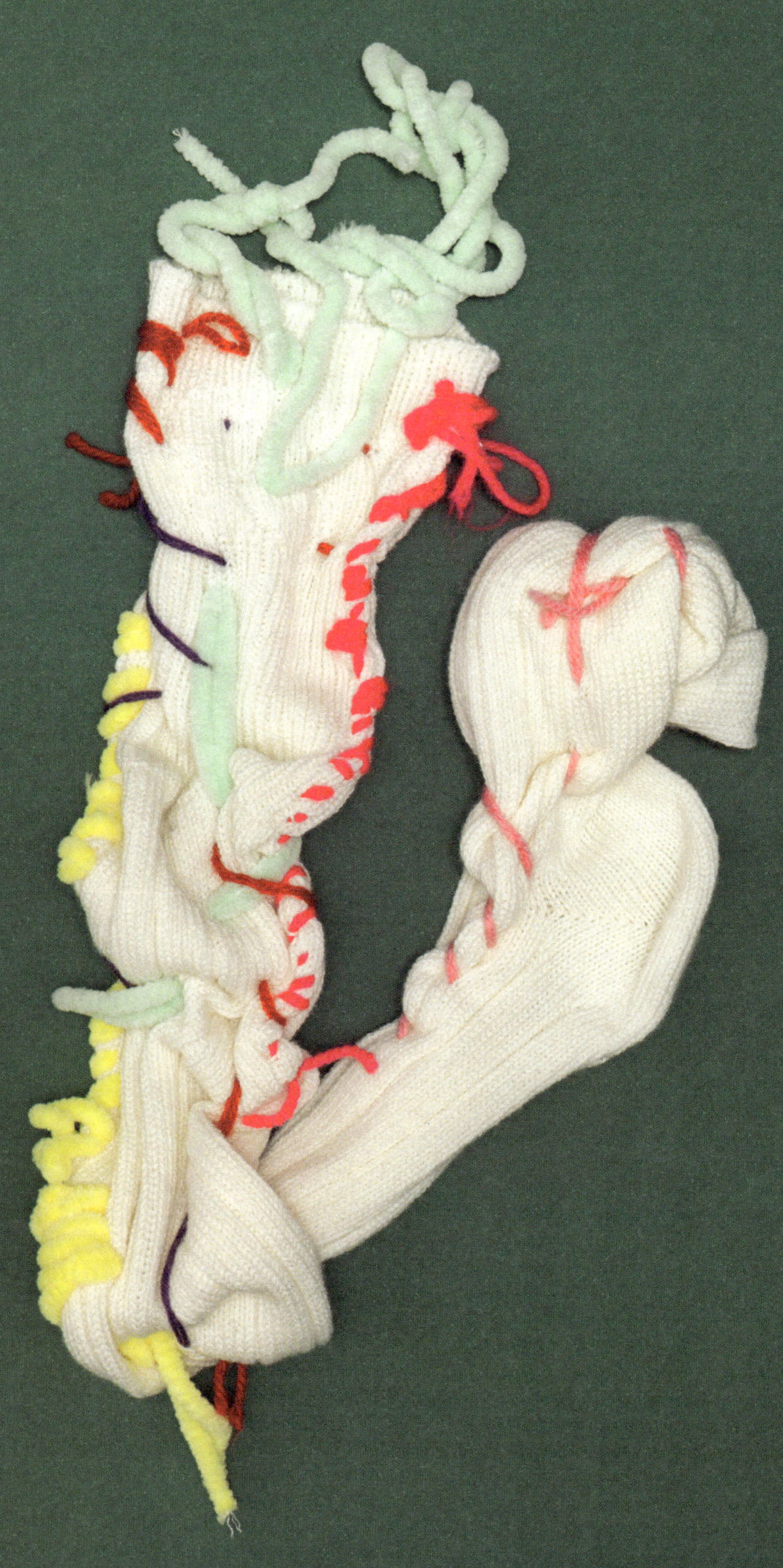

Ameena

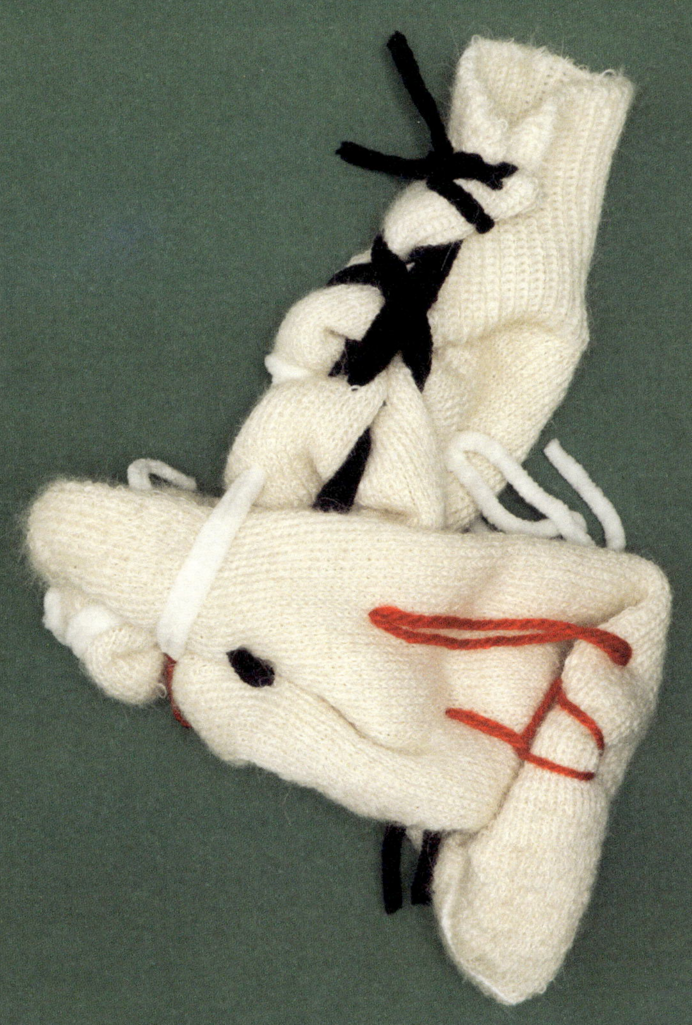

Muniat

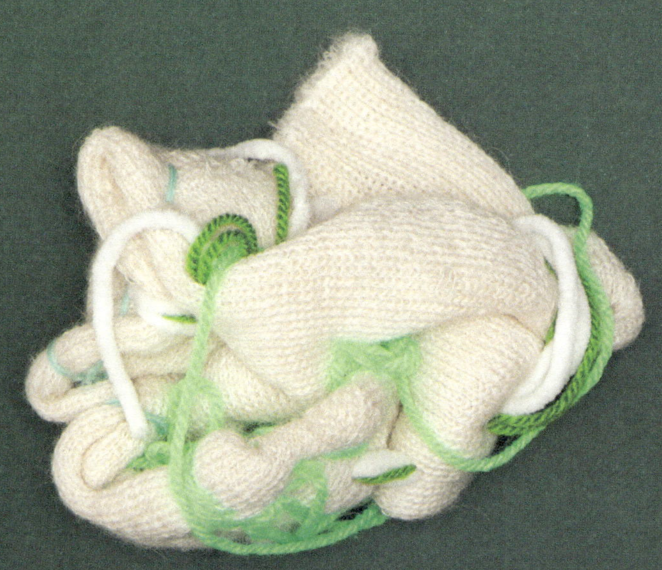

Kumari

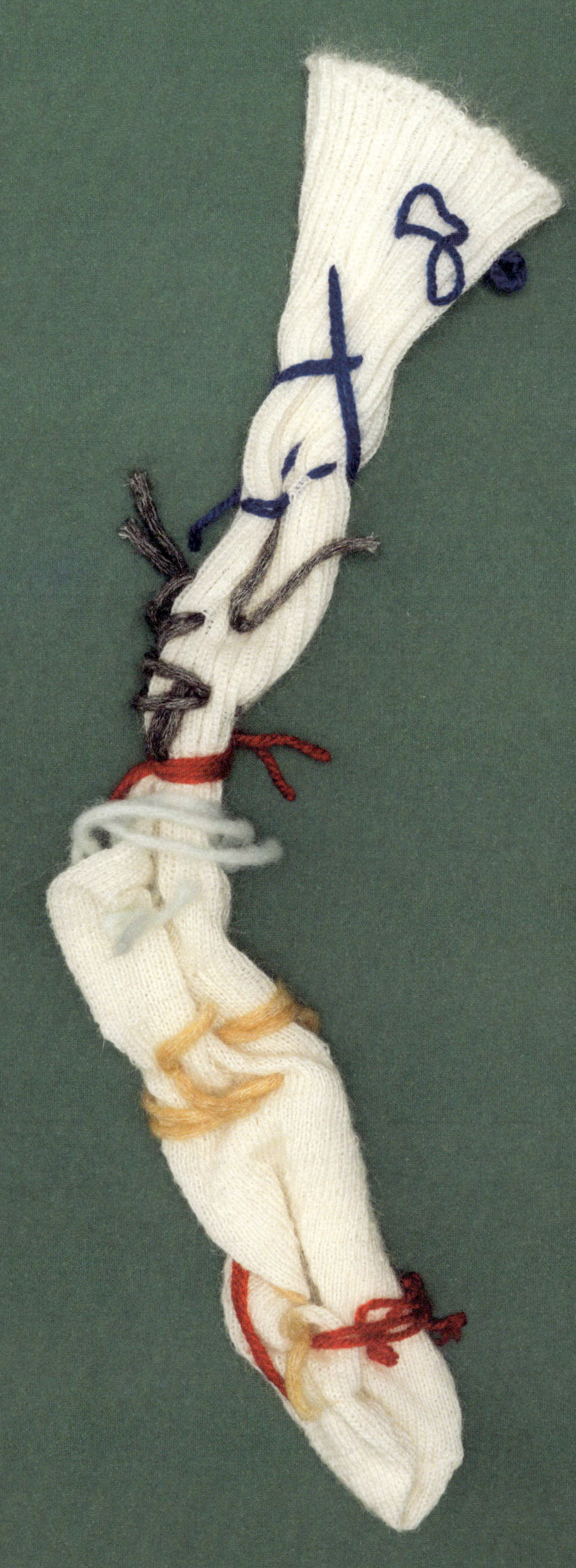

Shadave

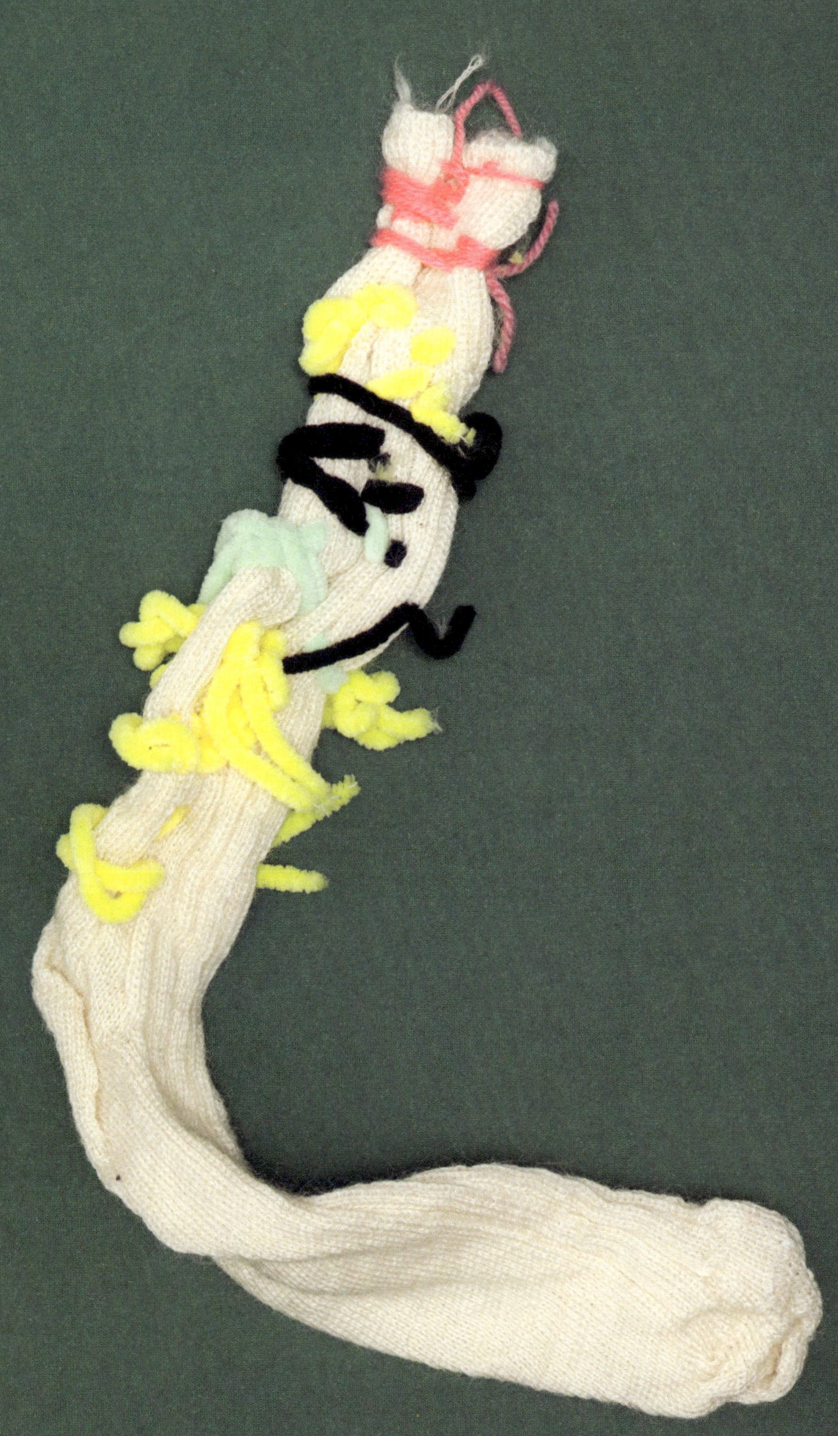

Indie

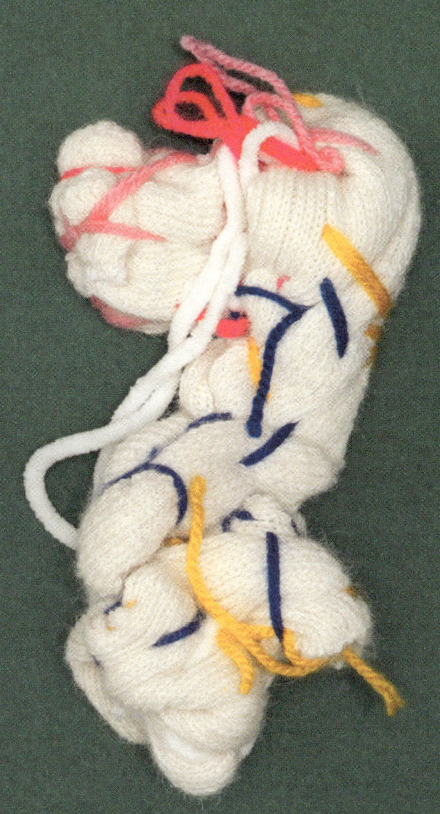

Alaia

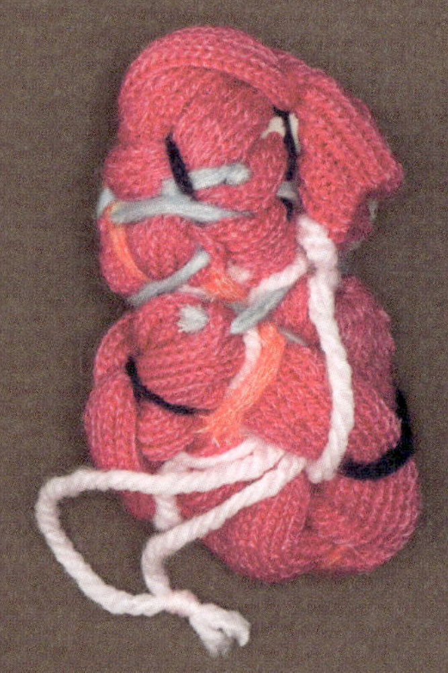

Tiwa

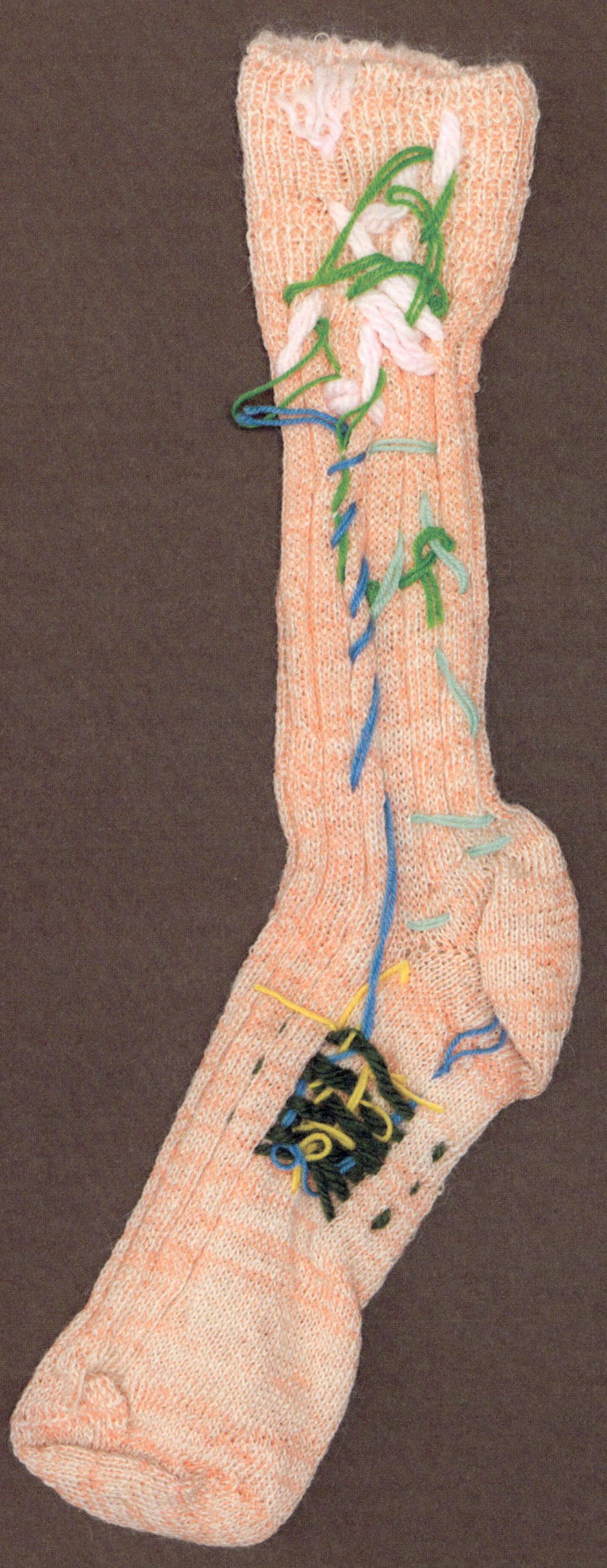

Kamara

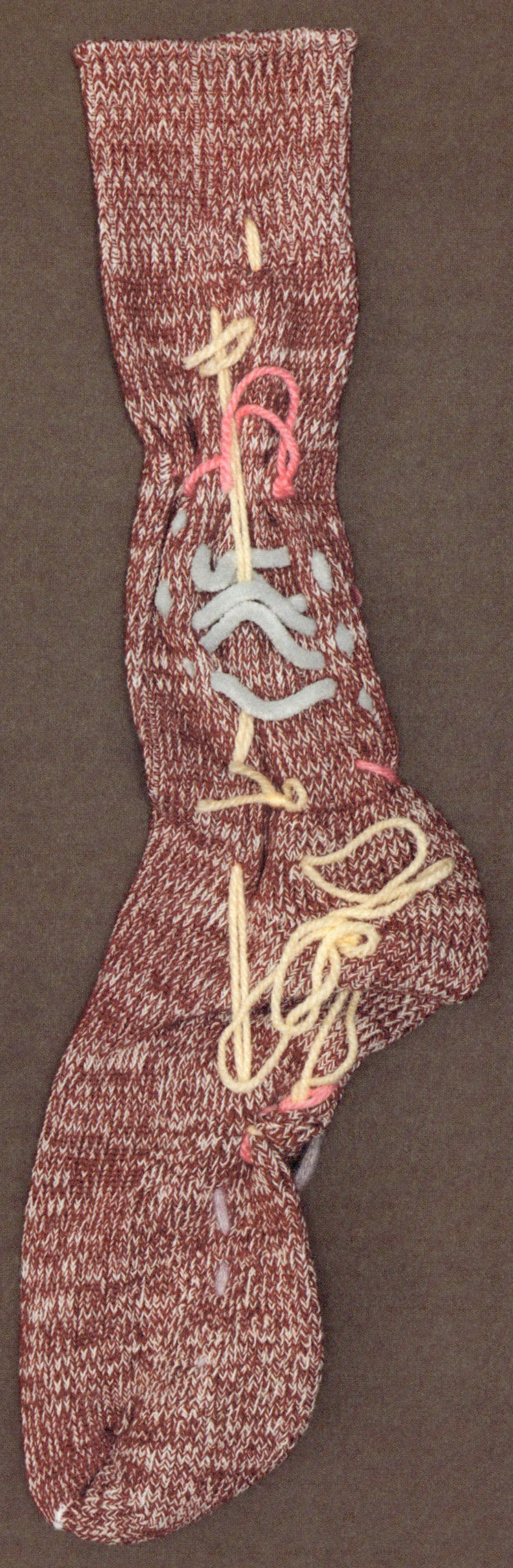

Kierra

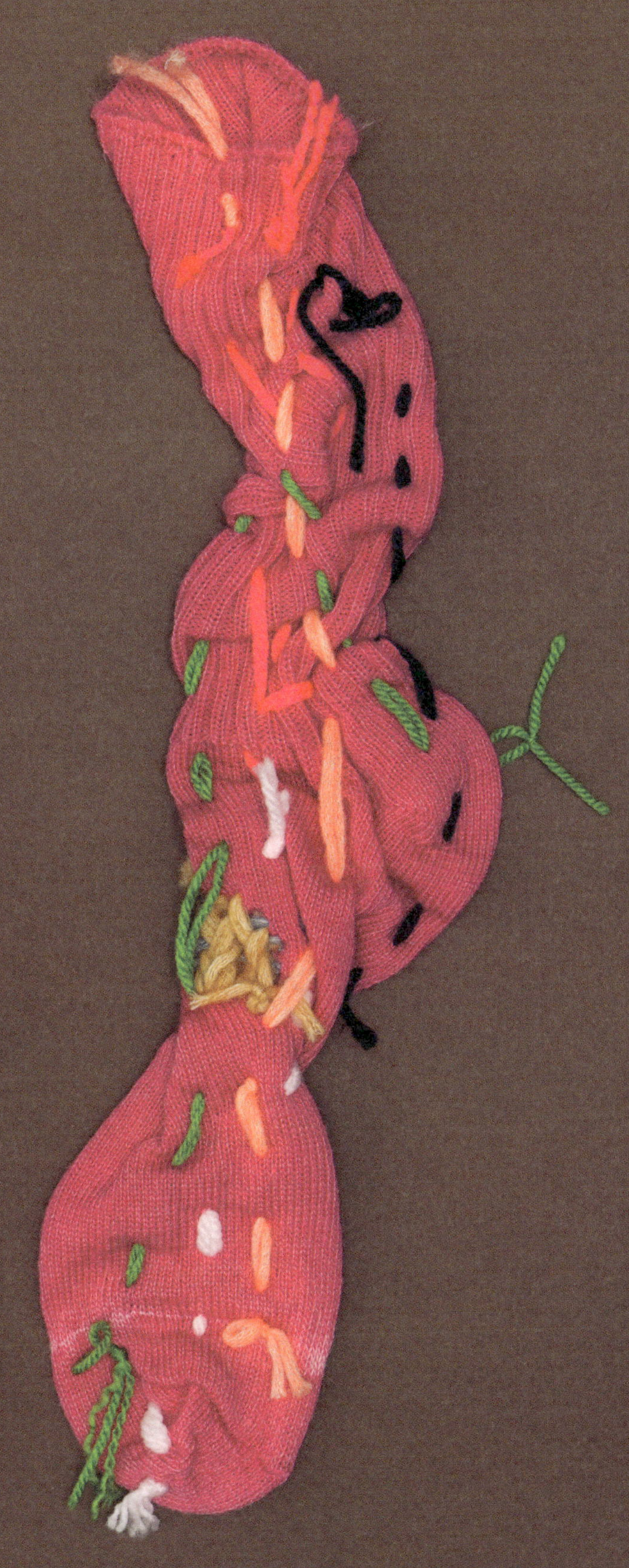

Dolcey

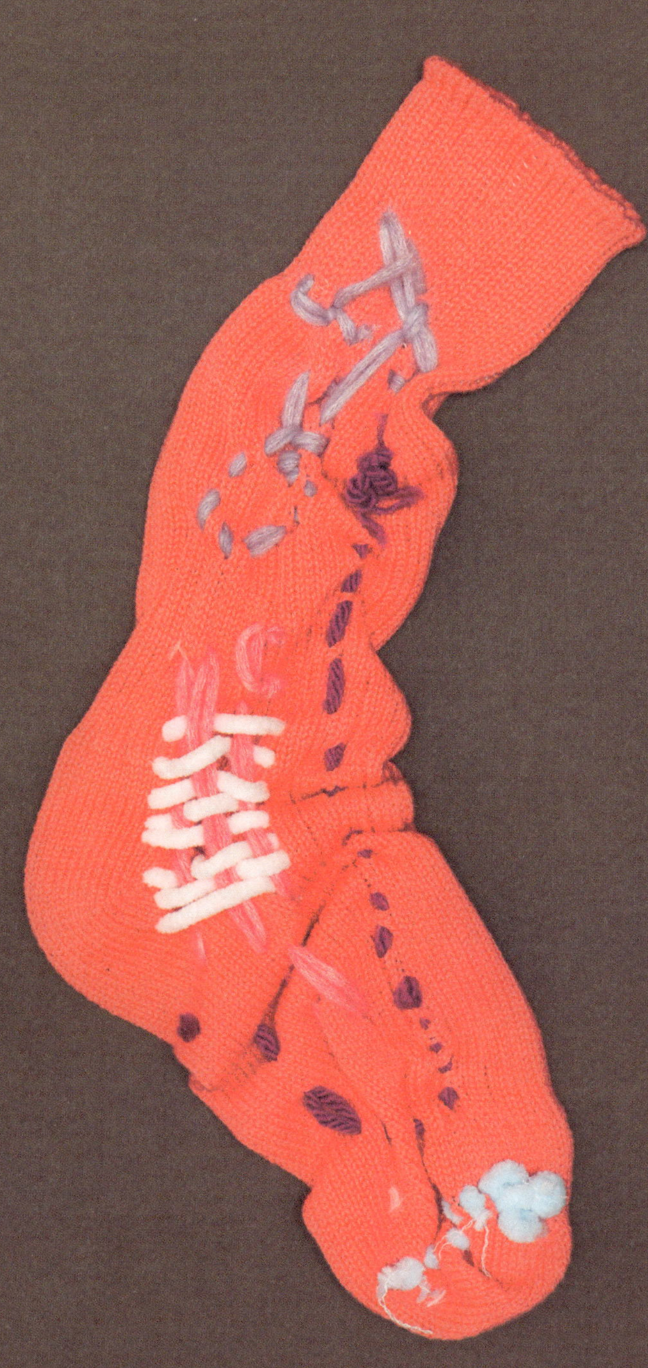

Kylie

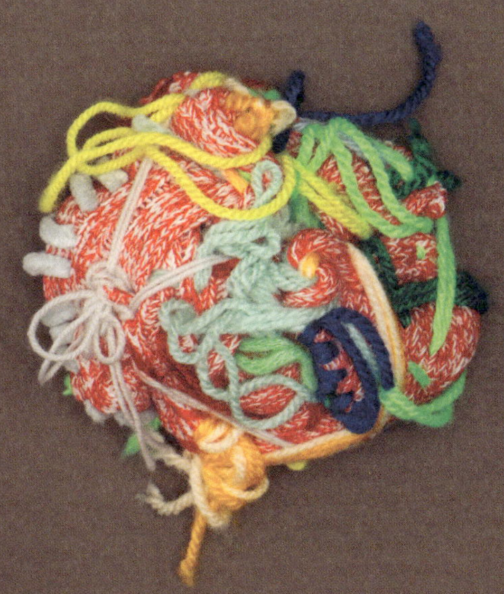

Juno

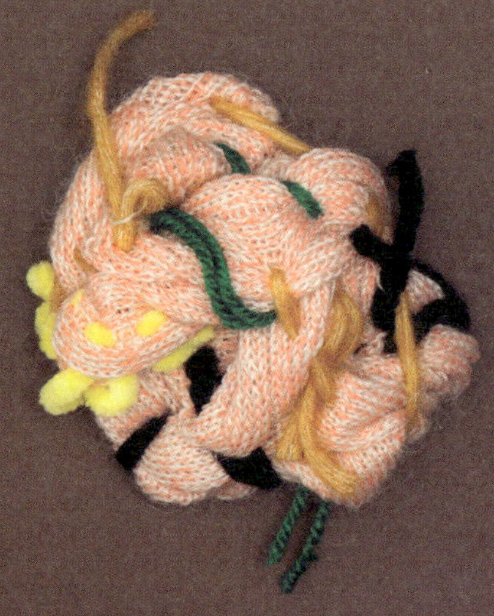

Reuben

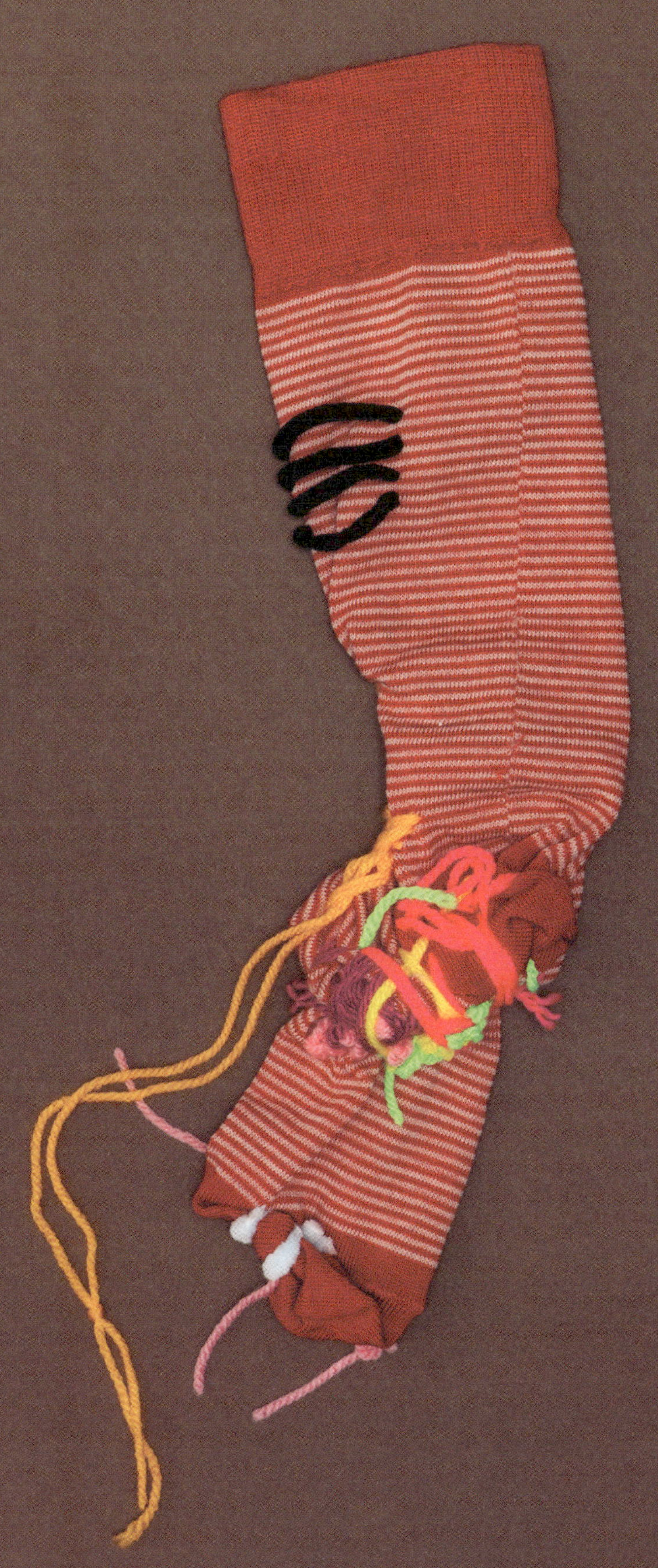

Helin

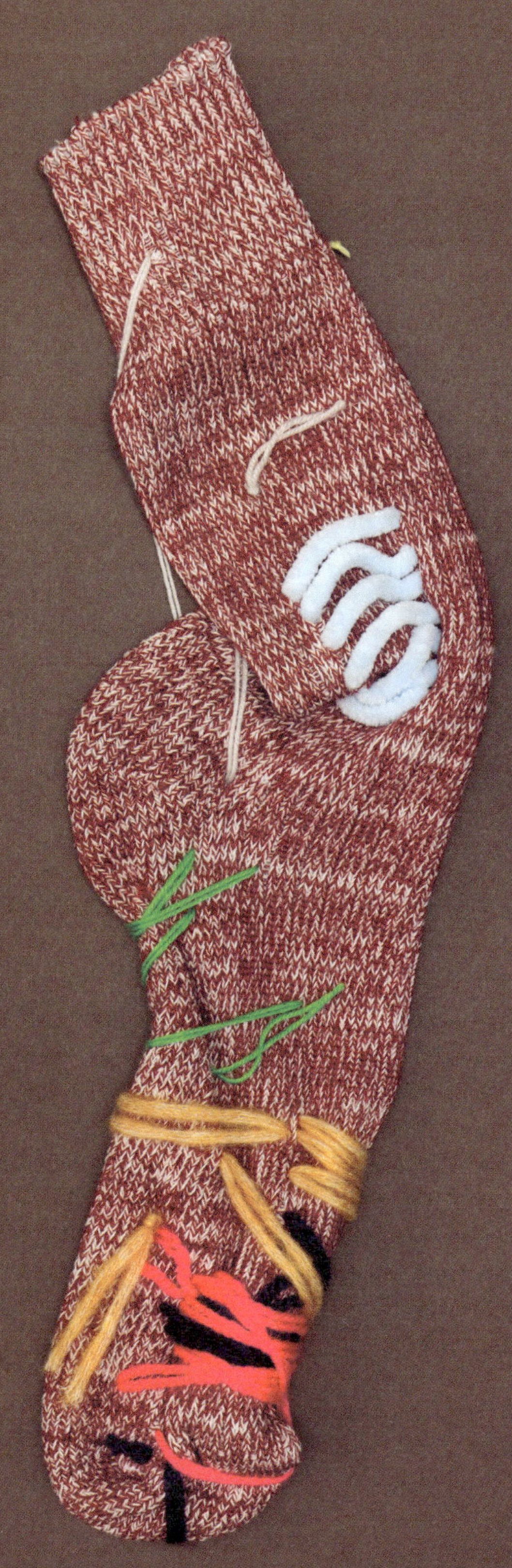

Anya

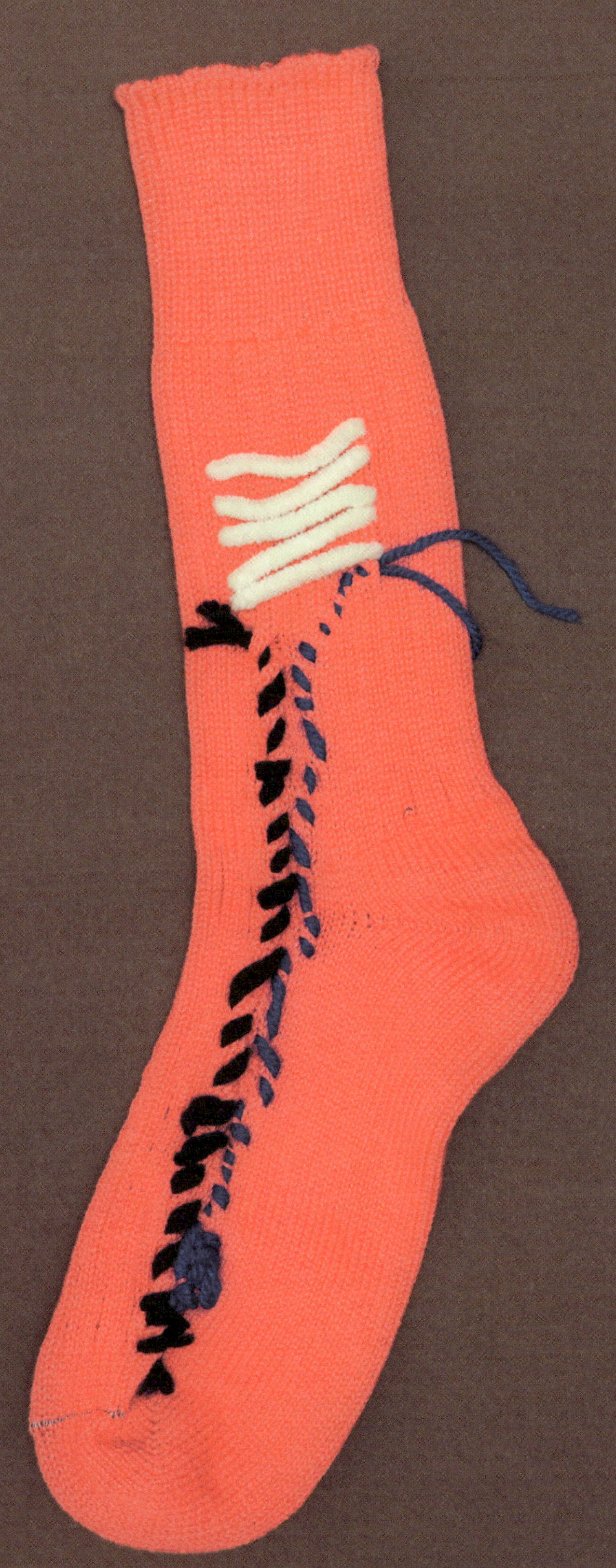

Raoof

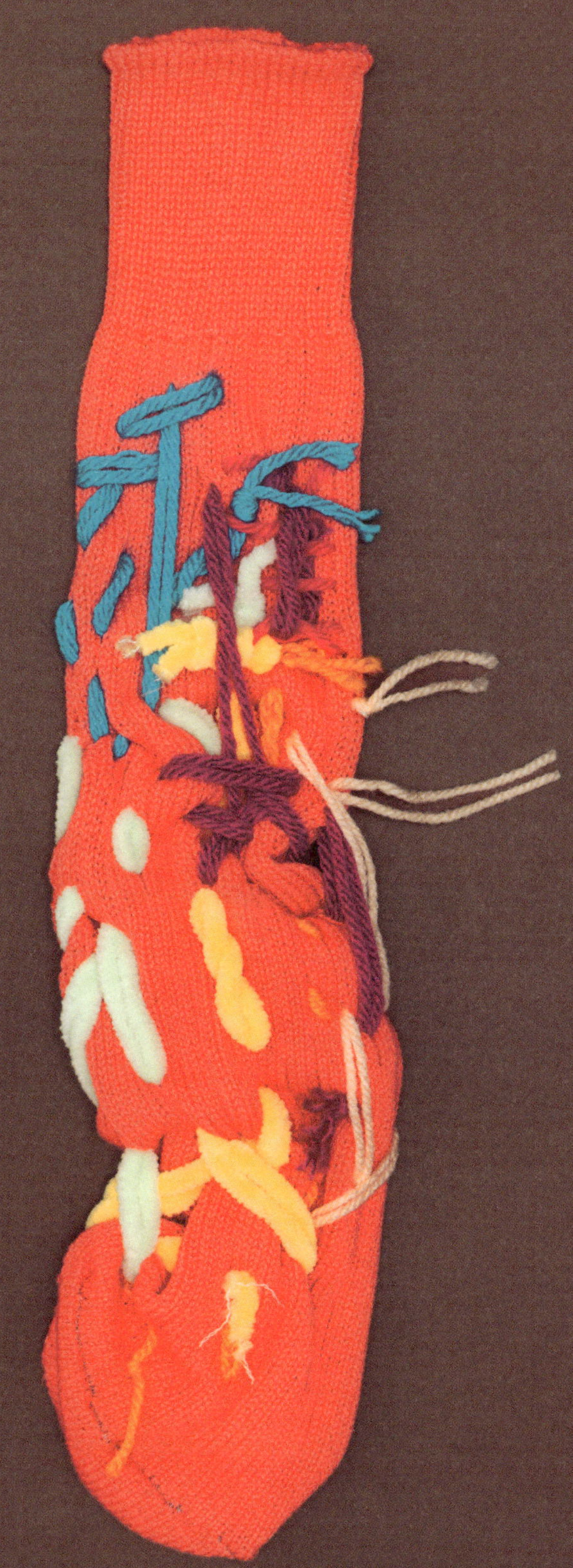

Iqra

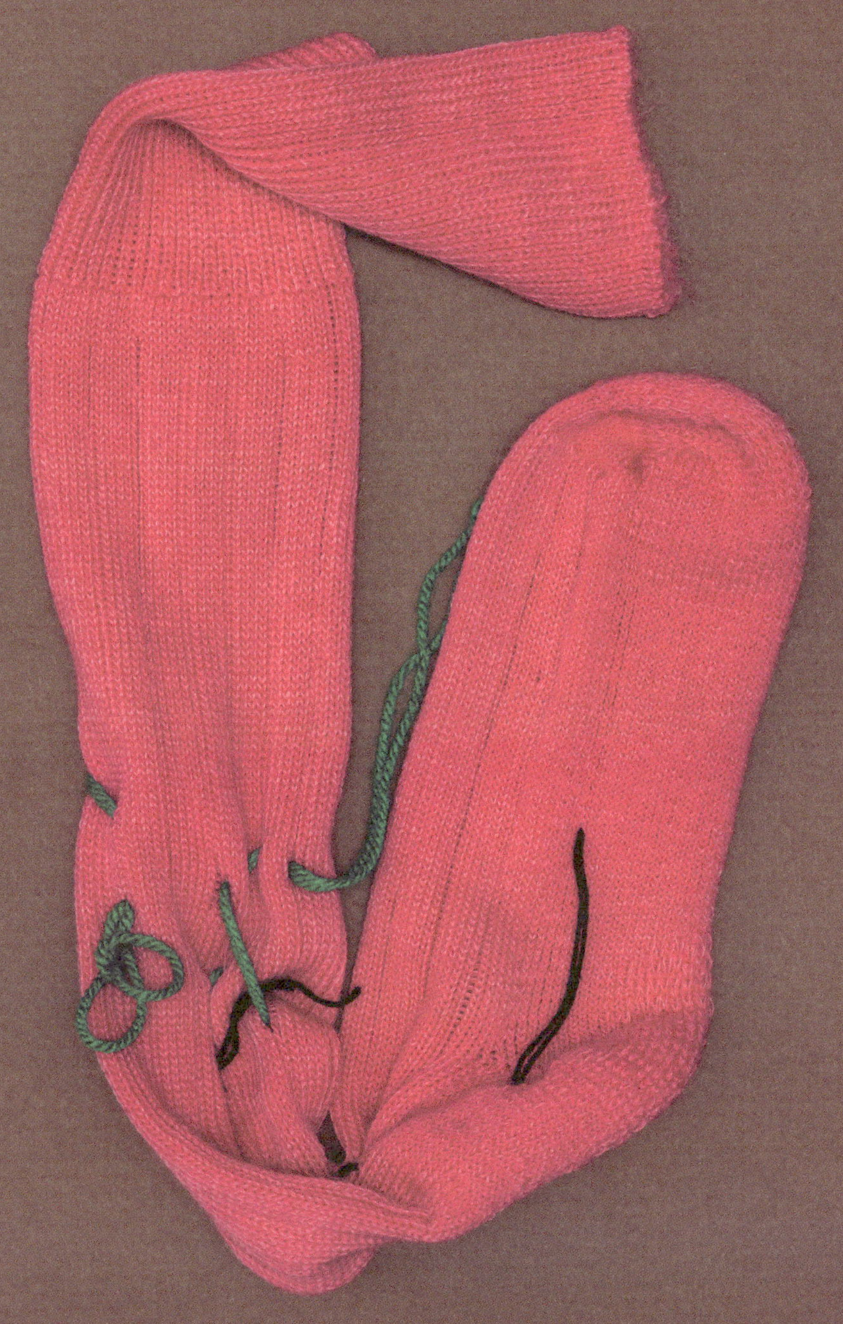

Omer

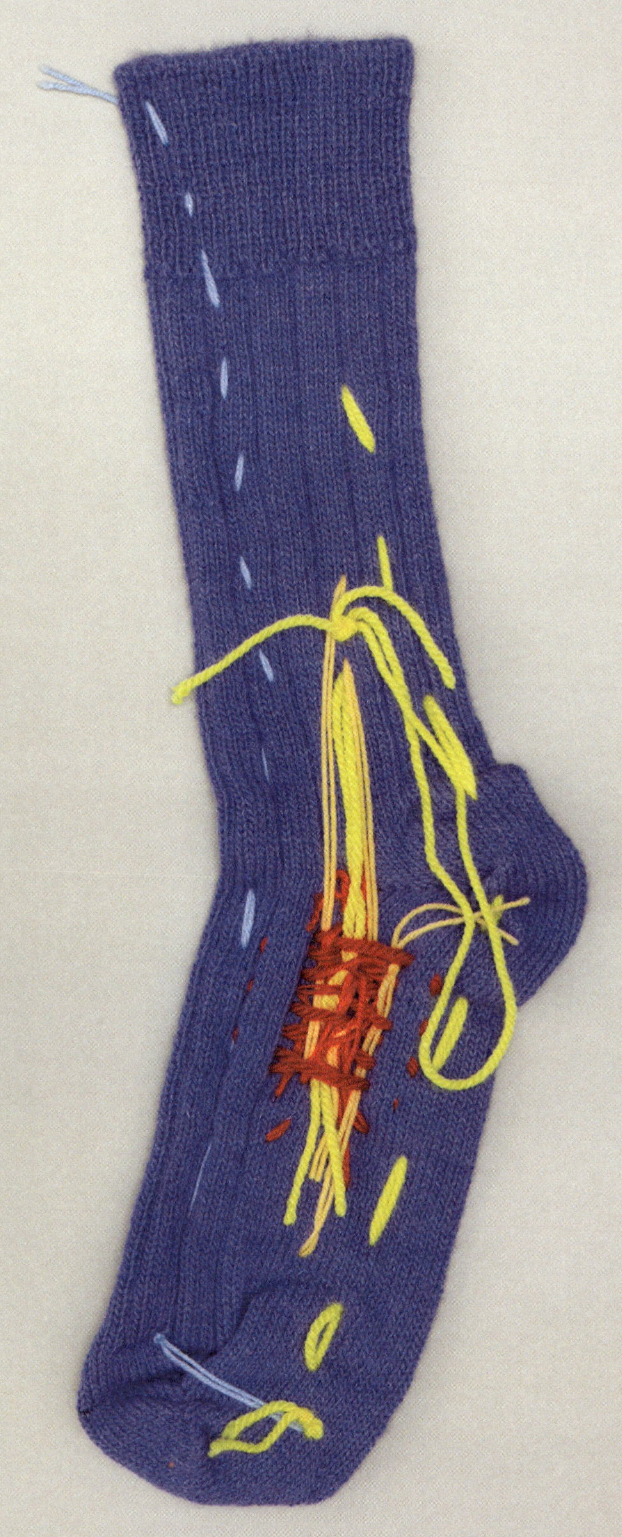

Kenny

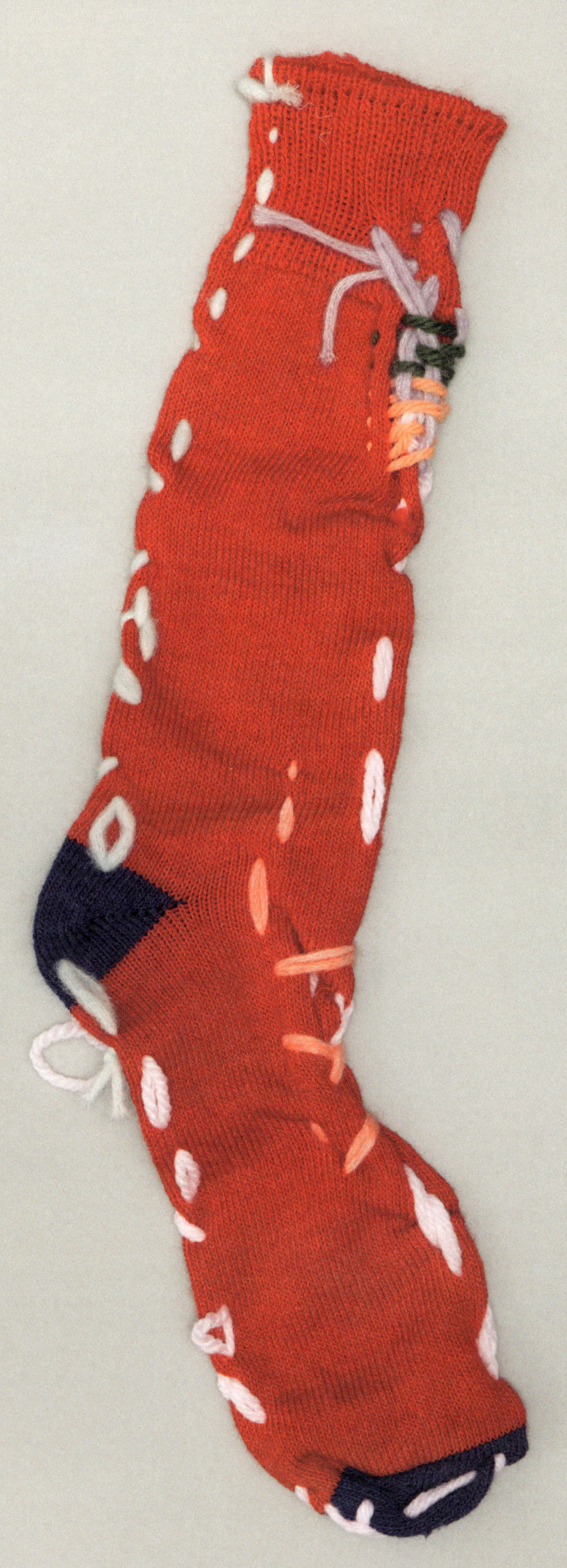

Aishah

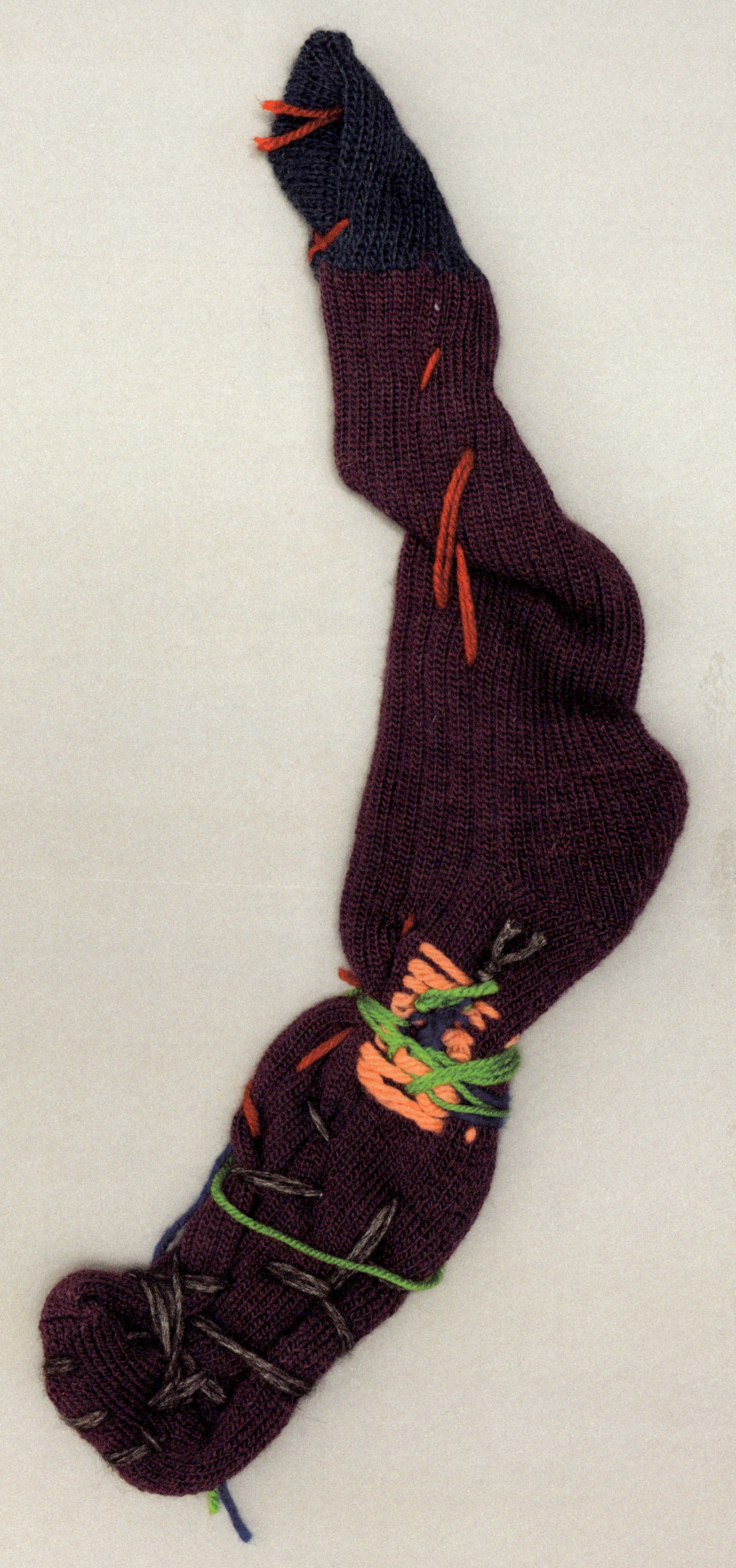

Badou

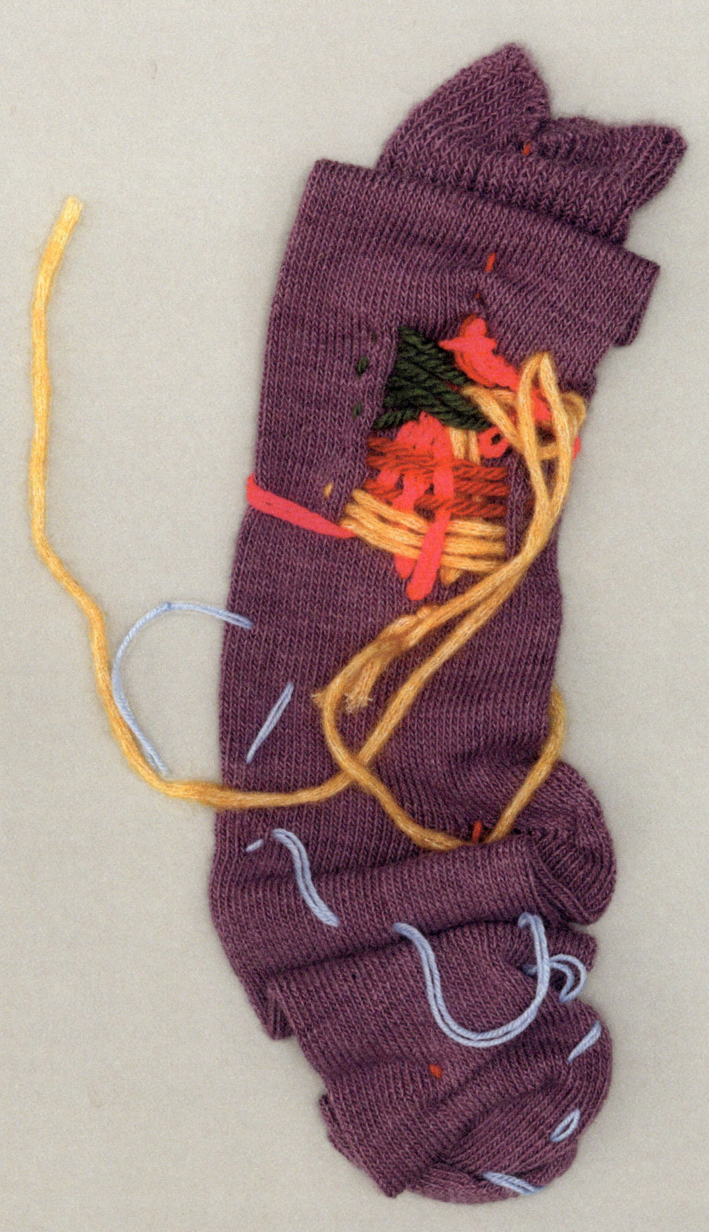

Marlena

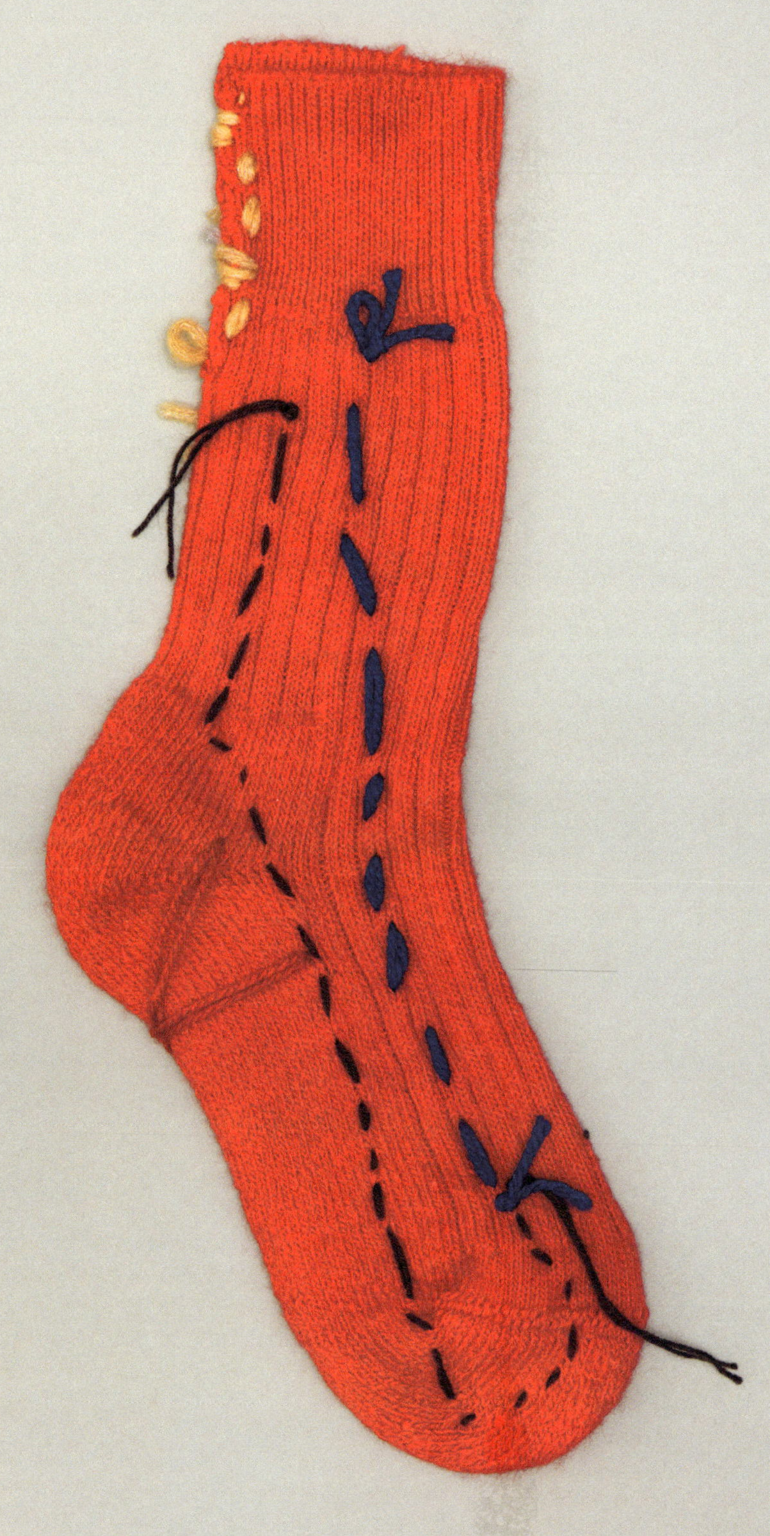

Jedidiah

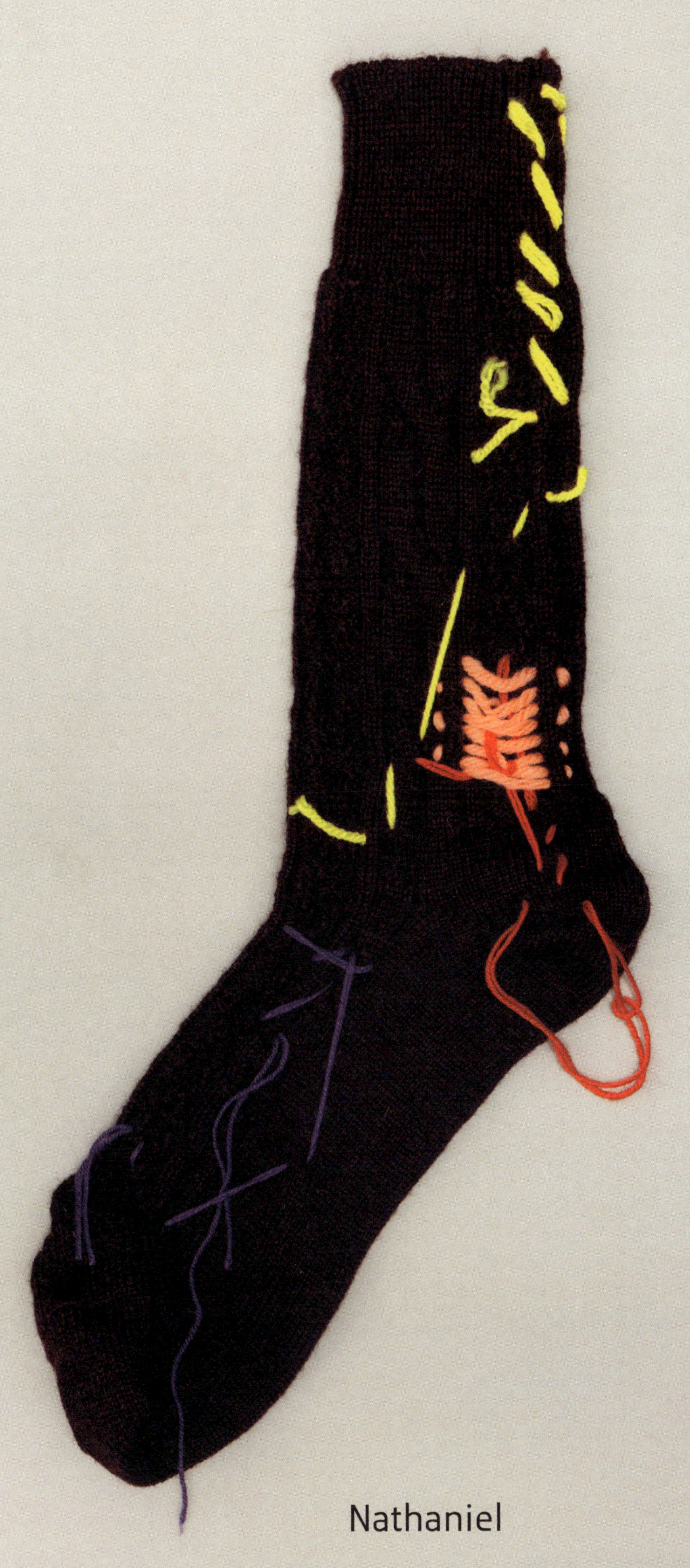

Nathaniel

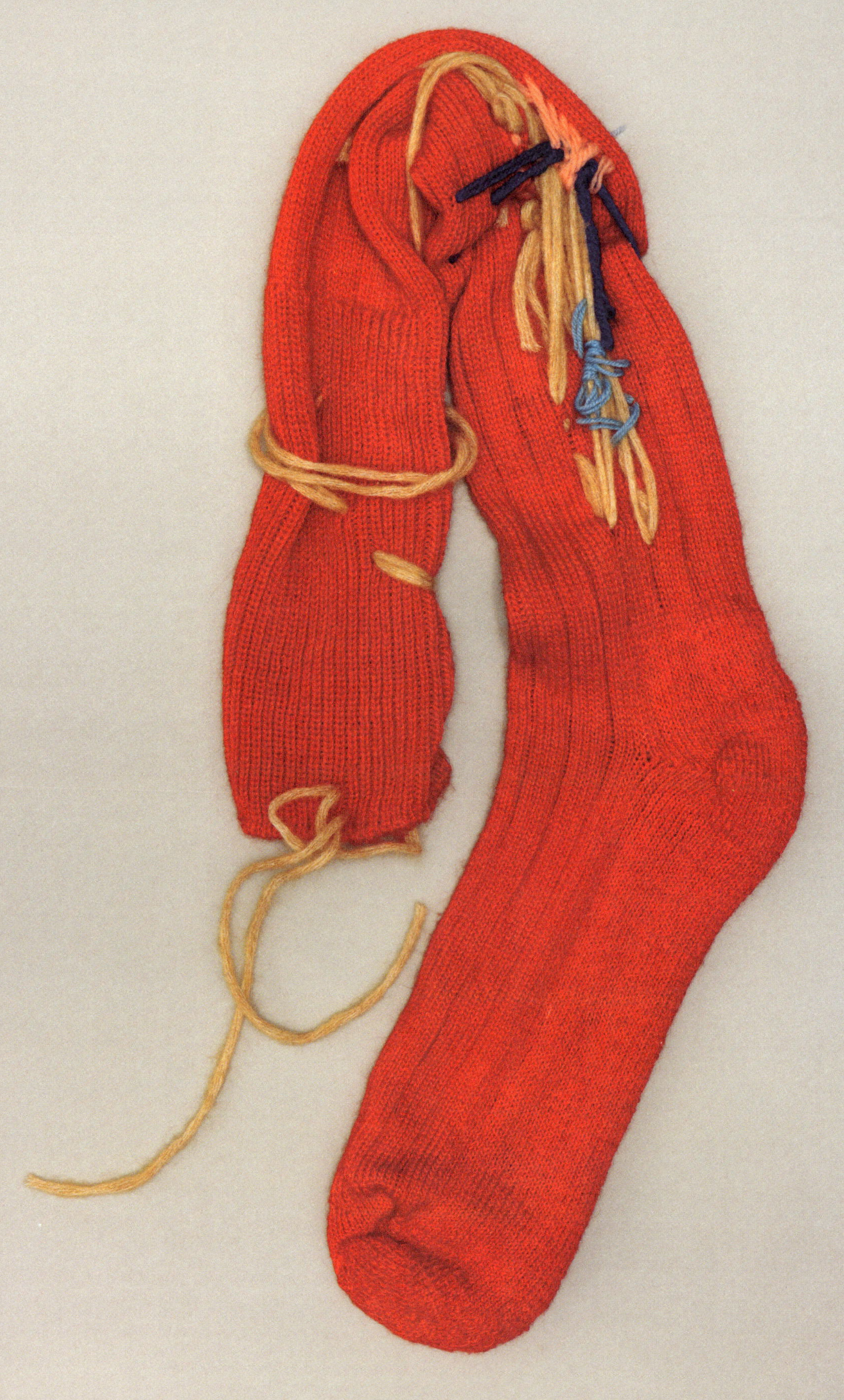

Hosain

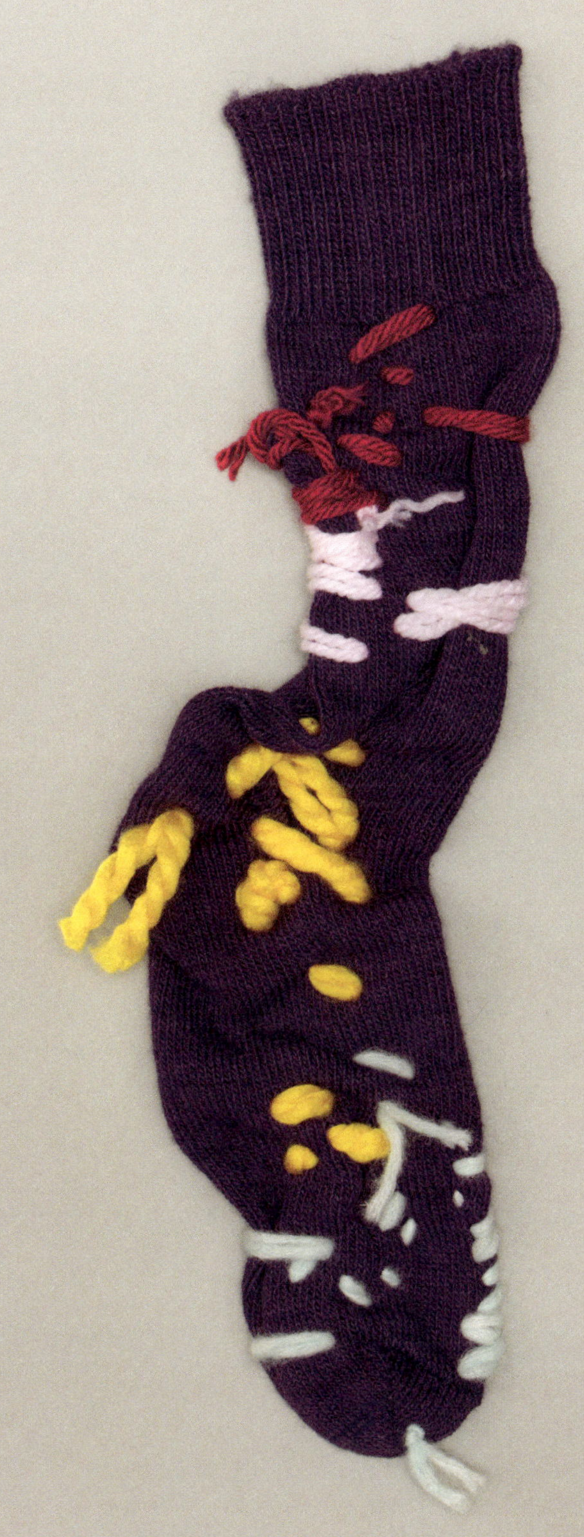

Aisha

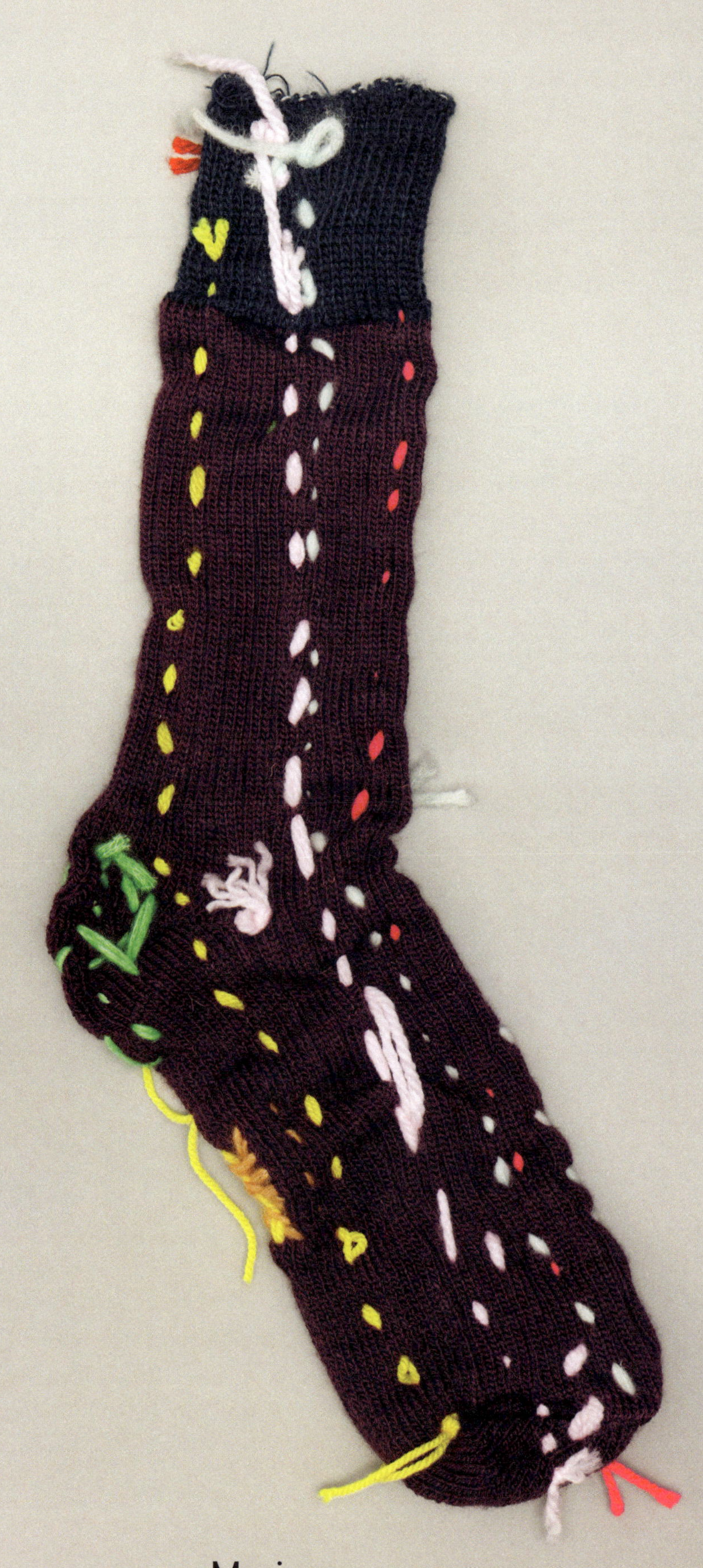

Mariam

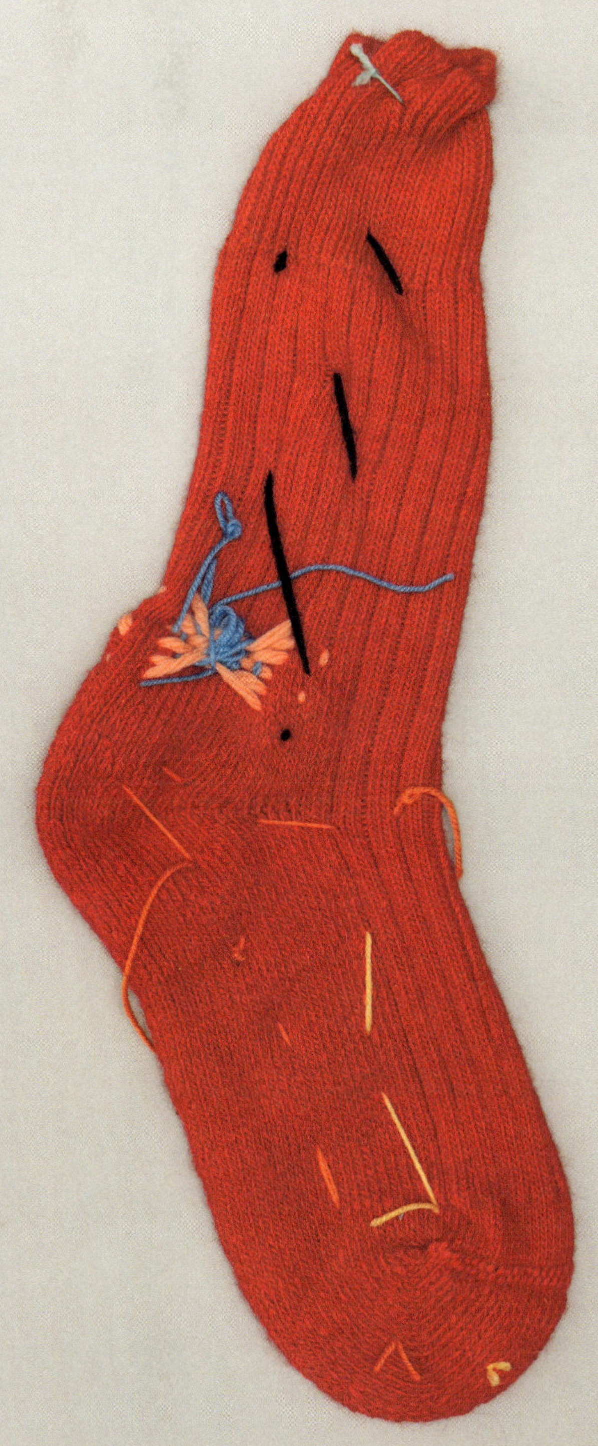

Kaydan

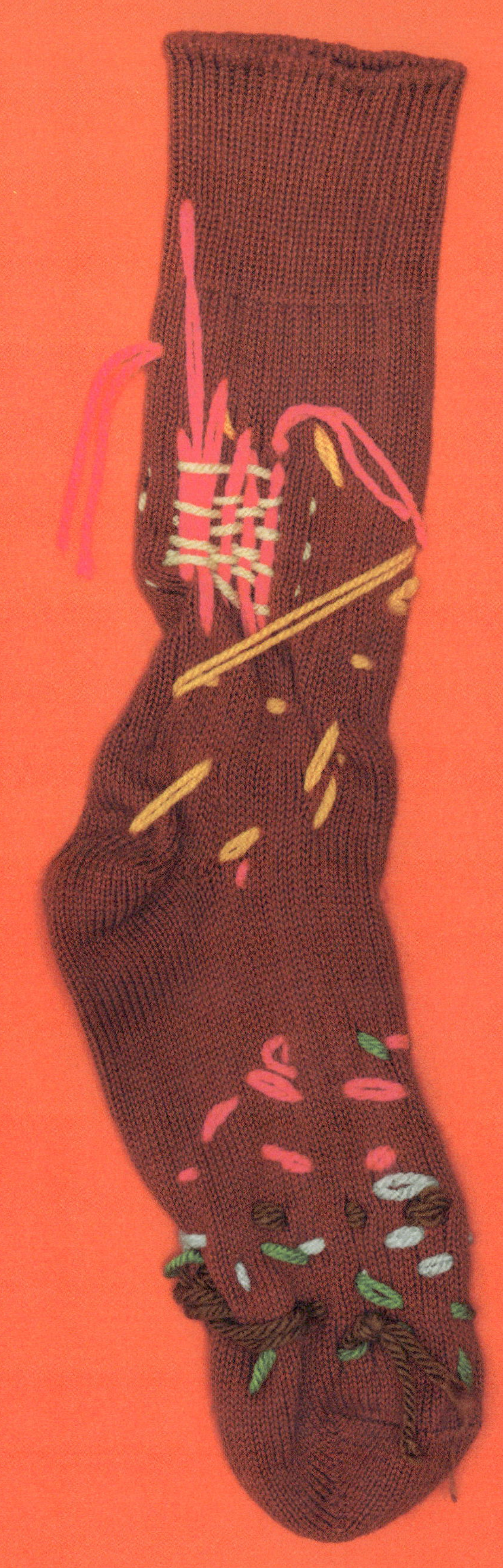

Rihaam

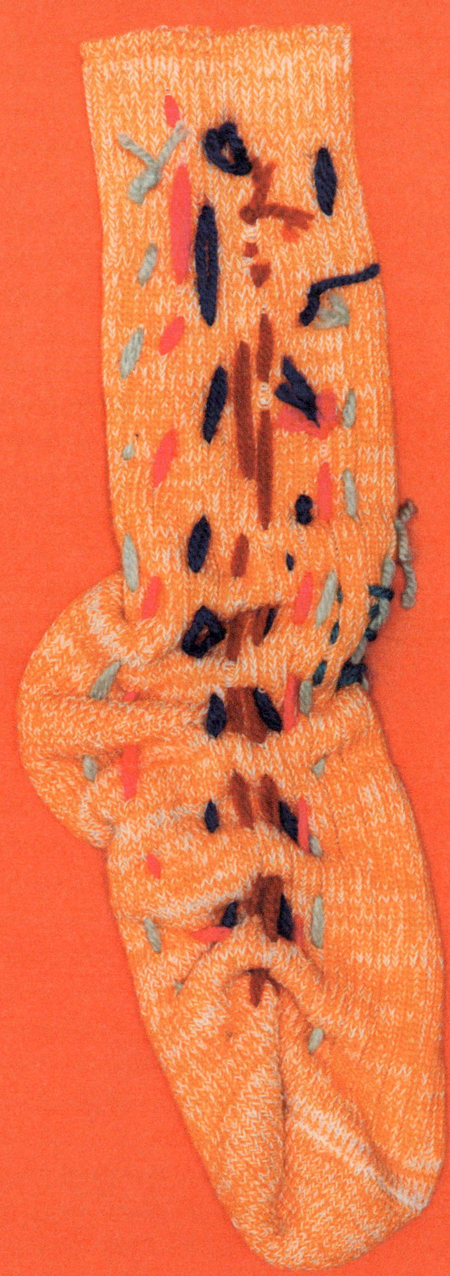

Loza

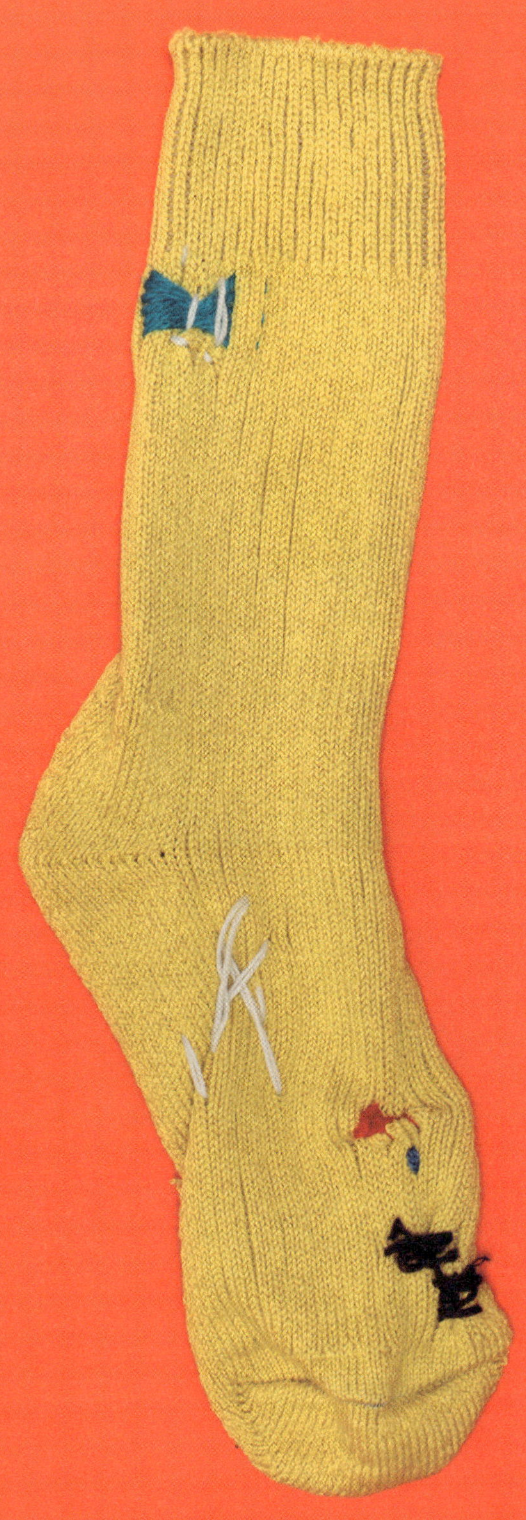

Abdurrahman

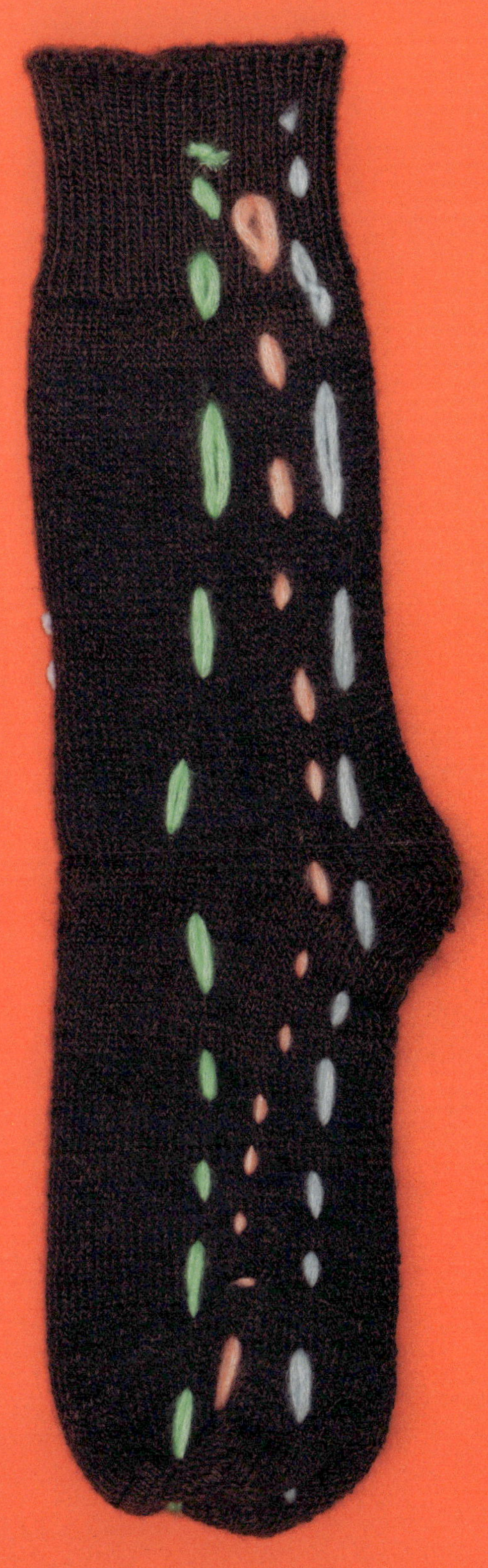

Makeda

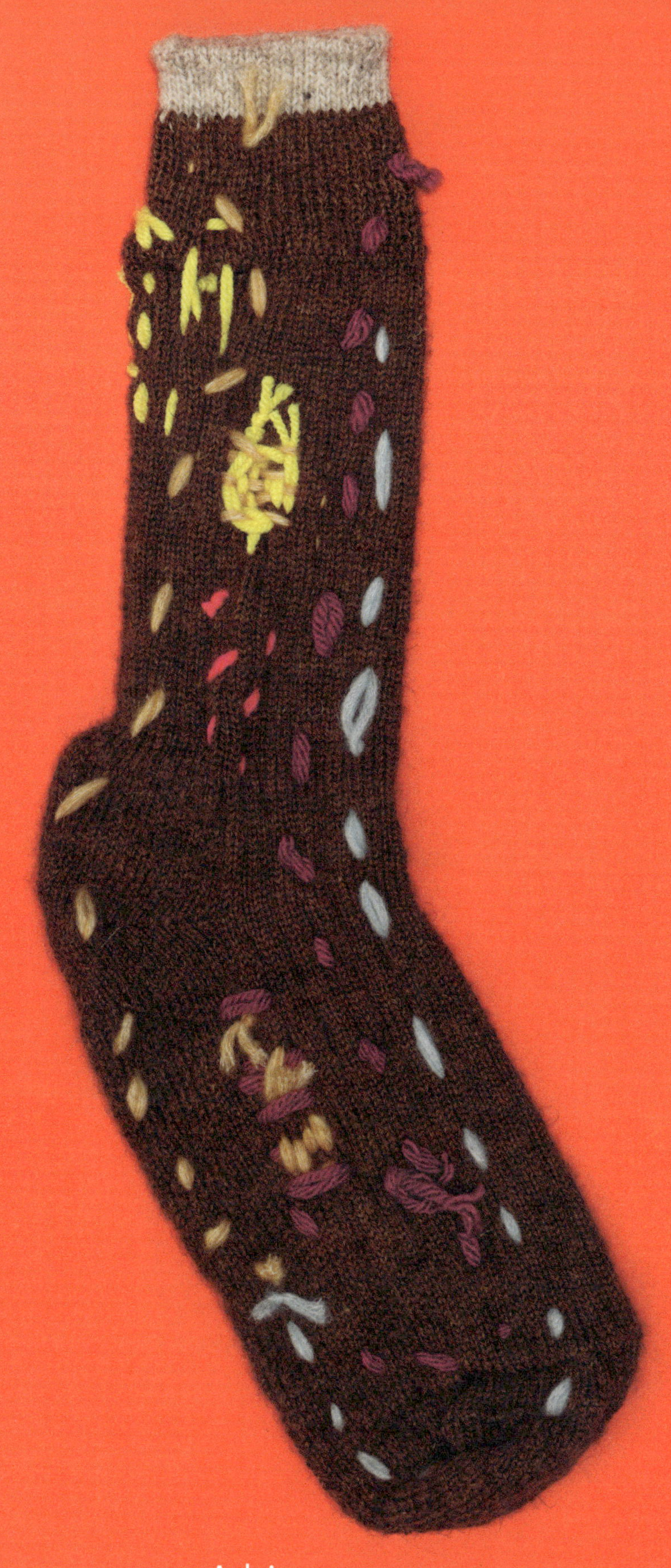

Adriana

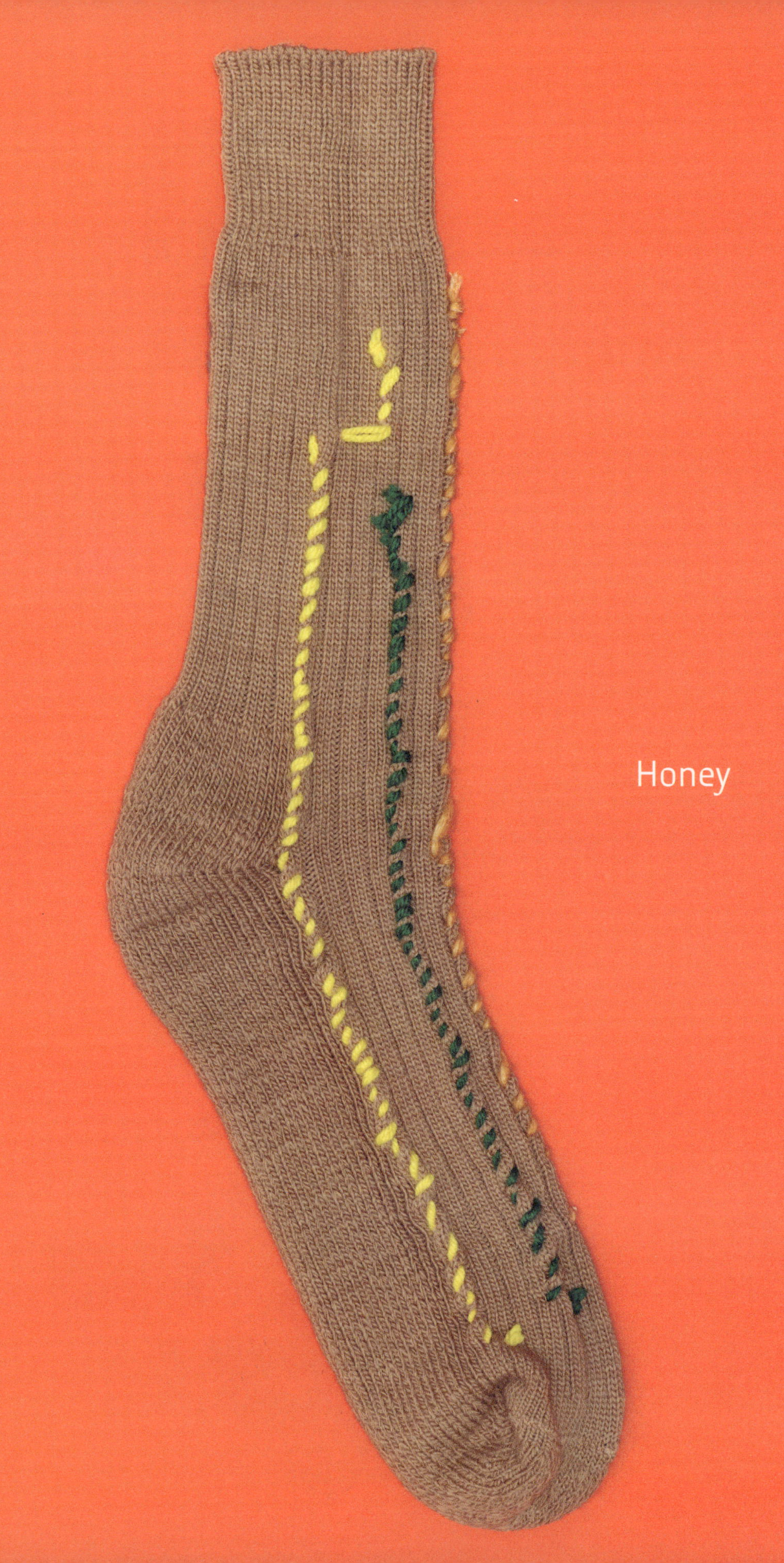

Honey

Paula

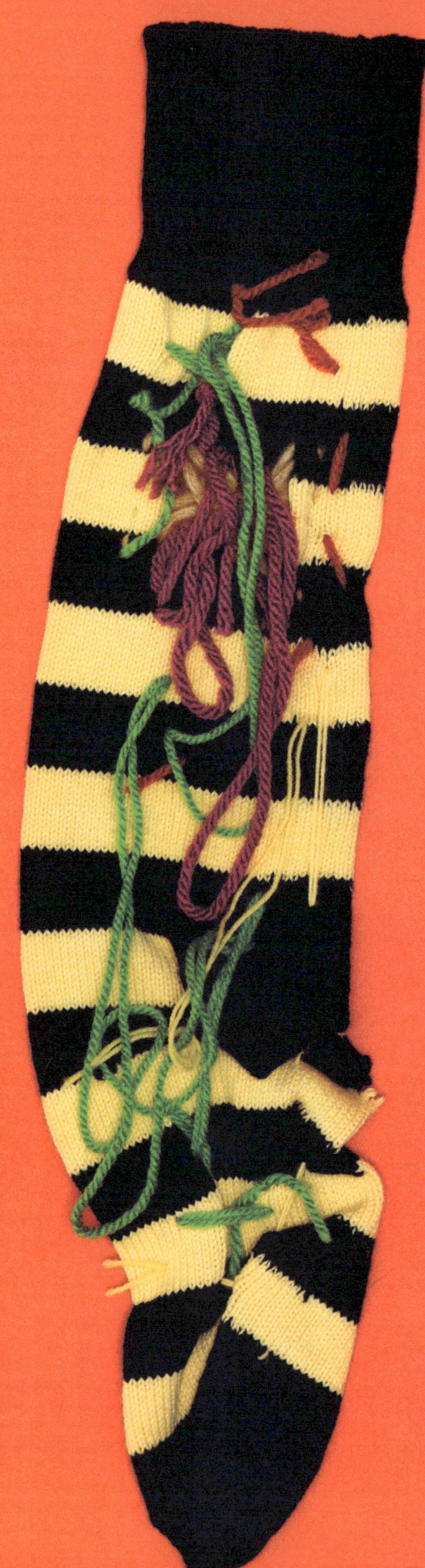

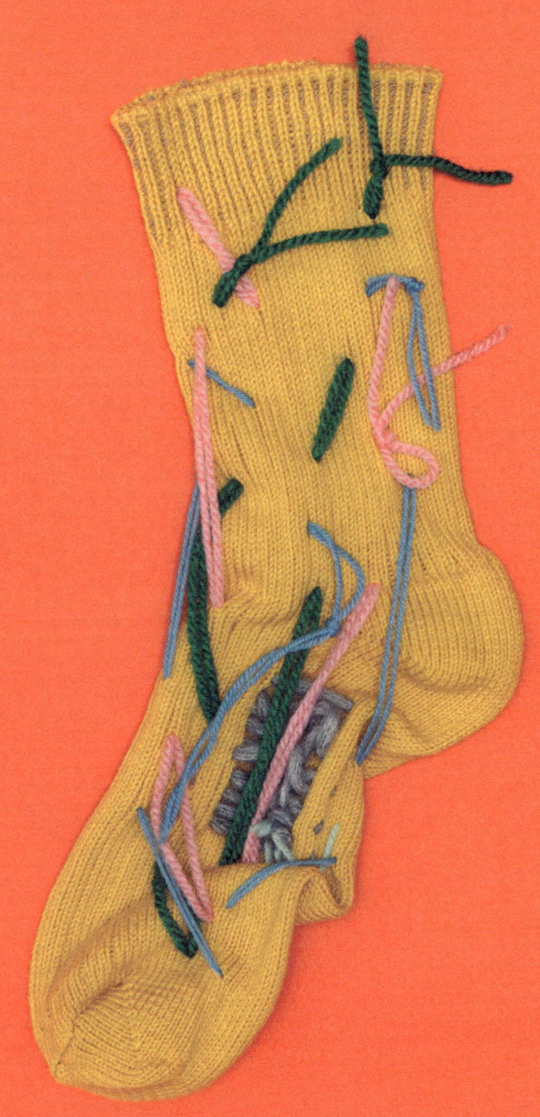

Nabila

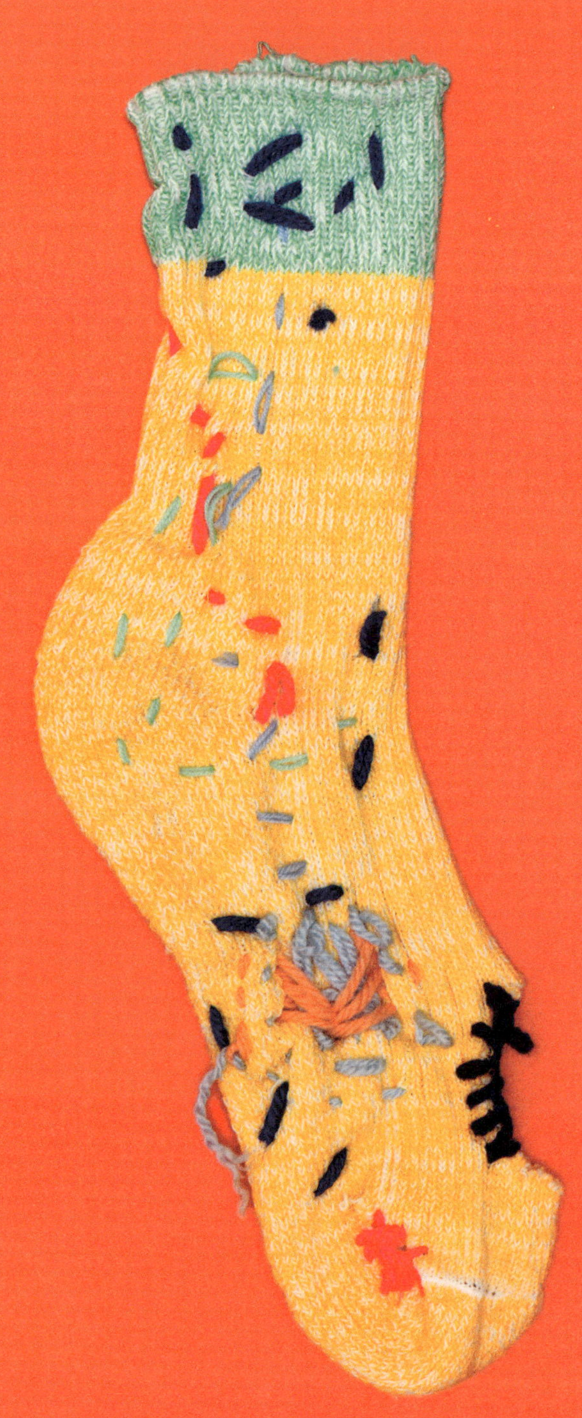

Maryam

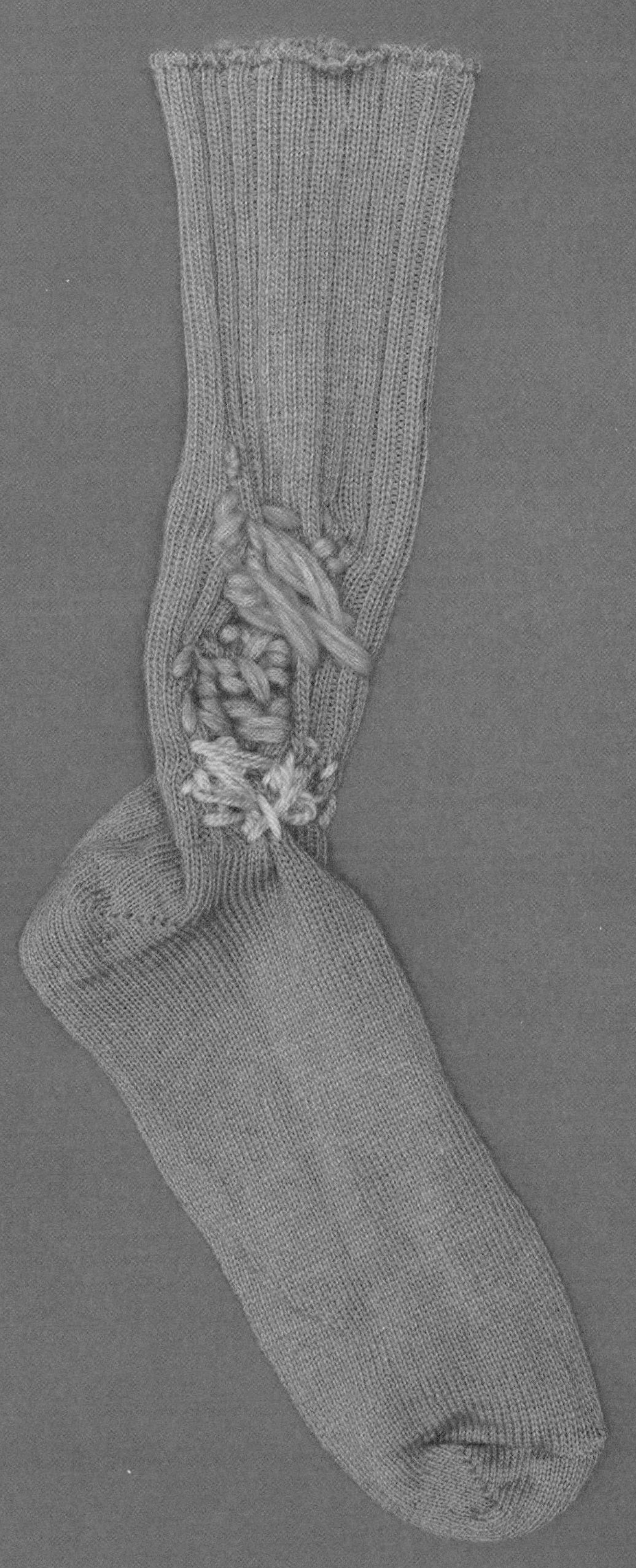

Eunice

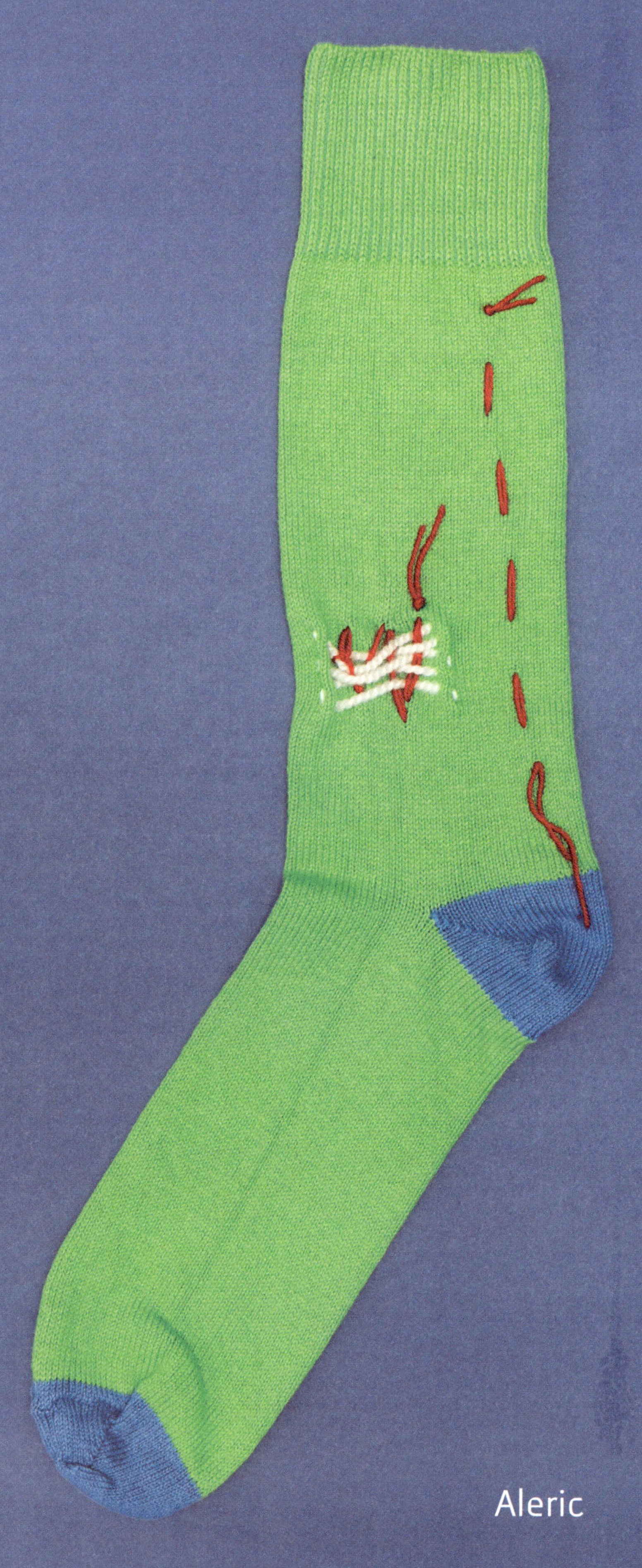

Aleric

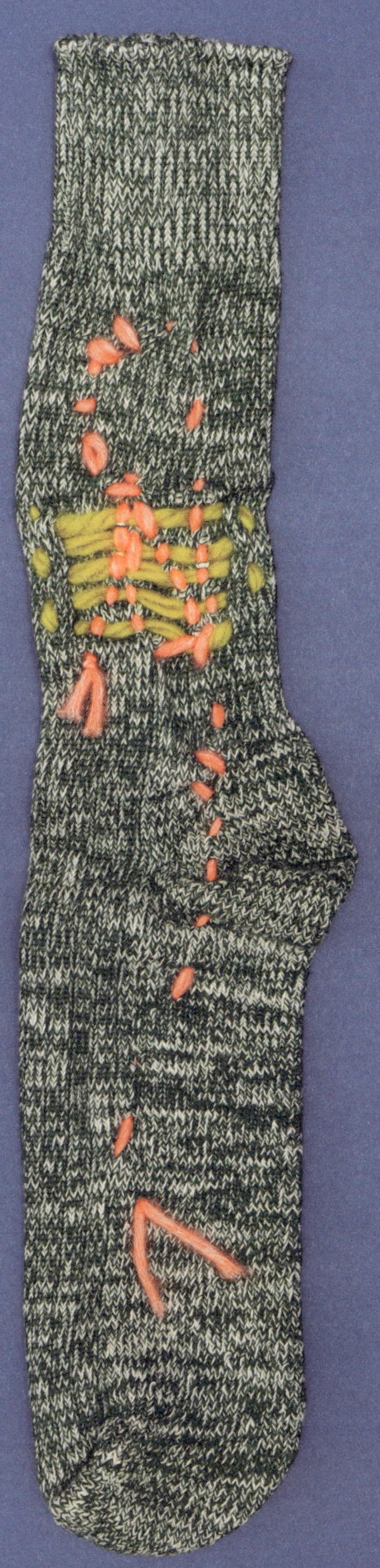

Naadir

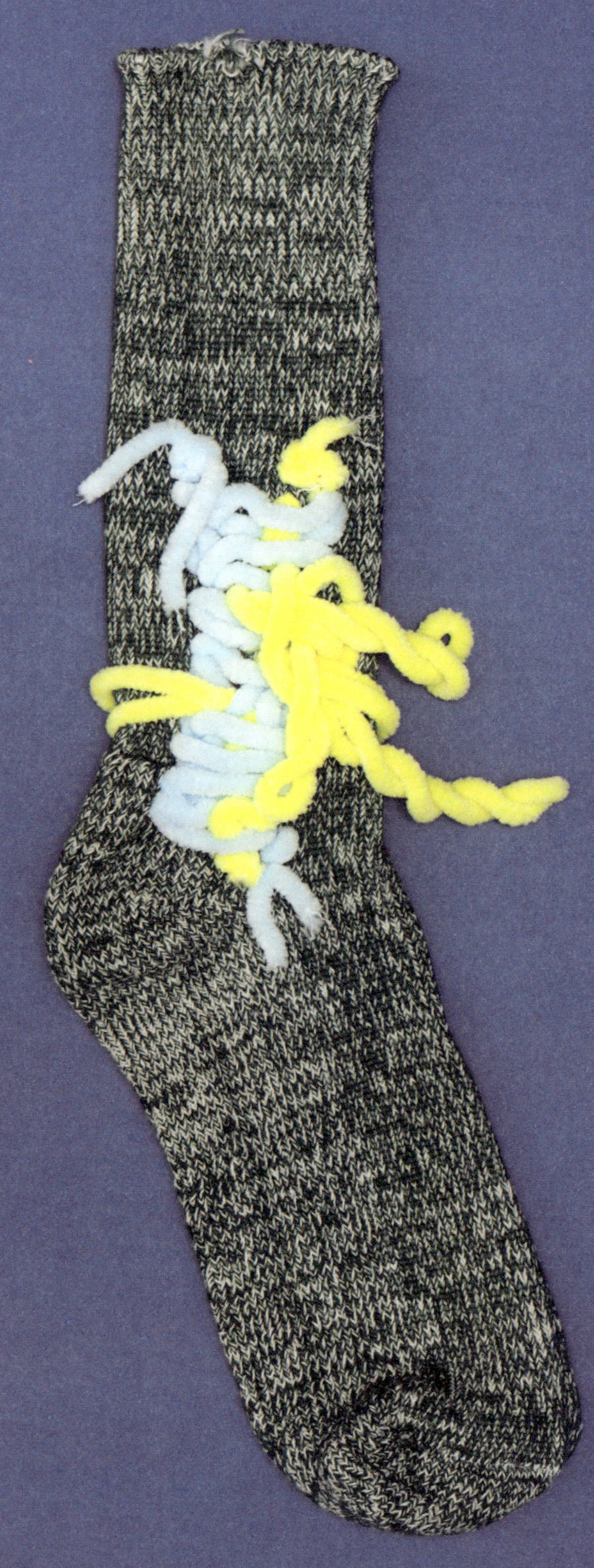

Artem

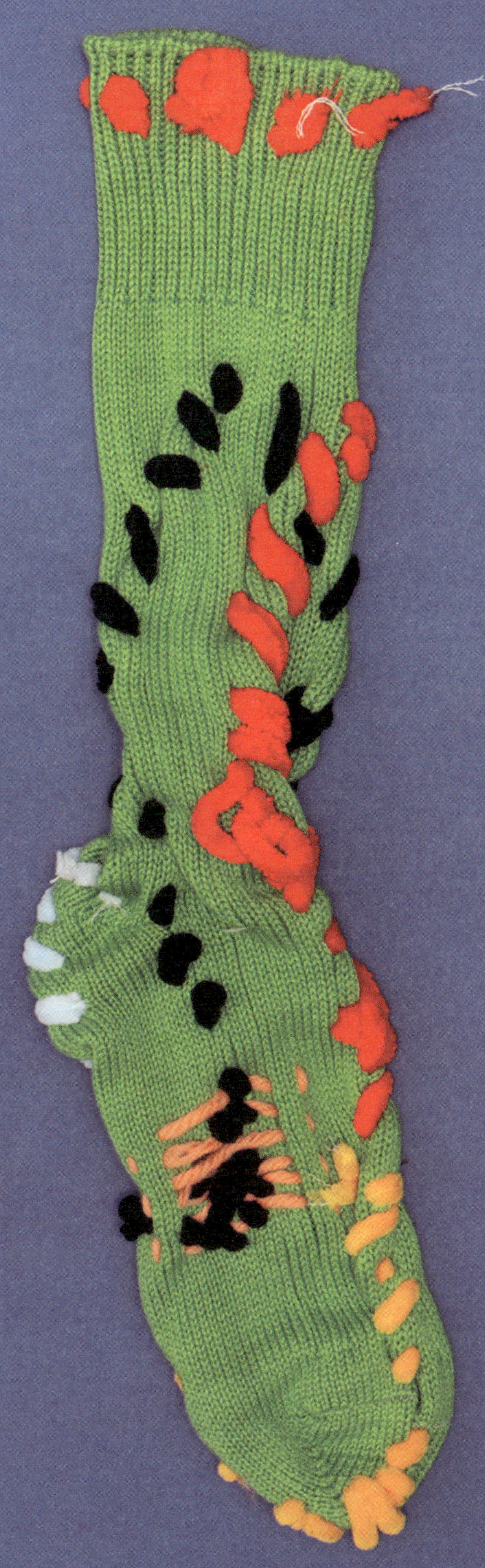

Halima

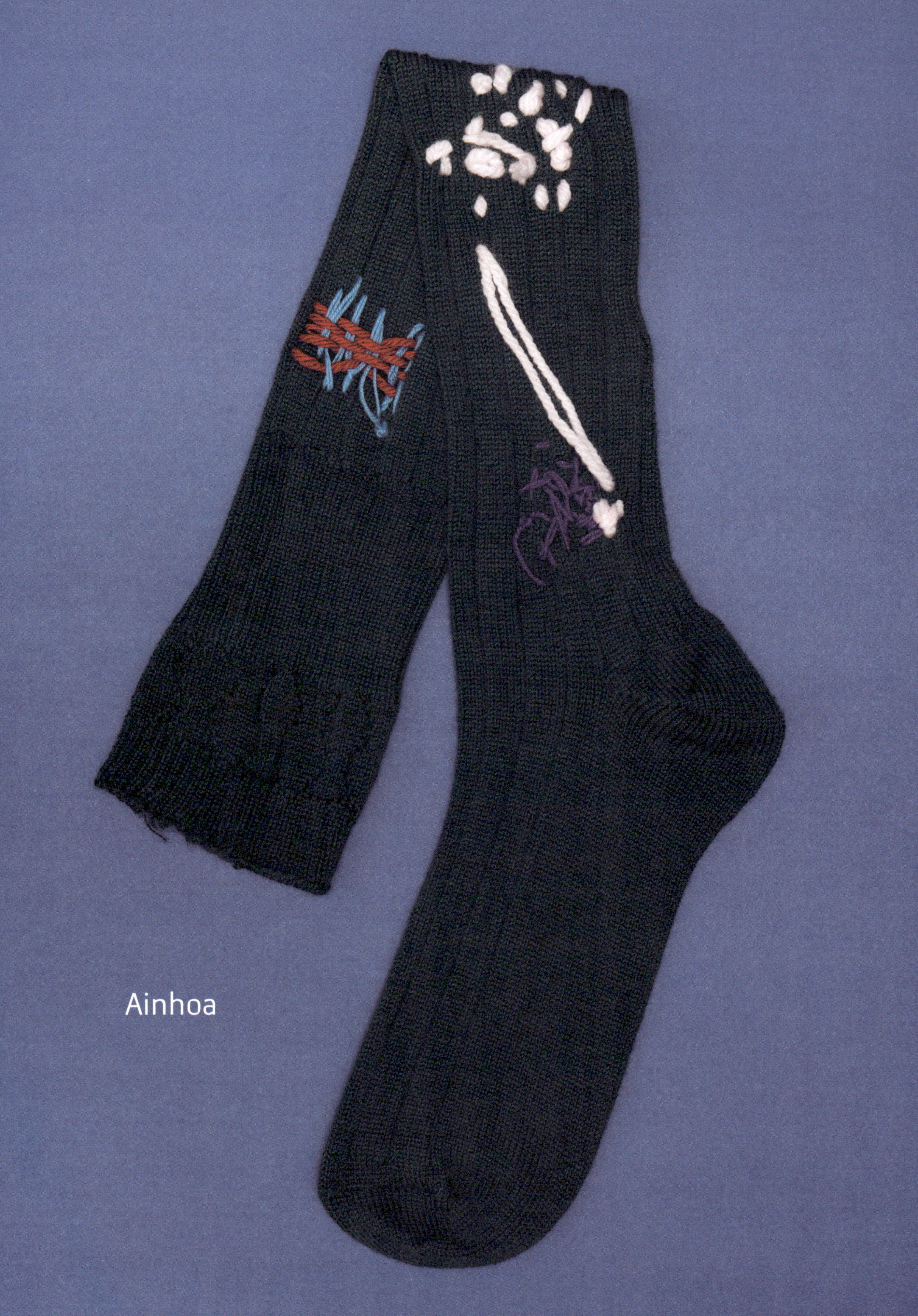

Ainhoa

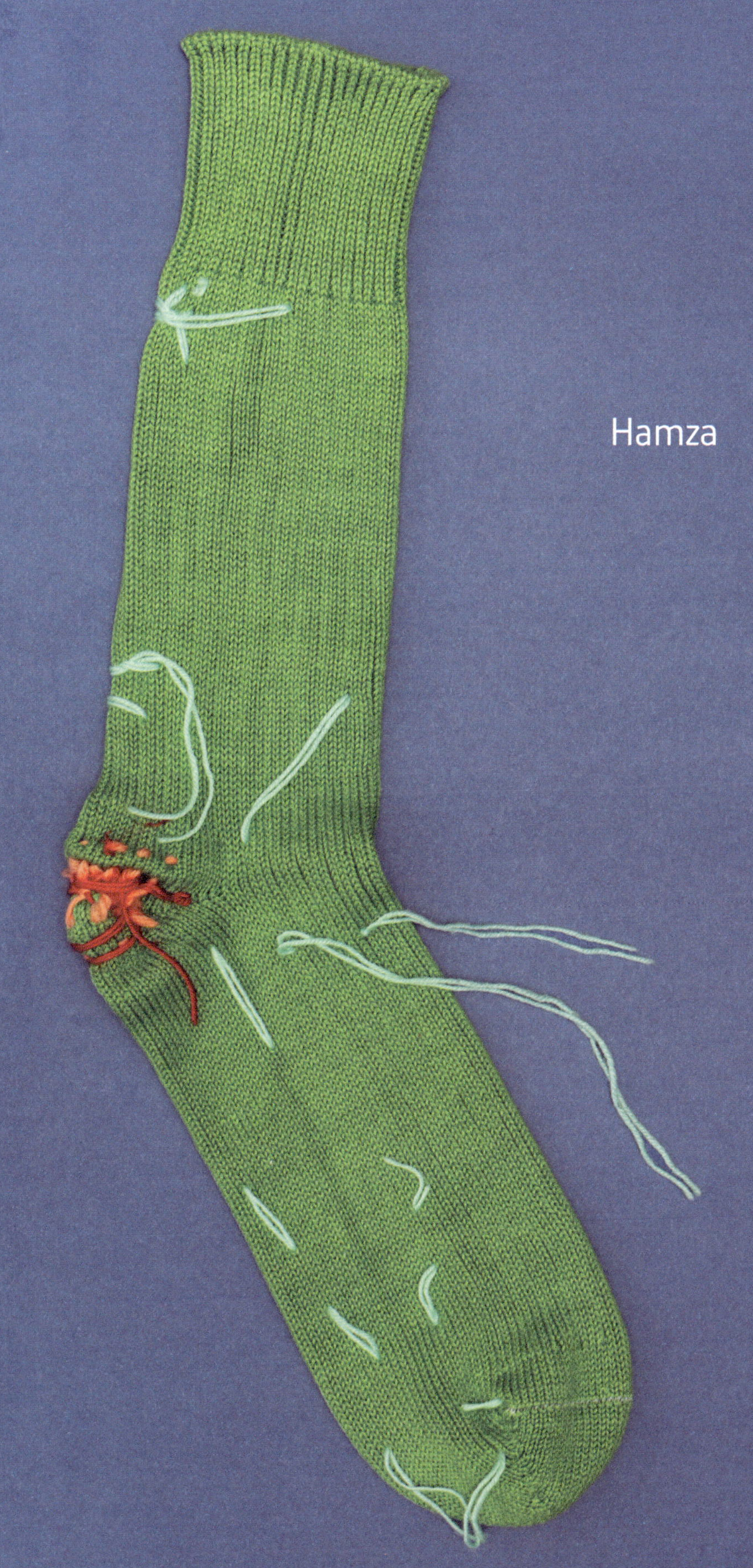

Hamza

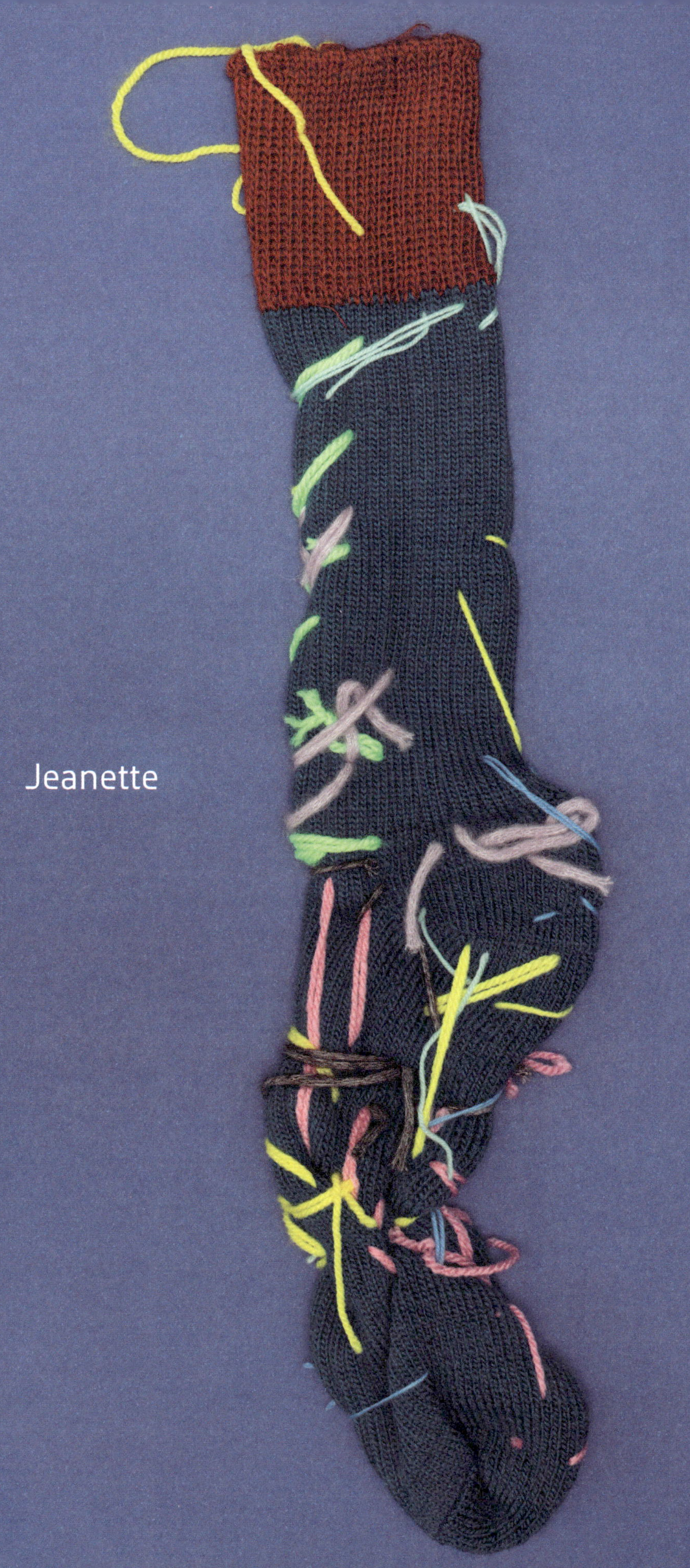

Jeanette

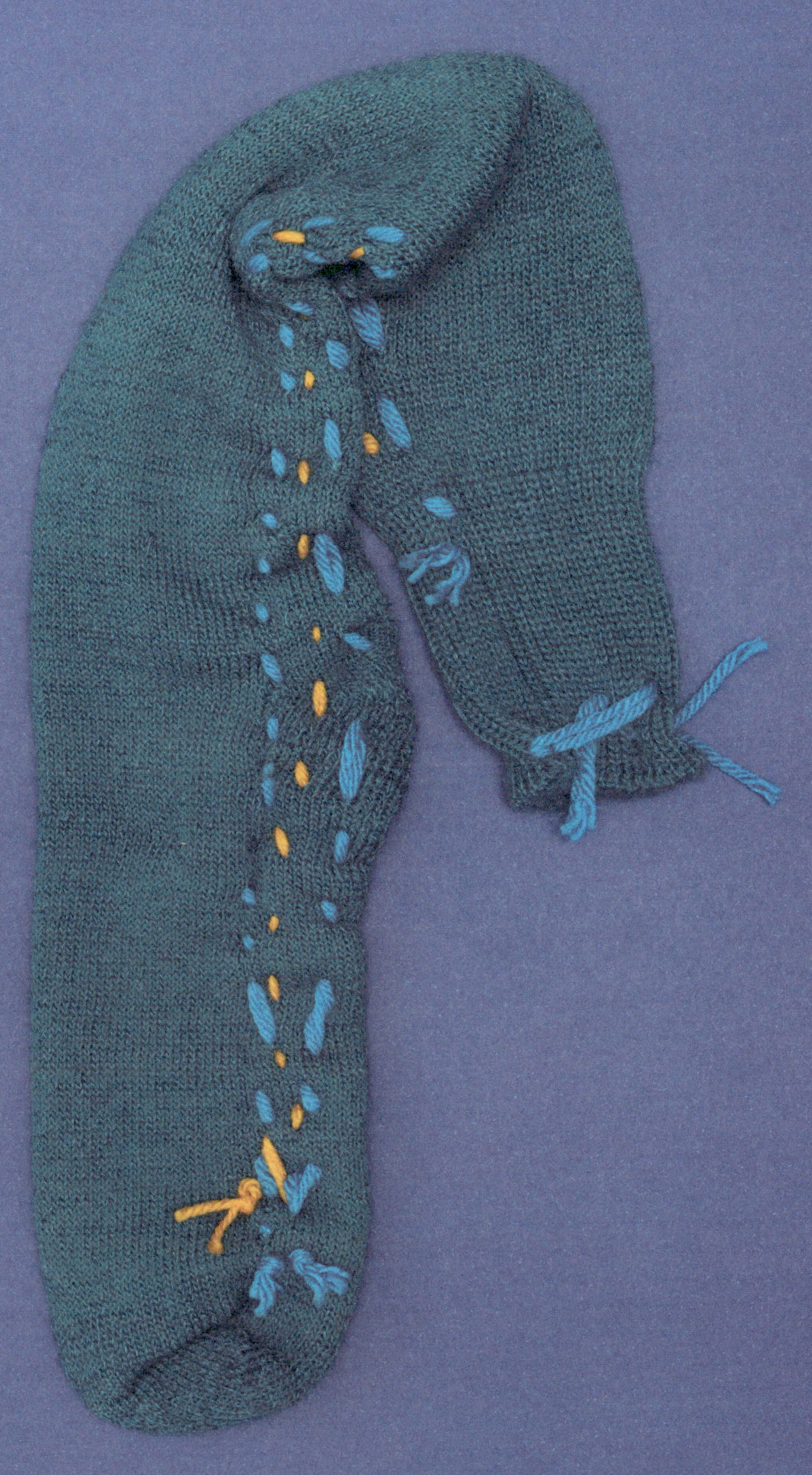

Naziah

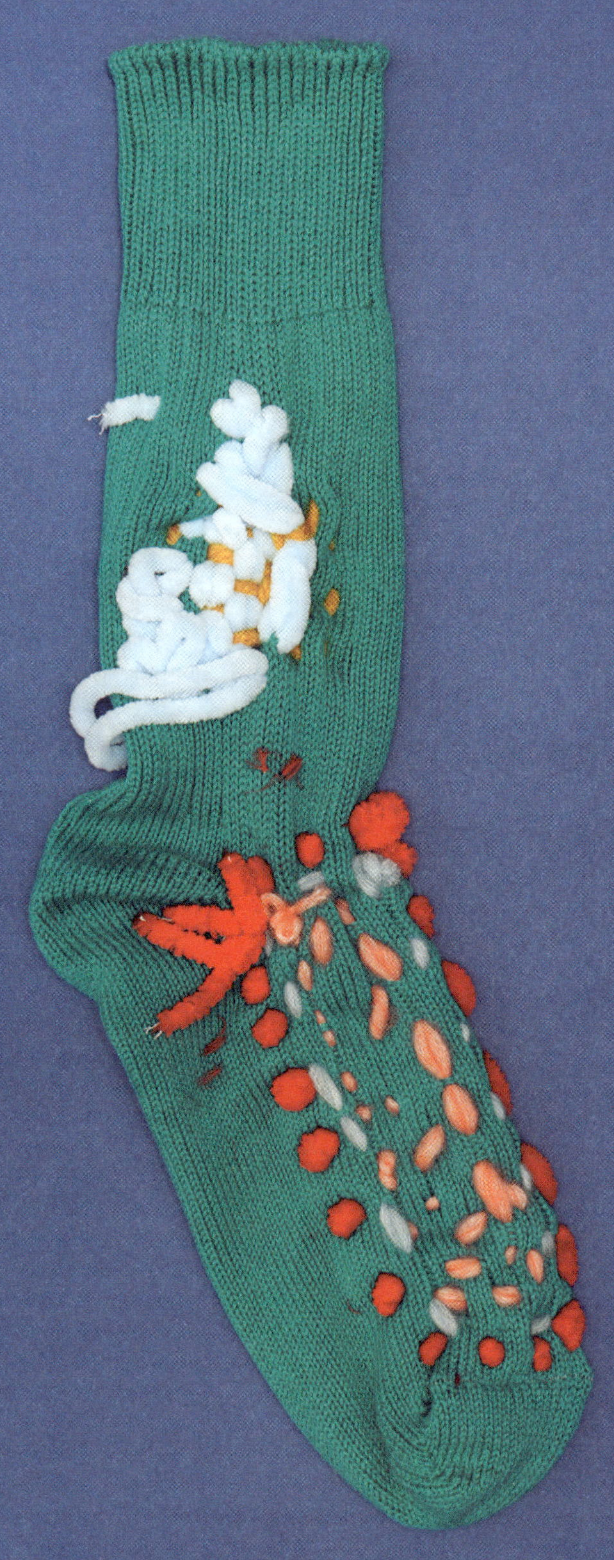

Allison

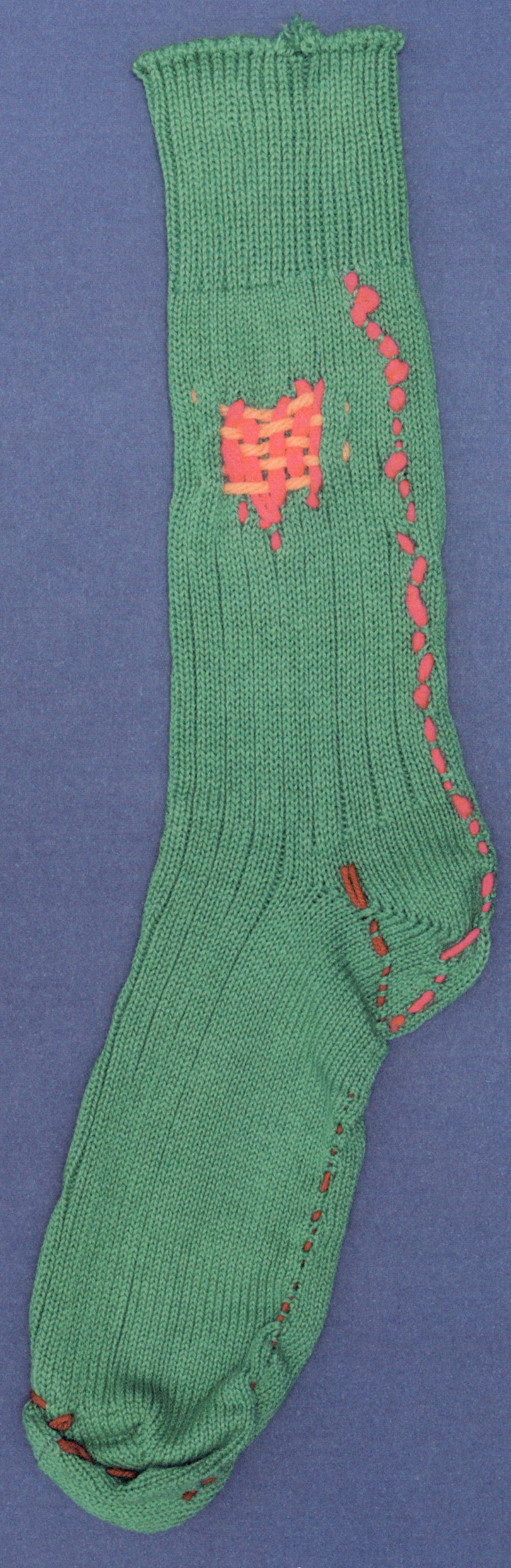

Kadija

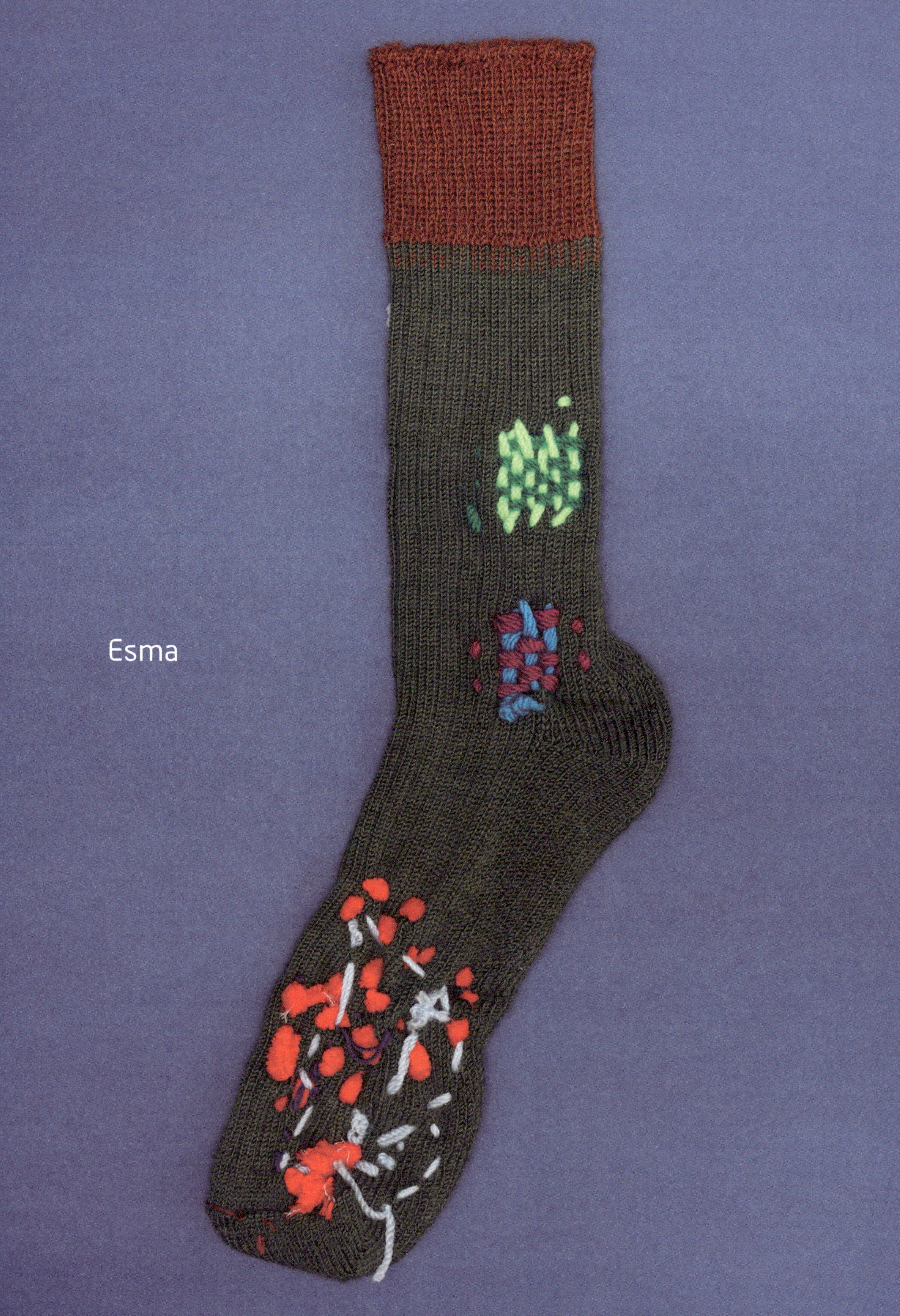

Esma

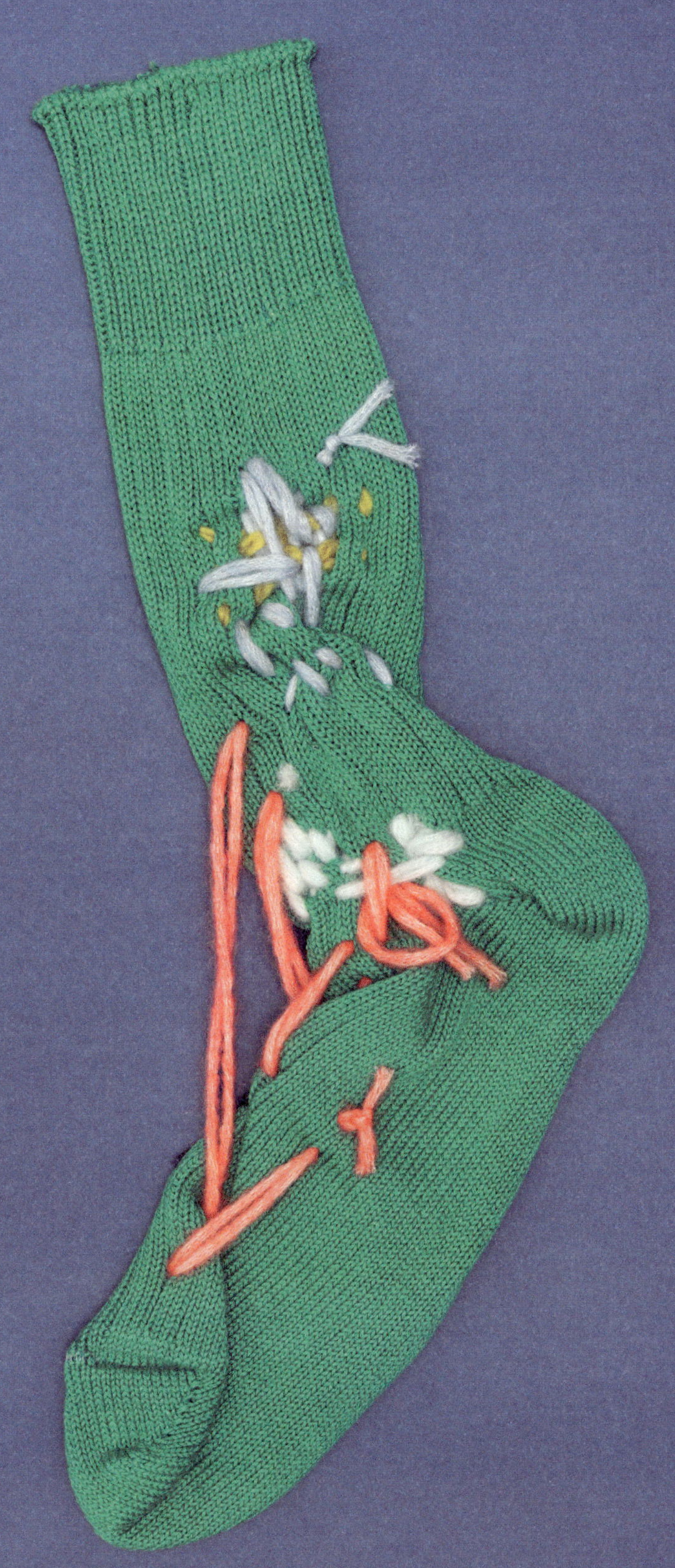

Maryam

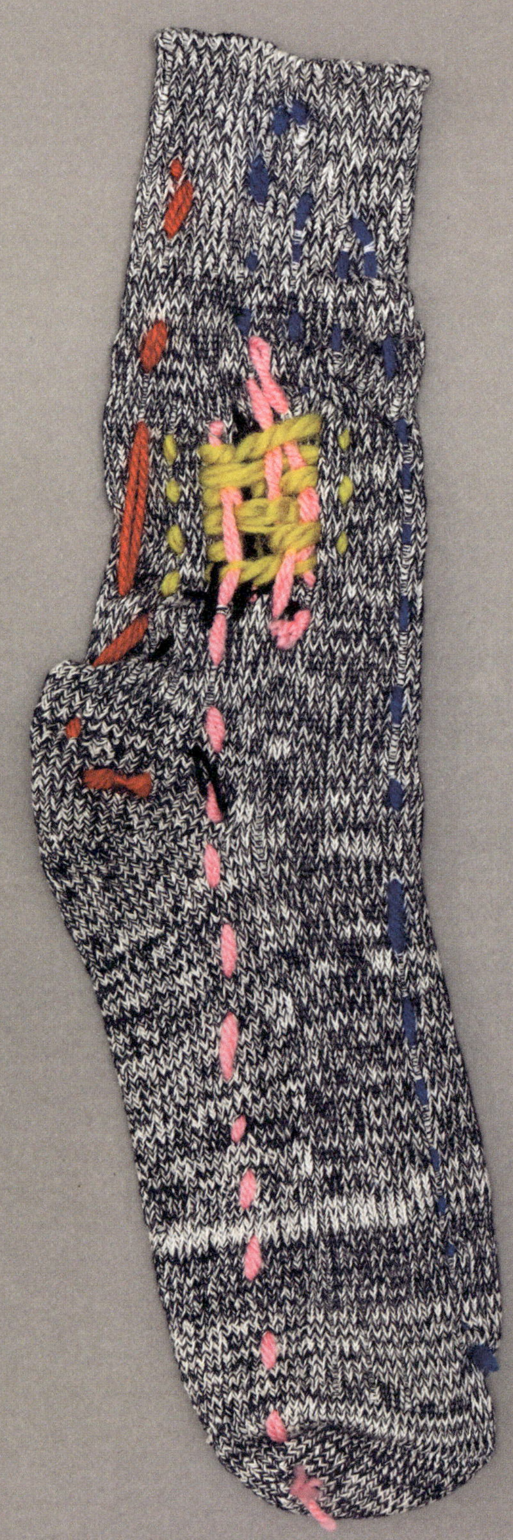

Omar

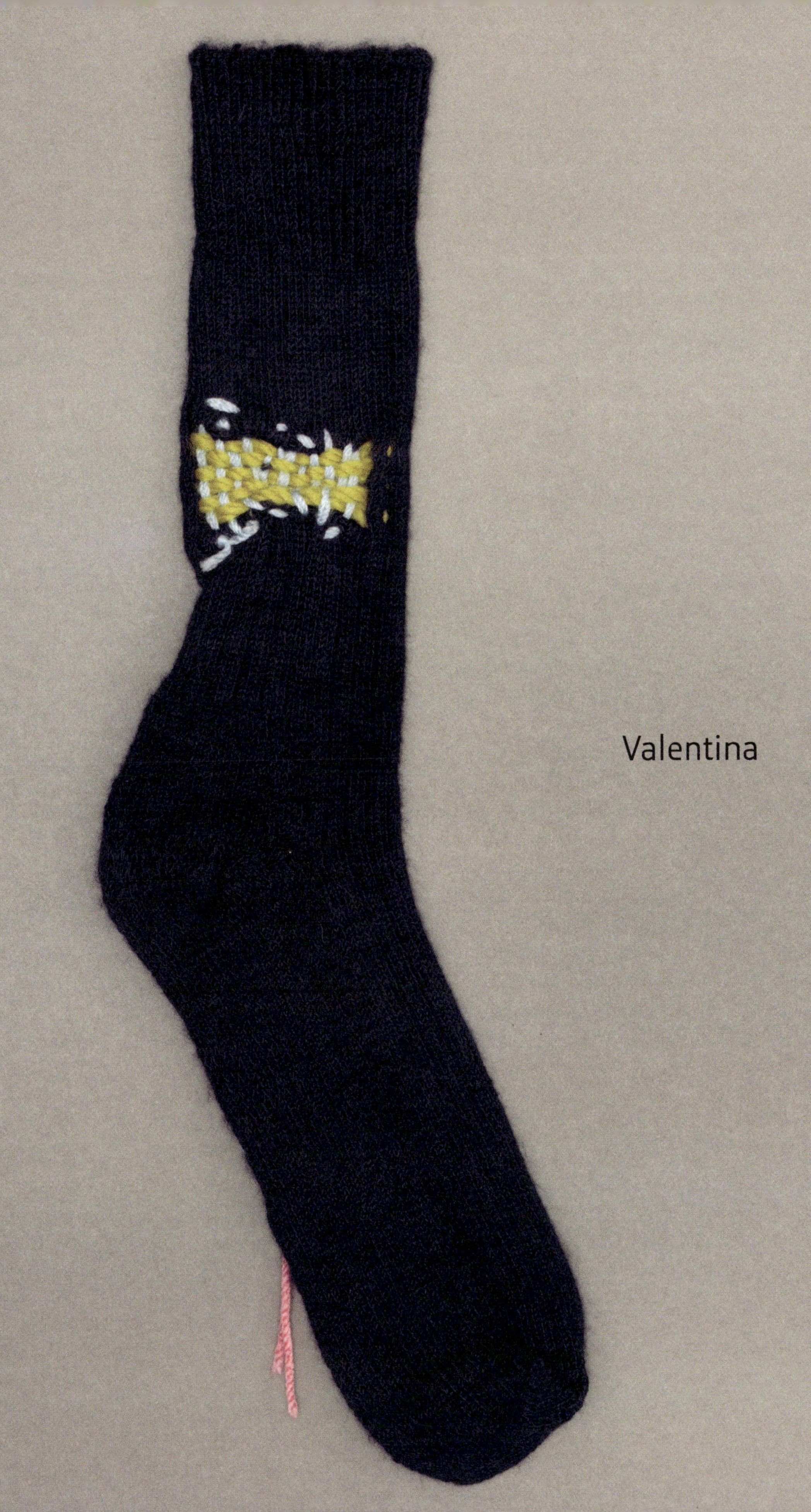

Valentina

Latifat

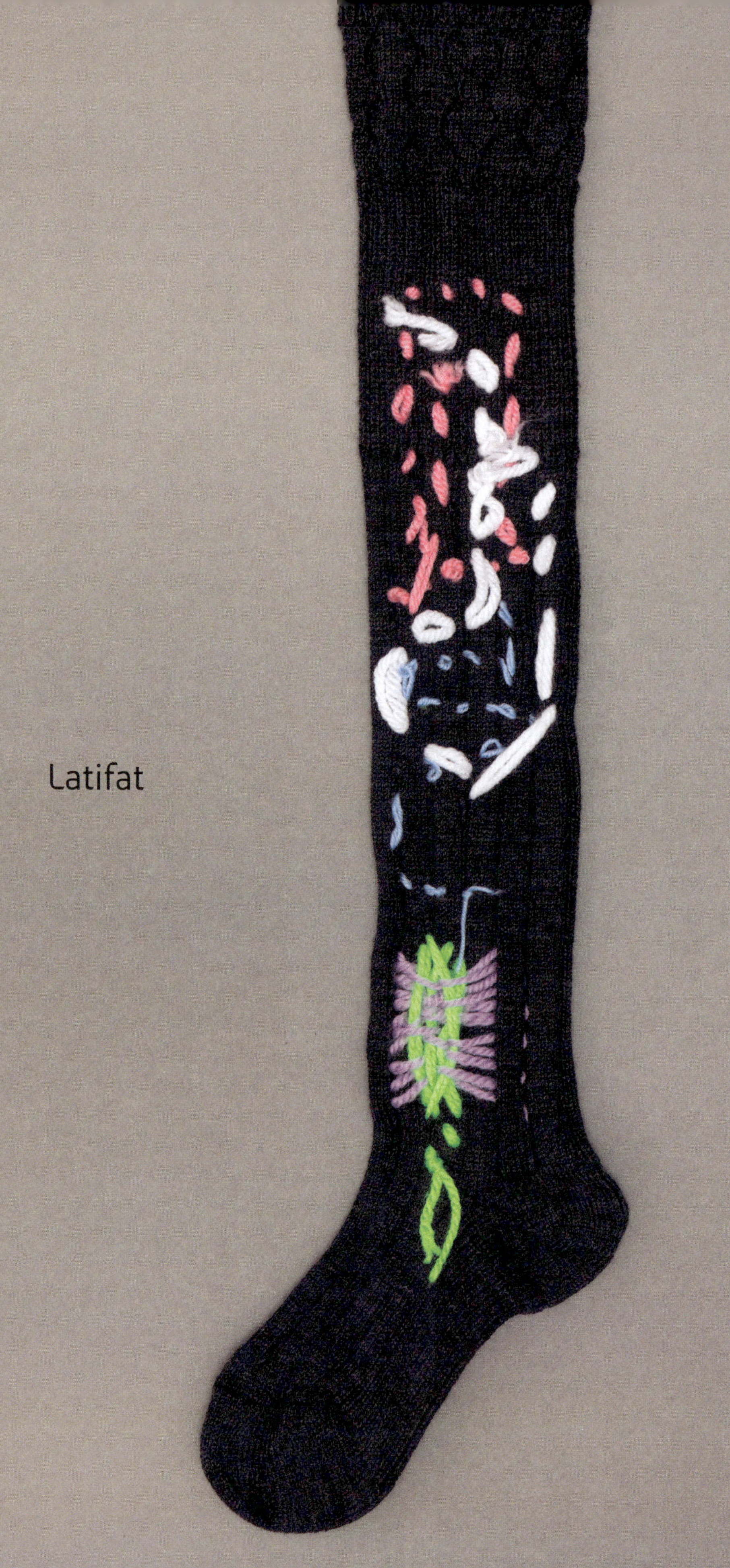

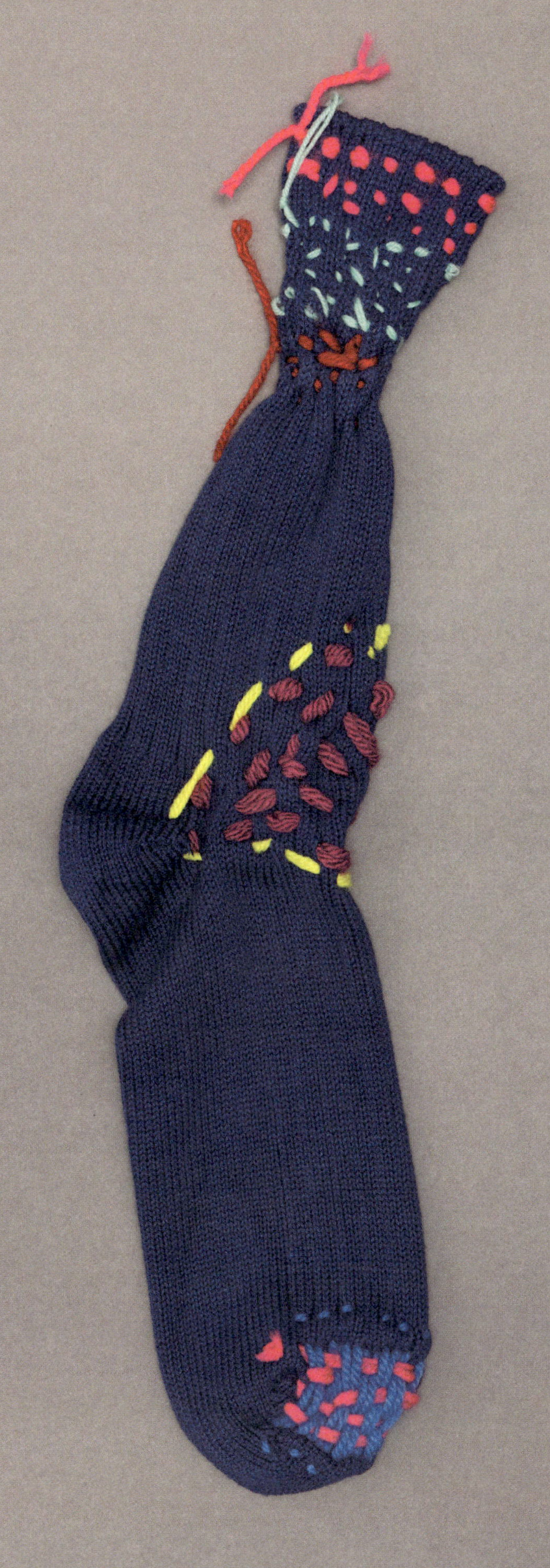

Ruth

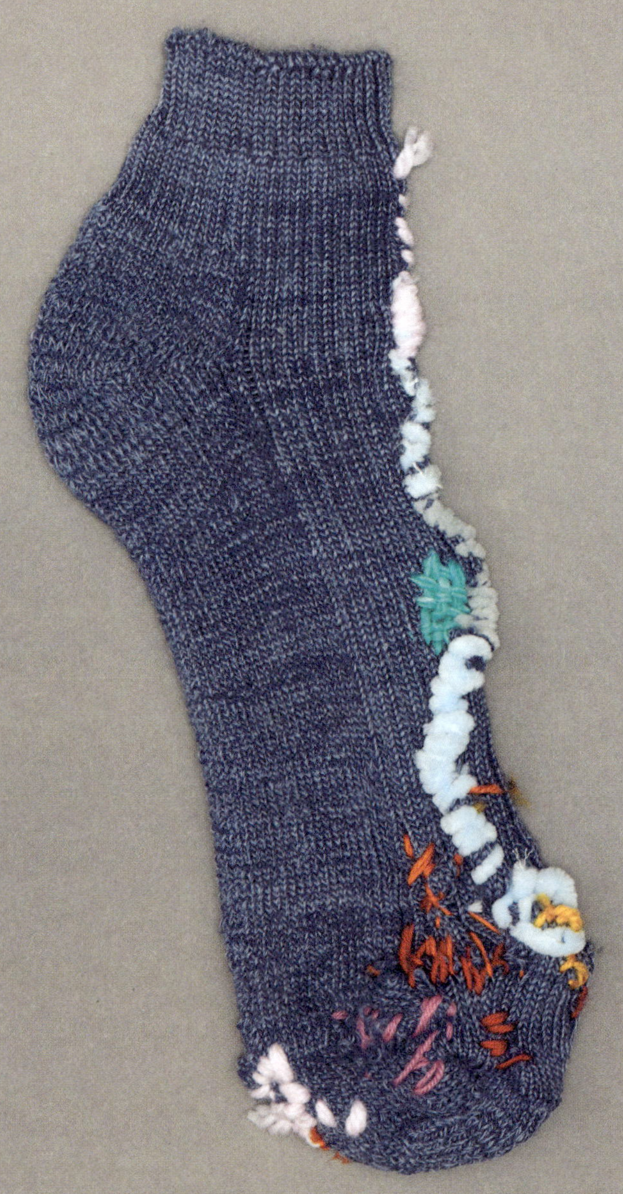

Raehanah

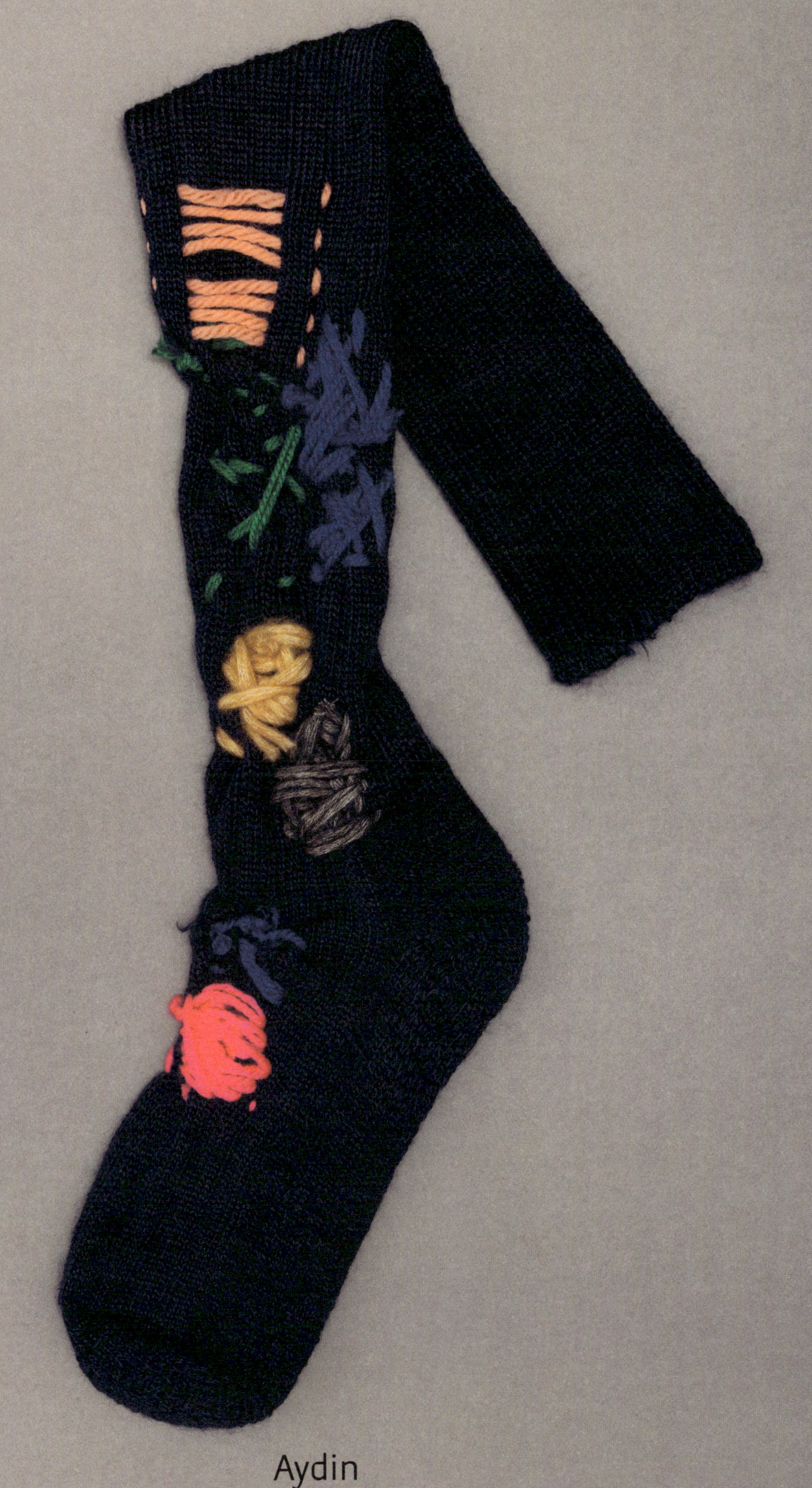

Aydin

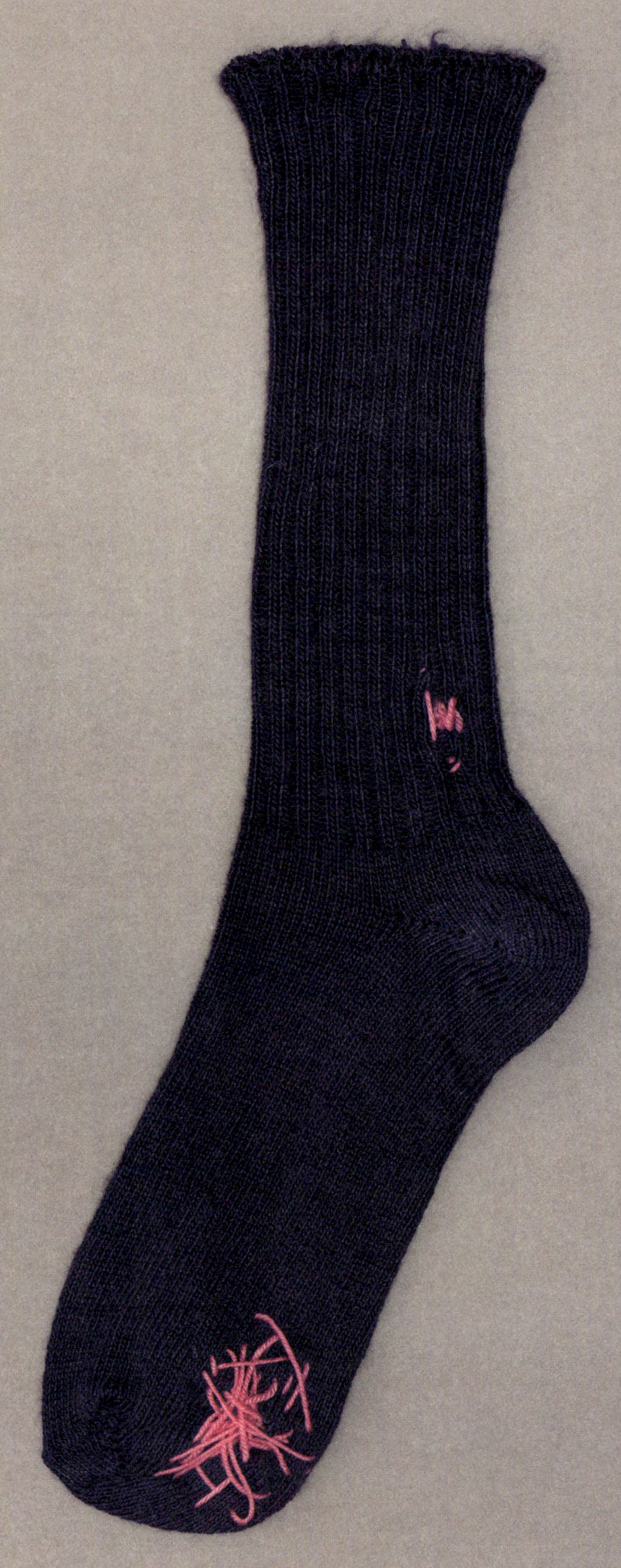

Lilliya

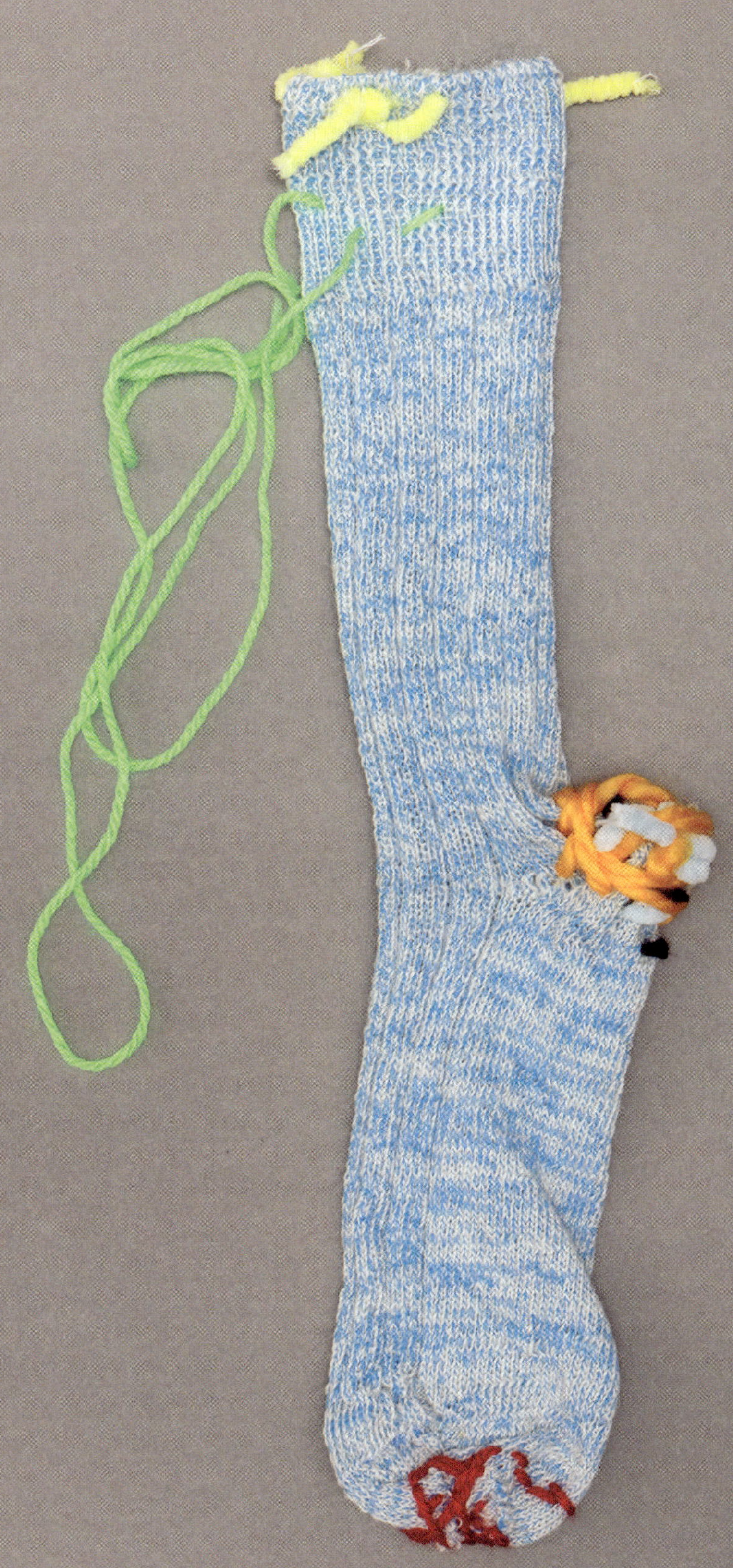

Ayaah

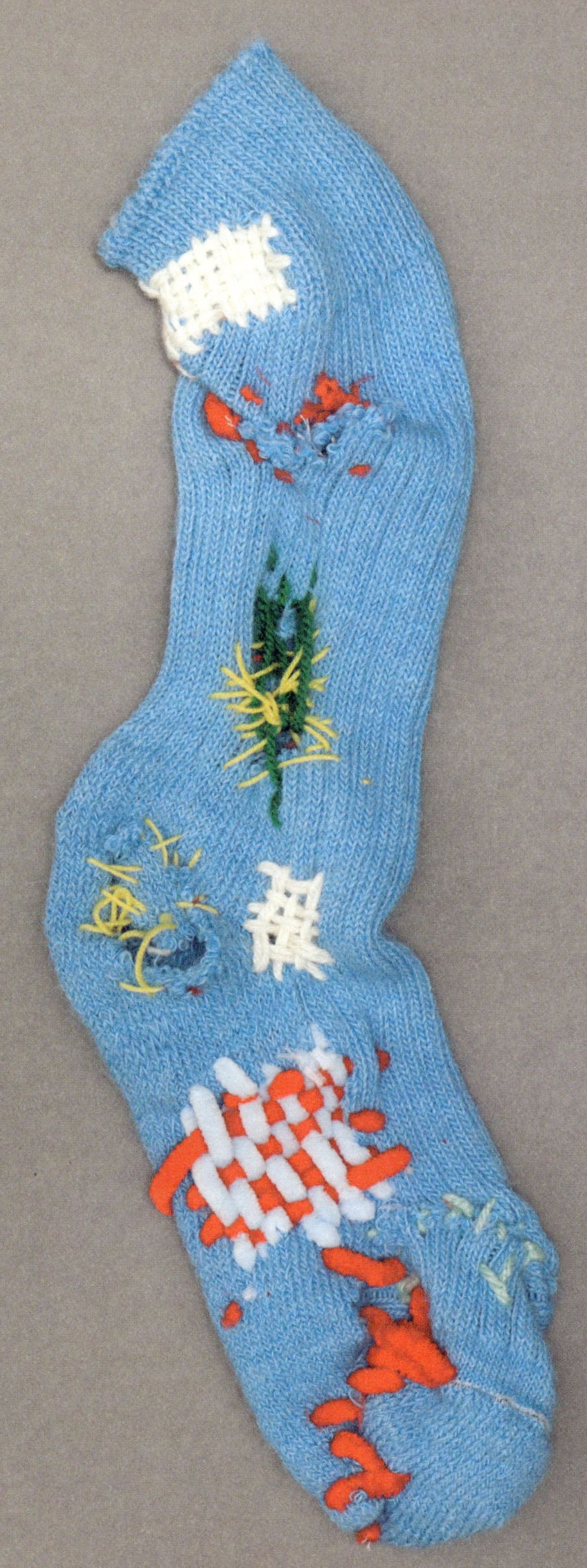

Aliyah

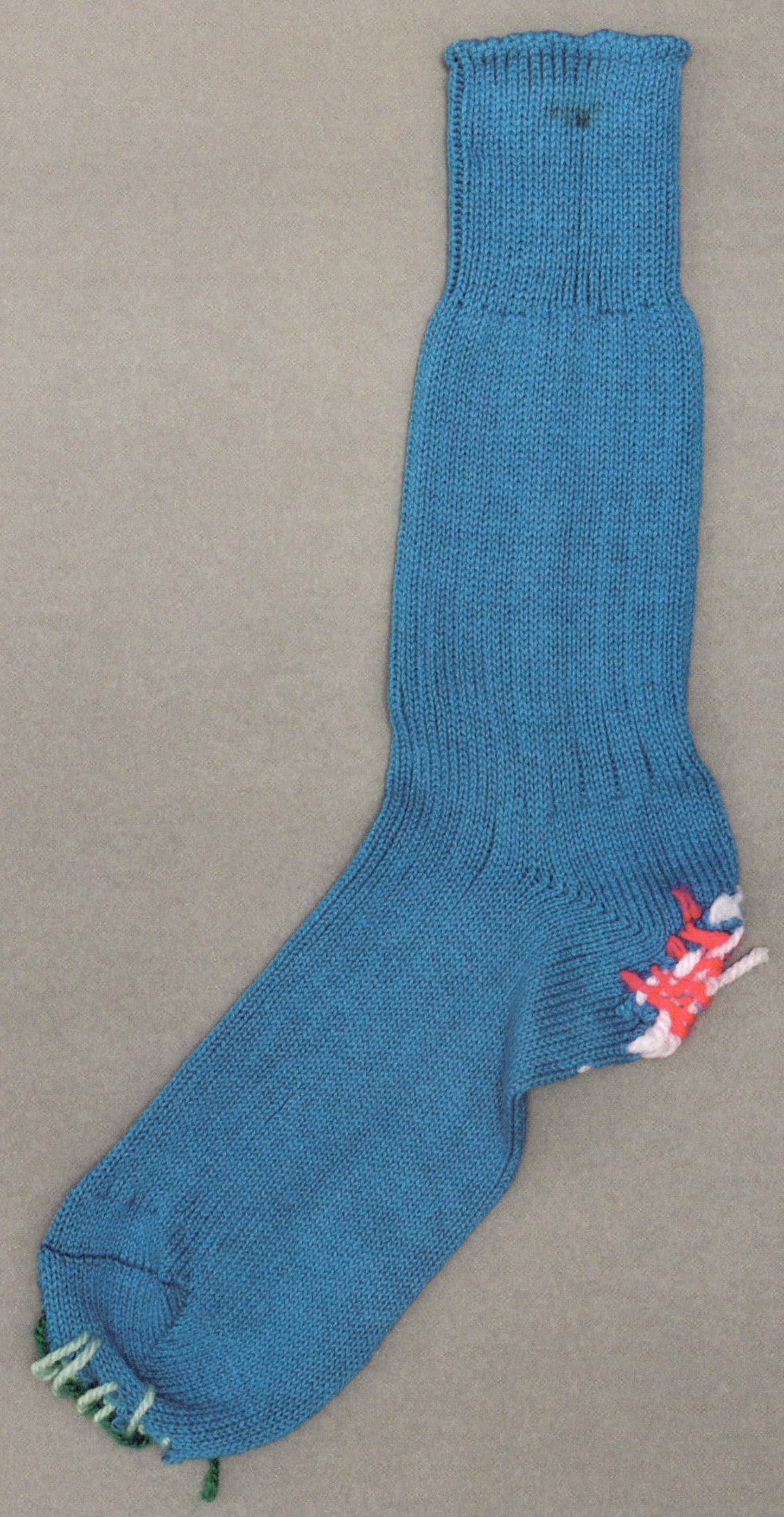

Ashraf

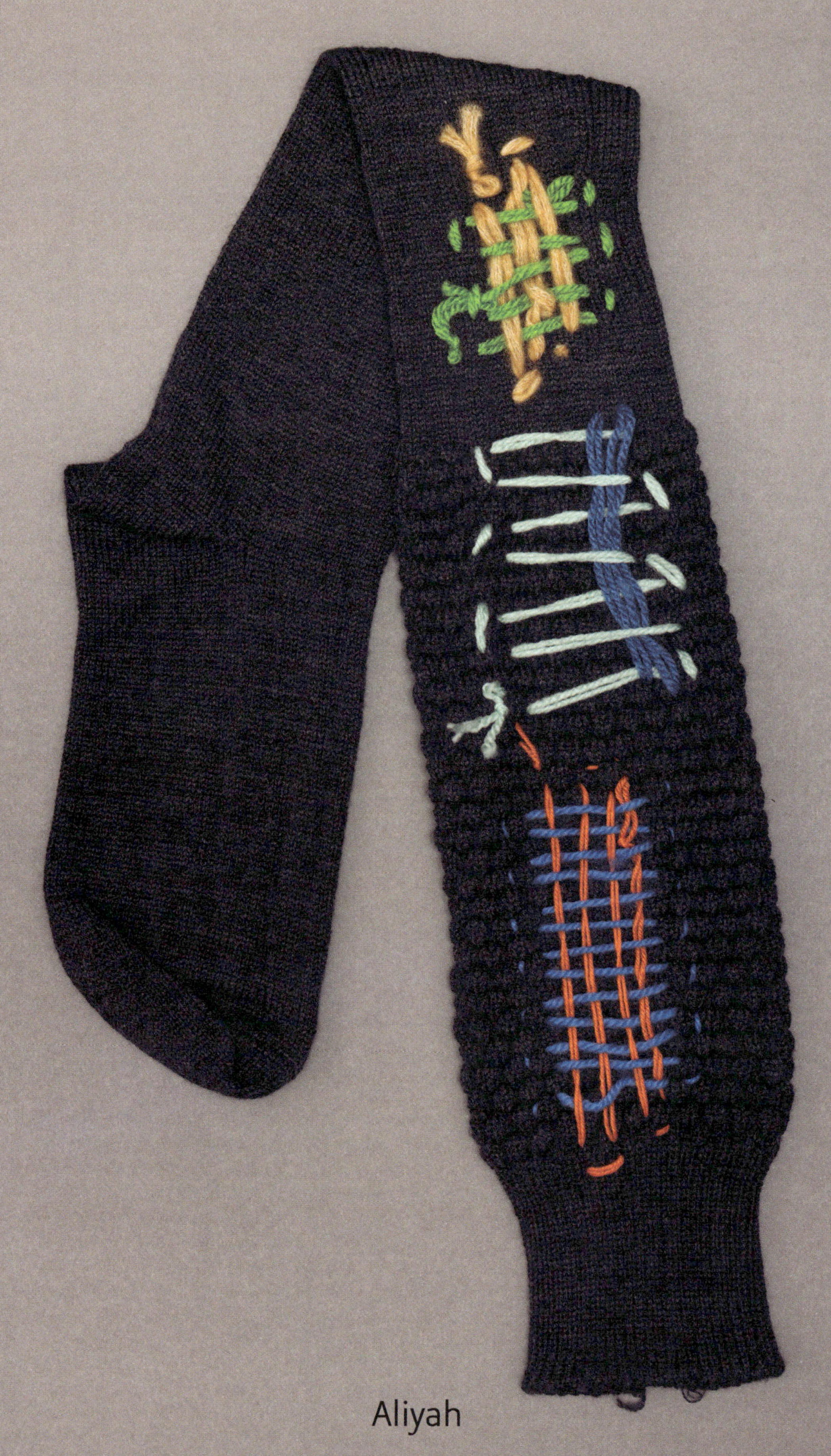

Aliyah

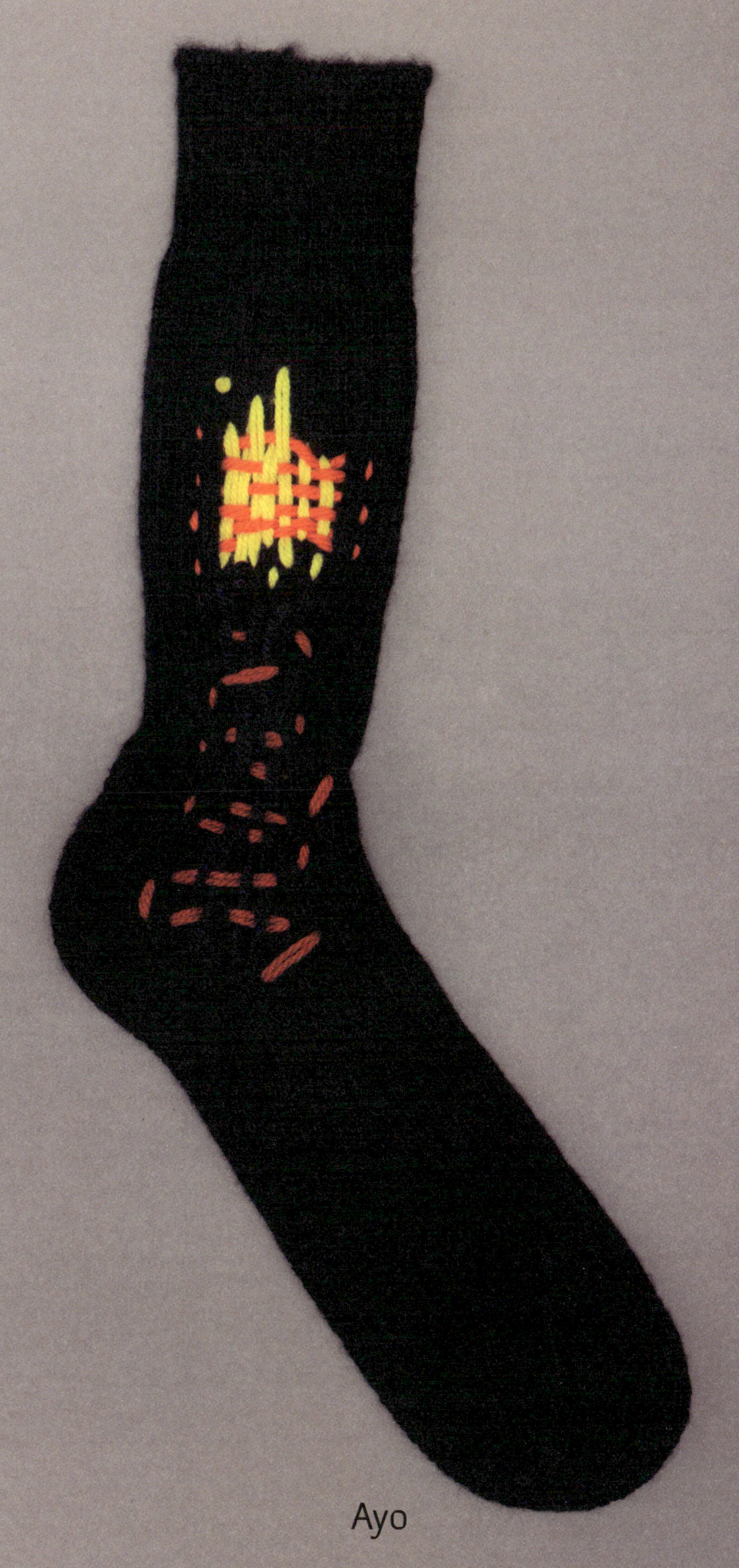

Ayo

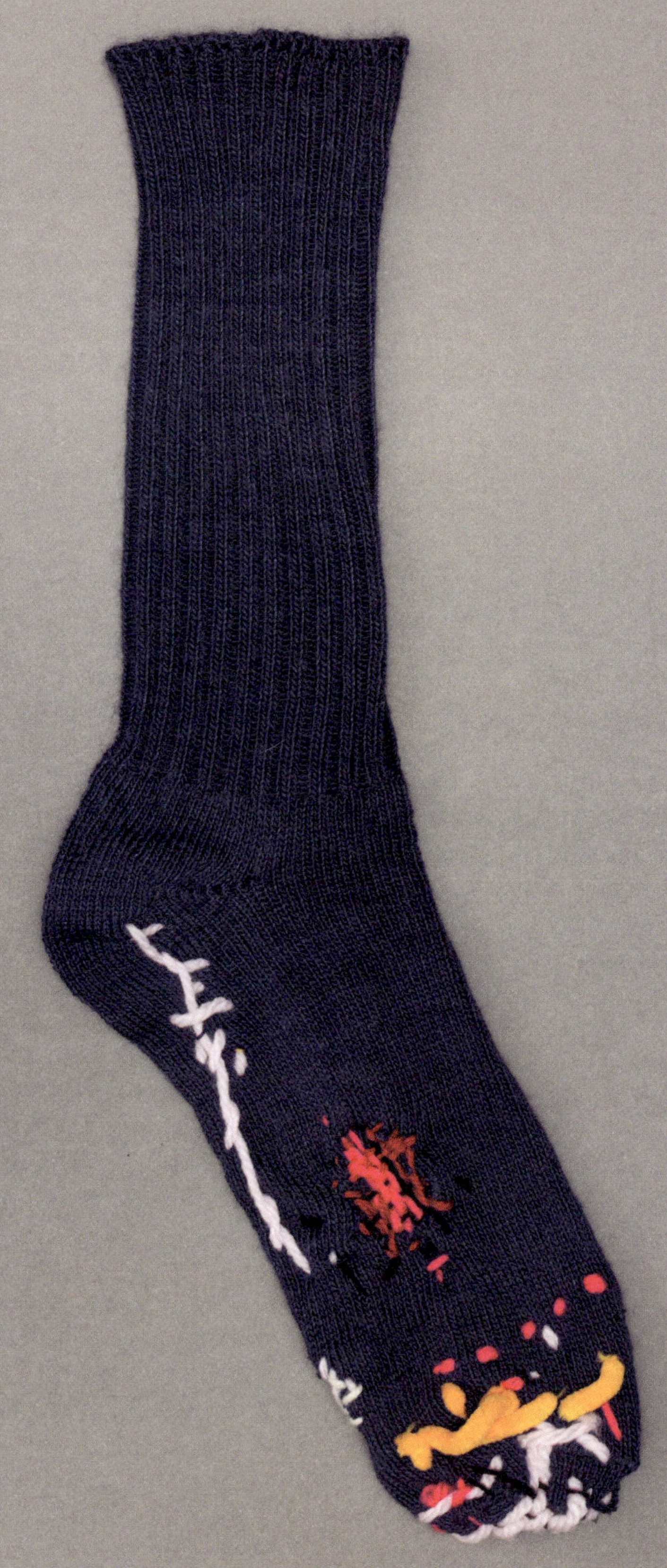

Latifat

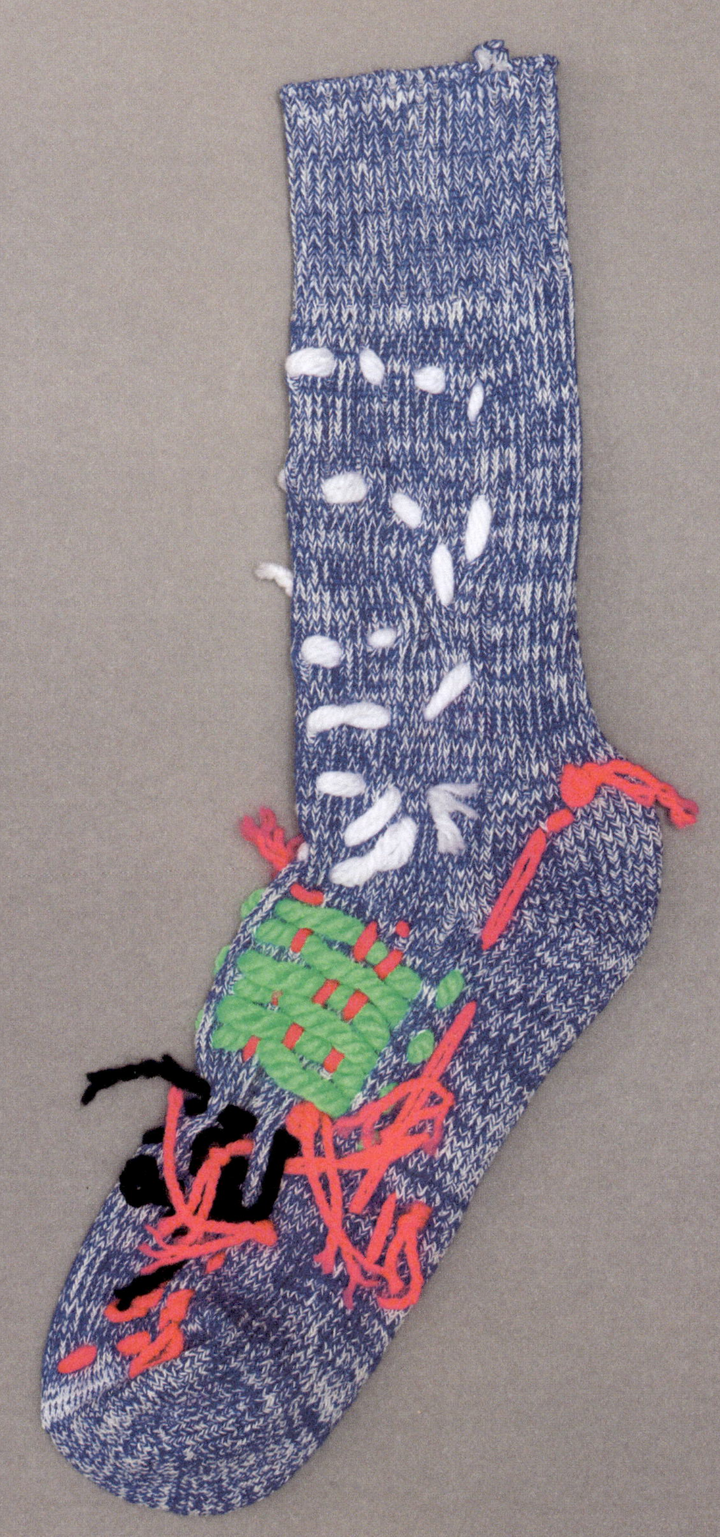

Kamiyah

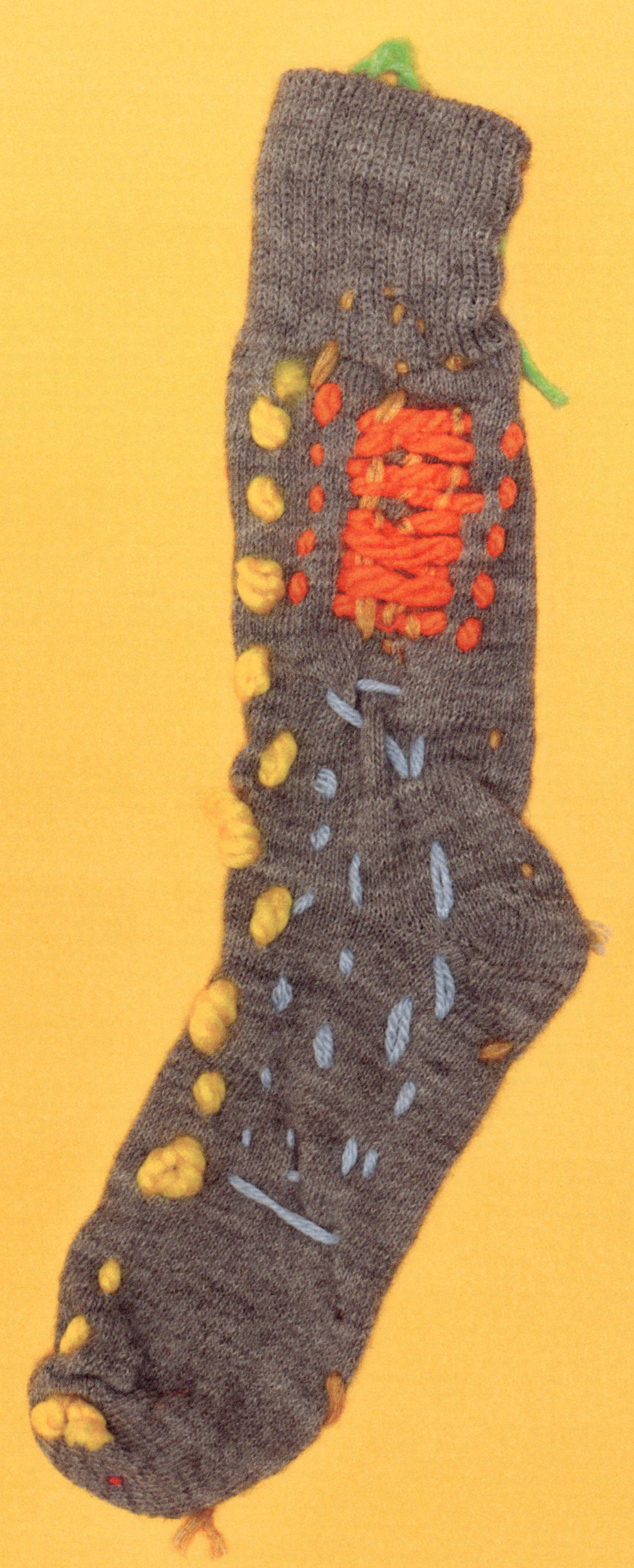

Diana

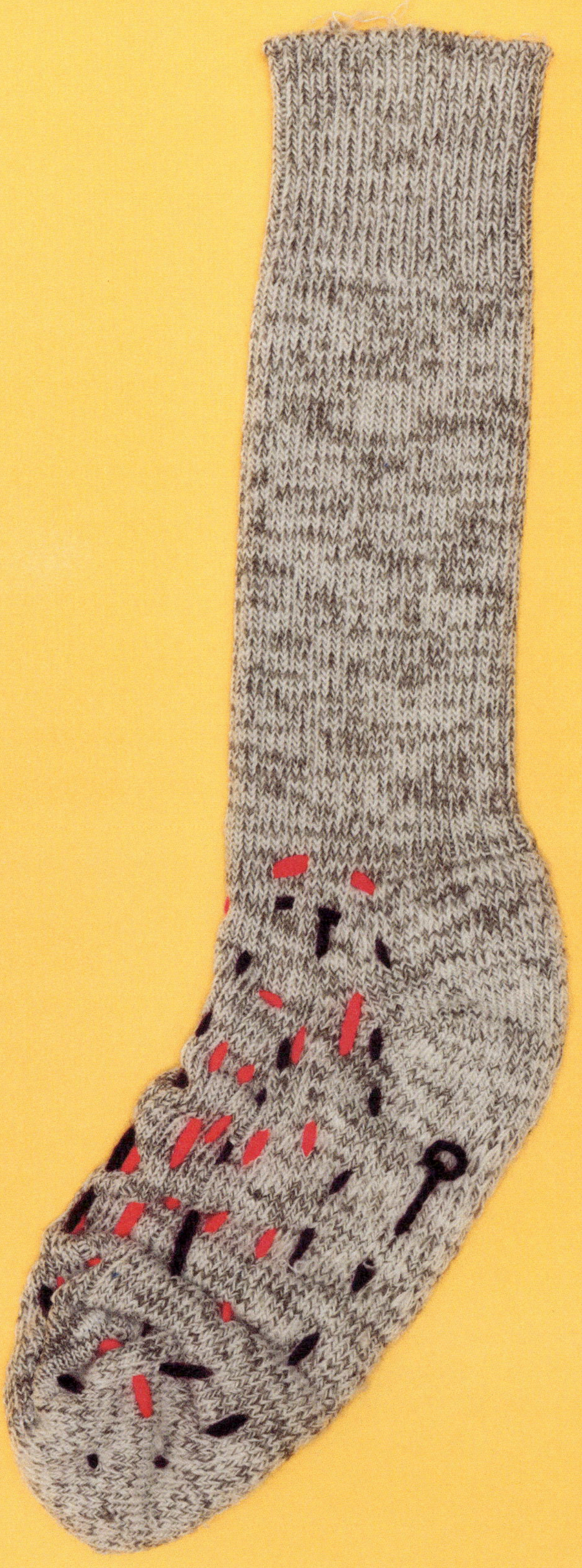

Fareedah

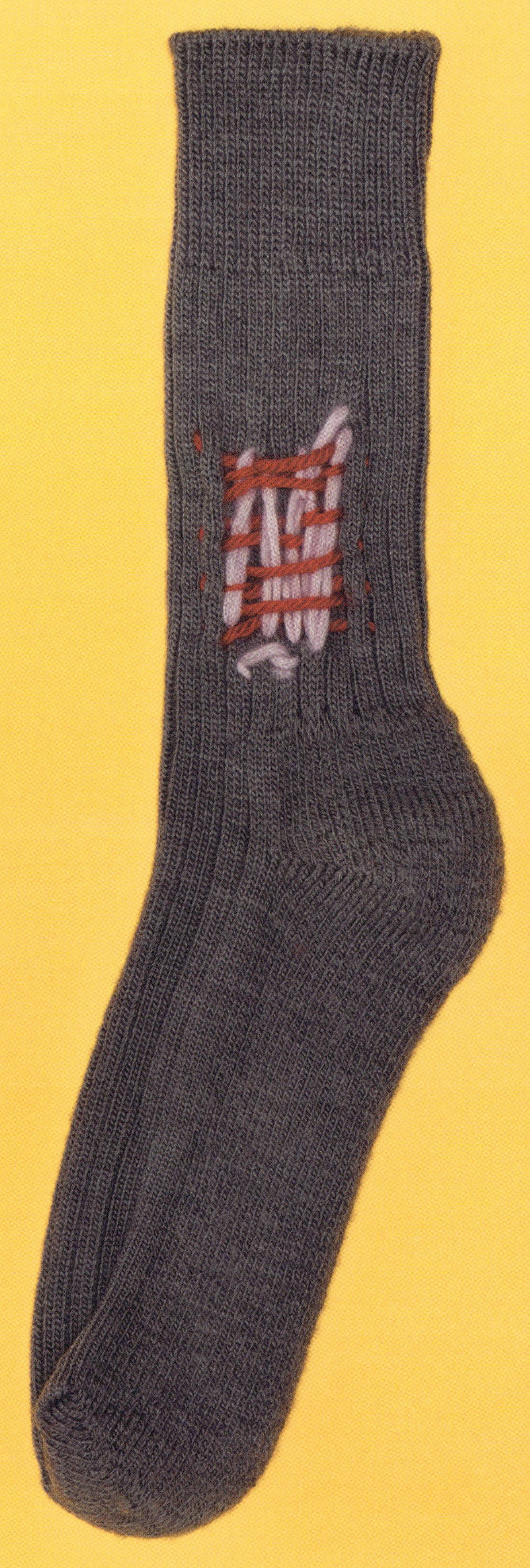

Samuel

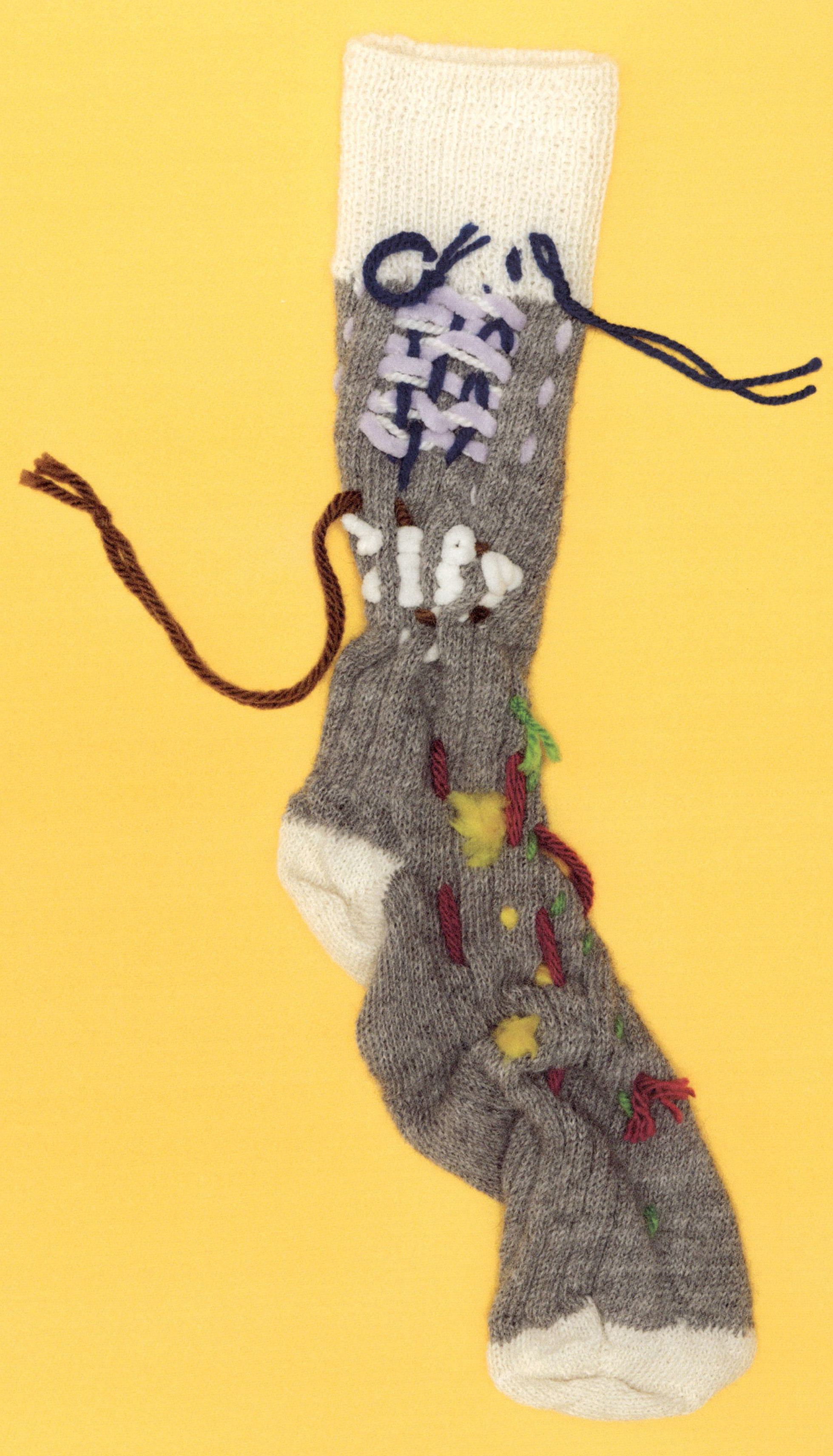

Lucas

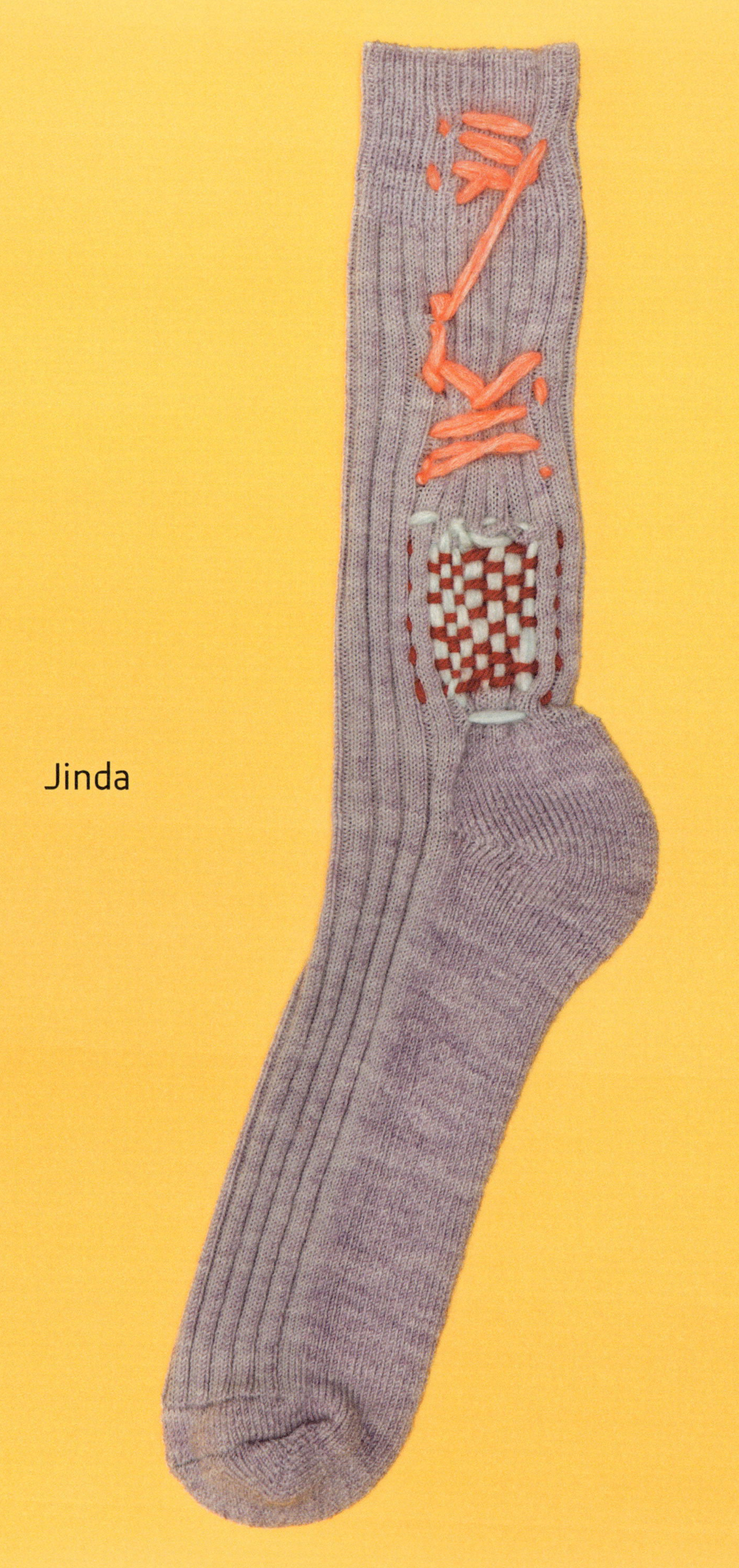

Jinda

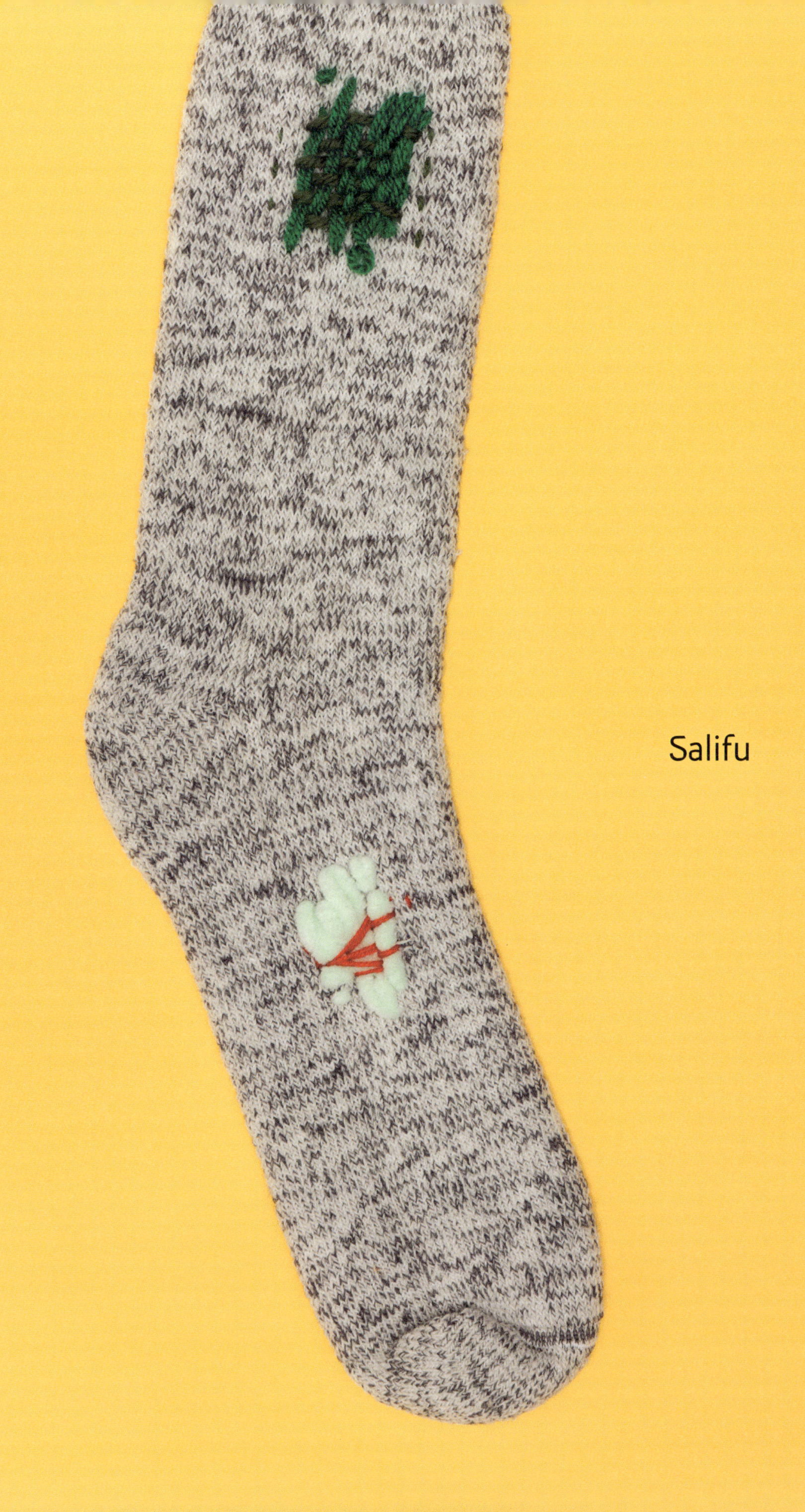

Salifu

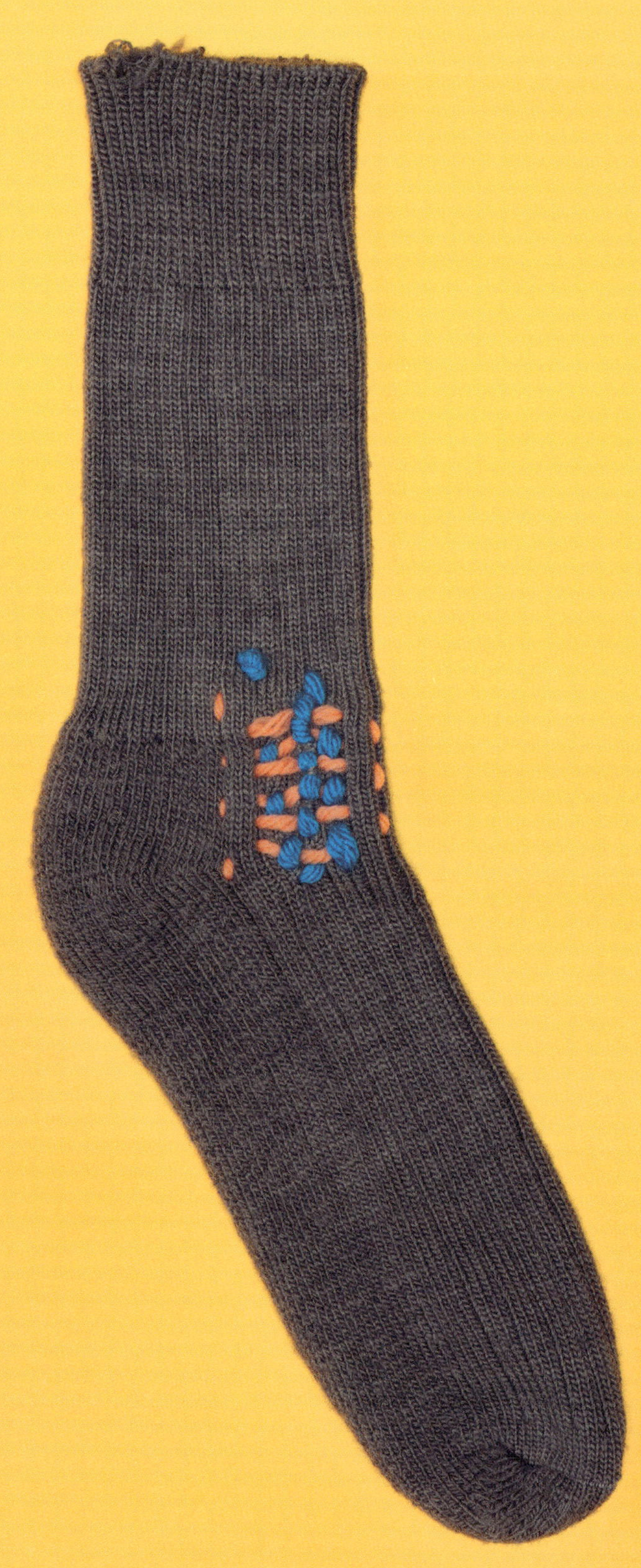

Daniel

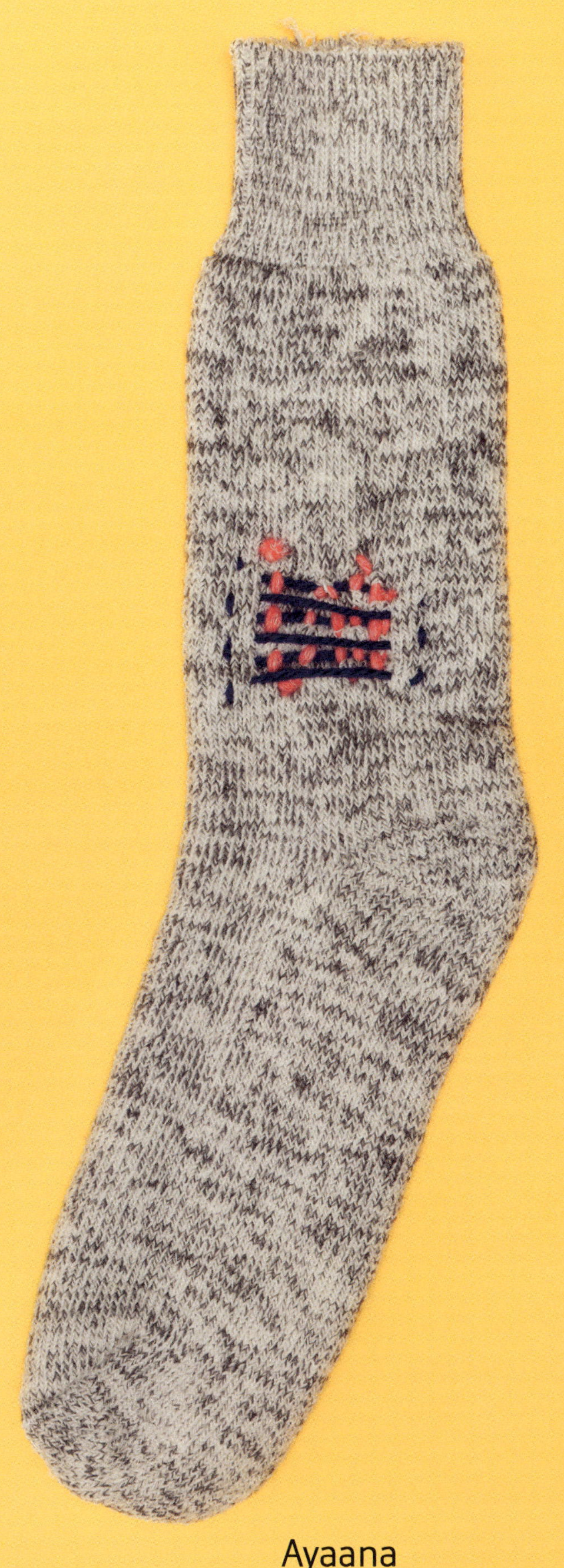

Ayaana

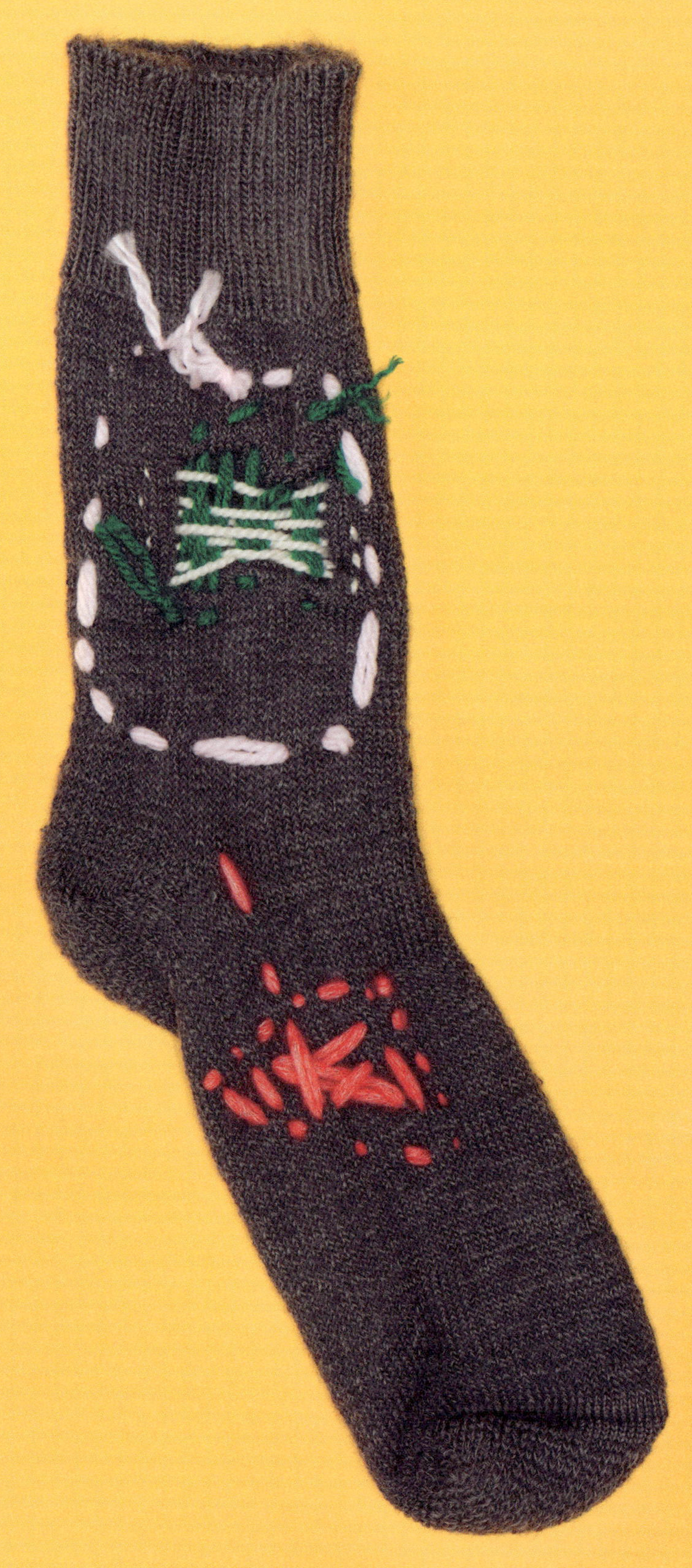

Adrian

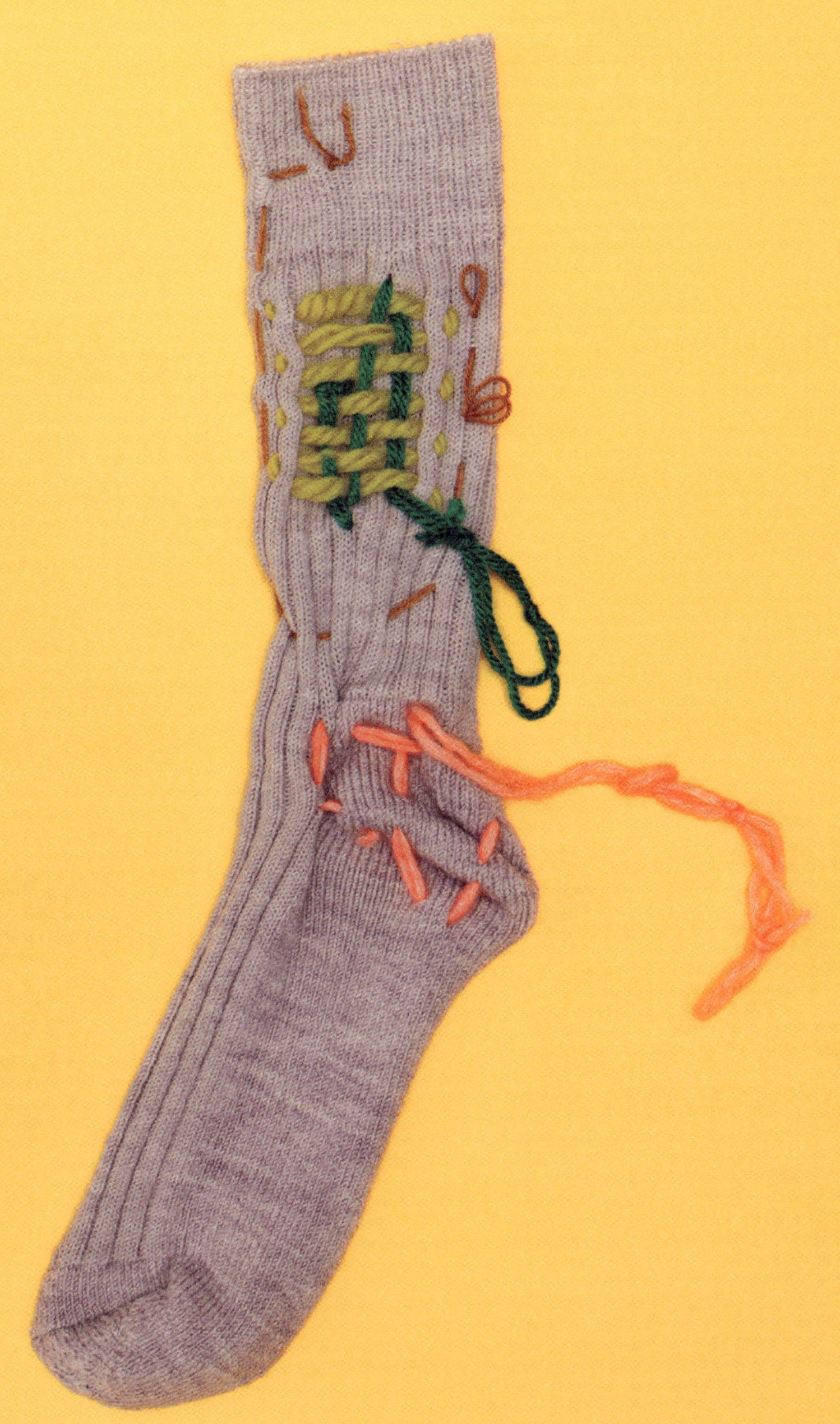

Avery

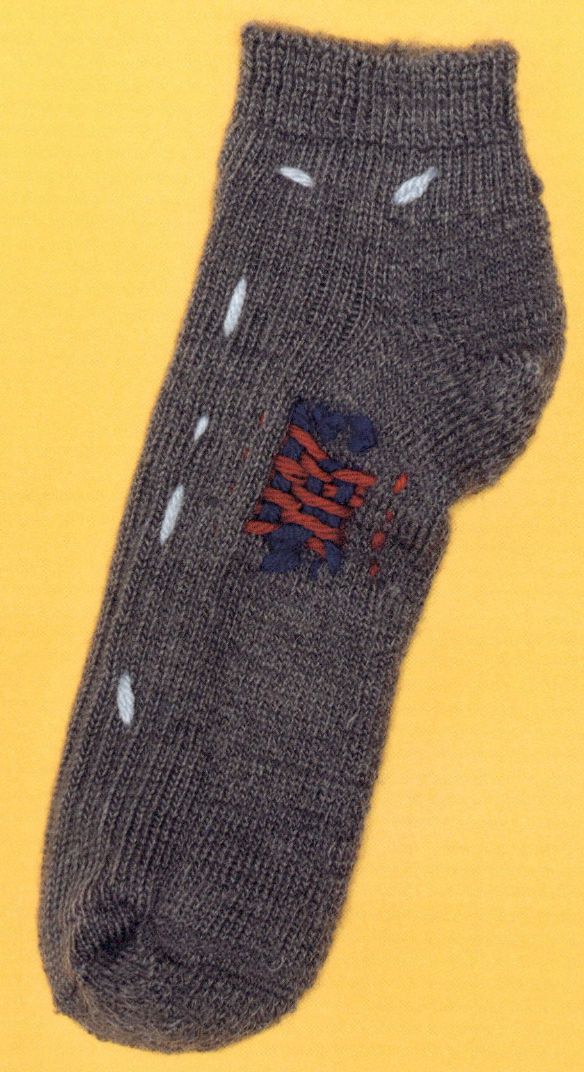

Star

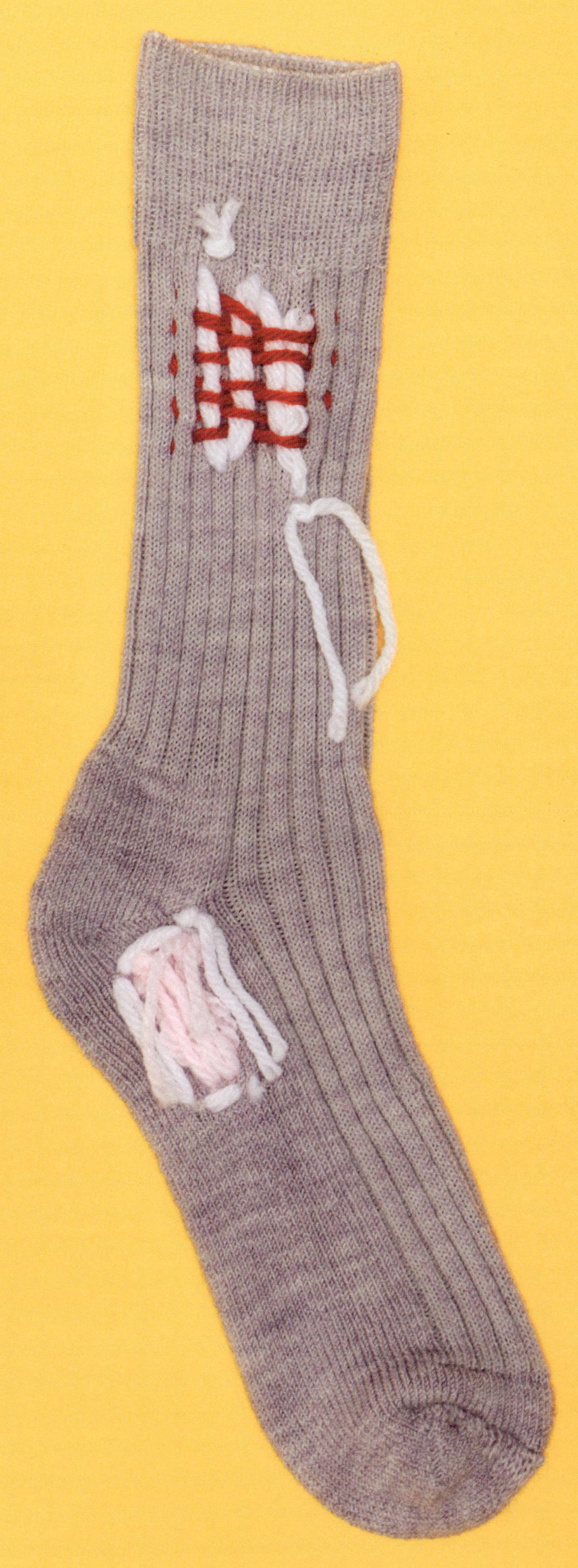

Aleena

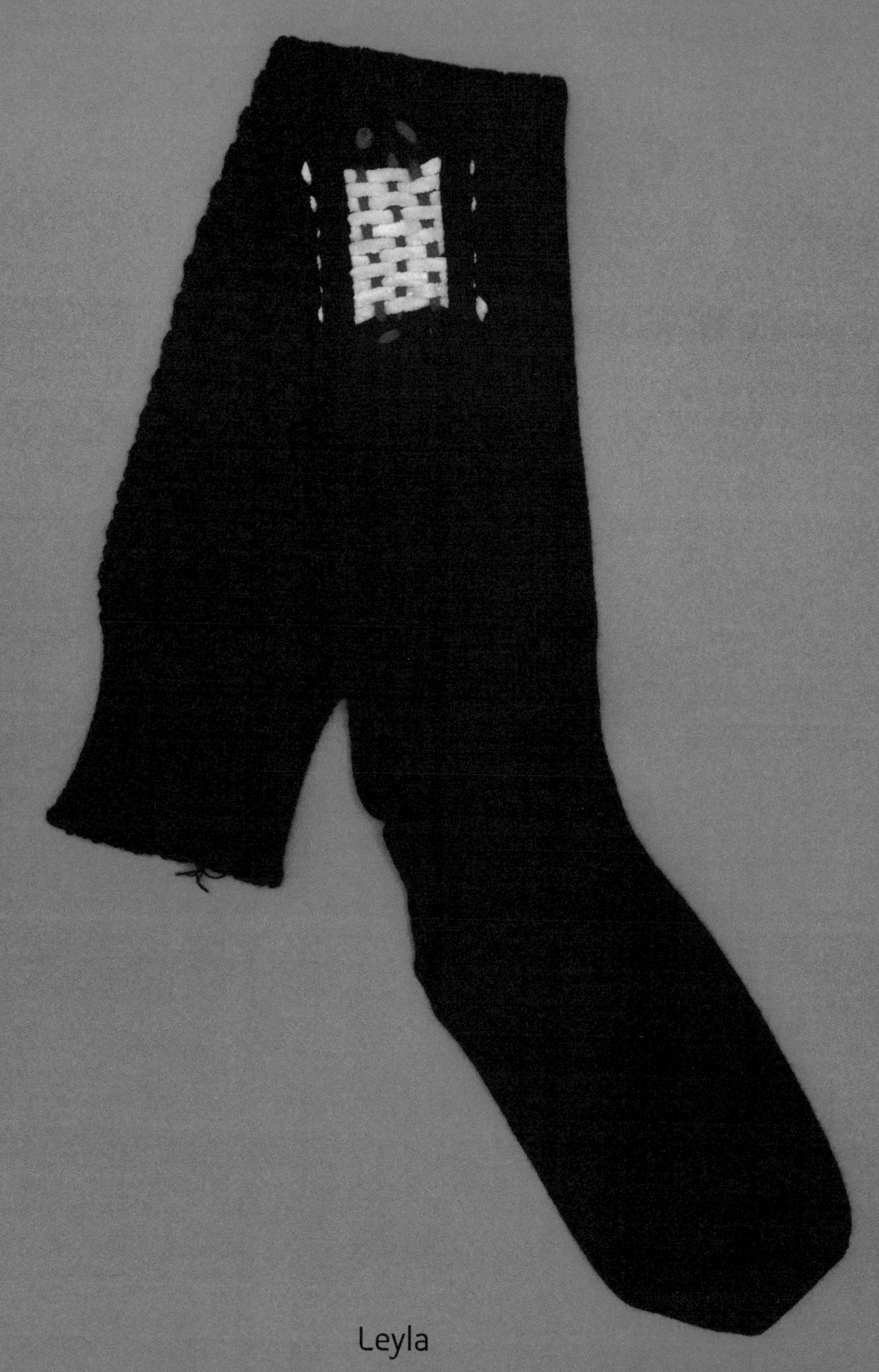

Leyla

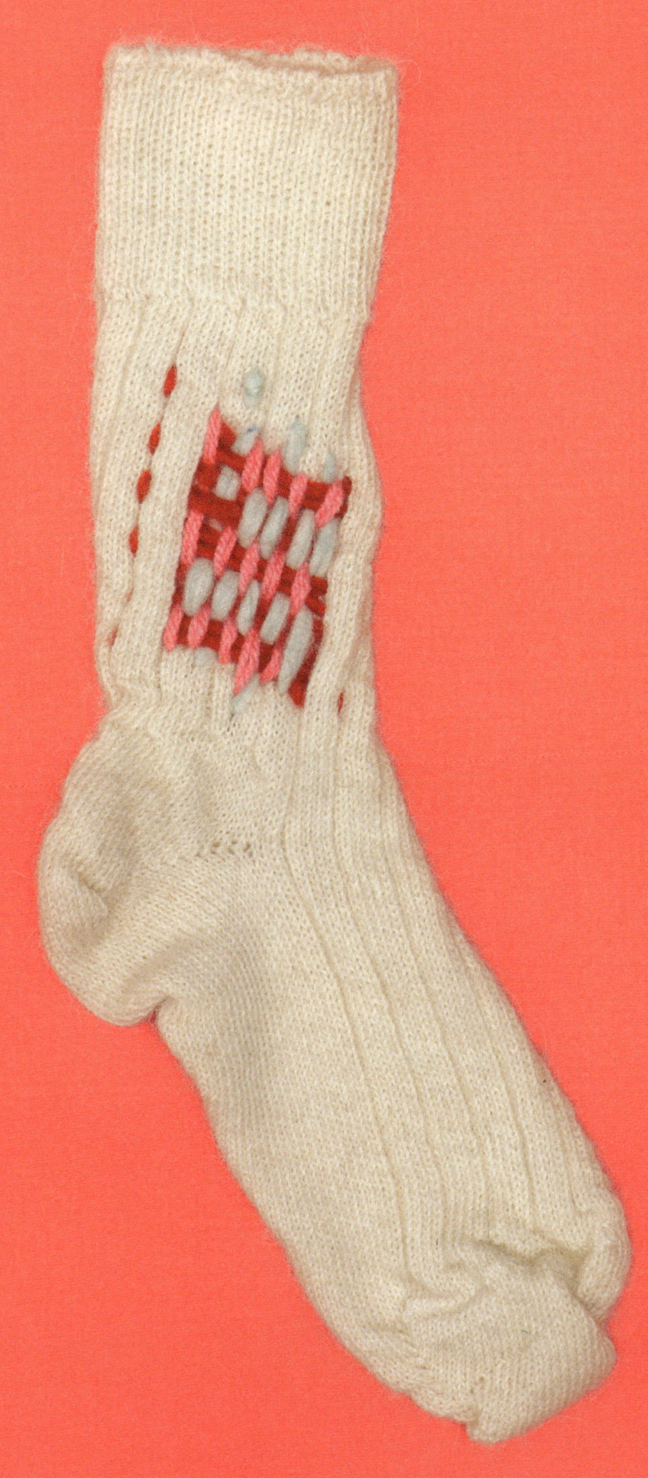

Aasim

Ariane

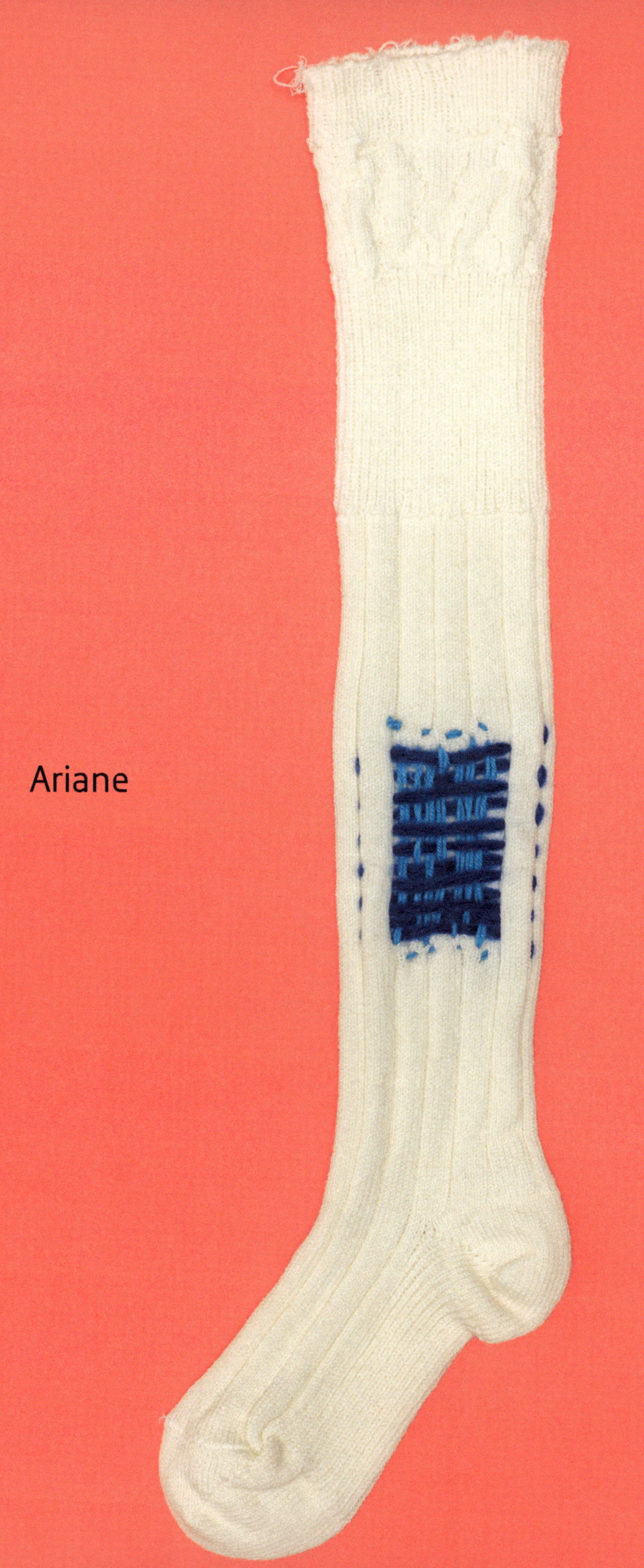

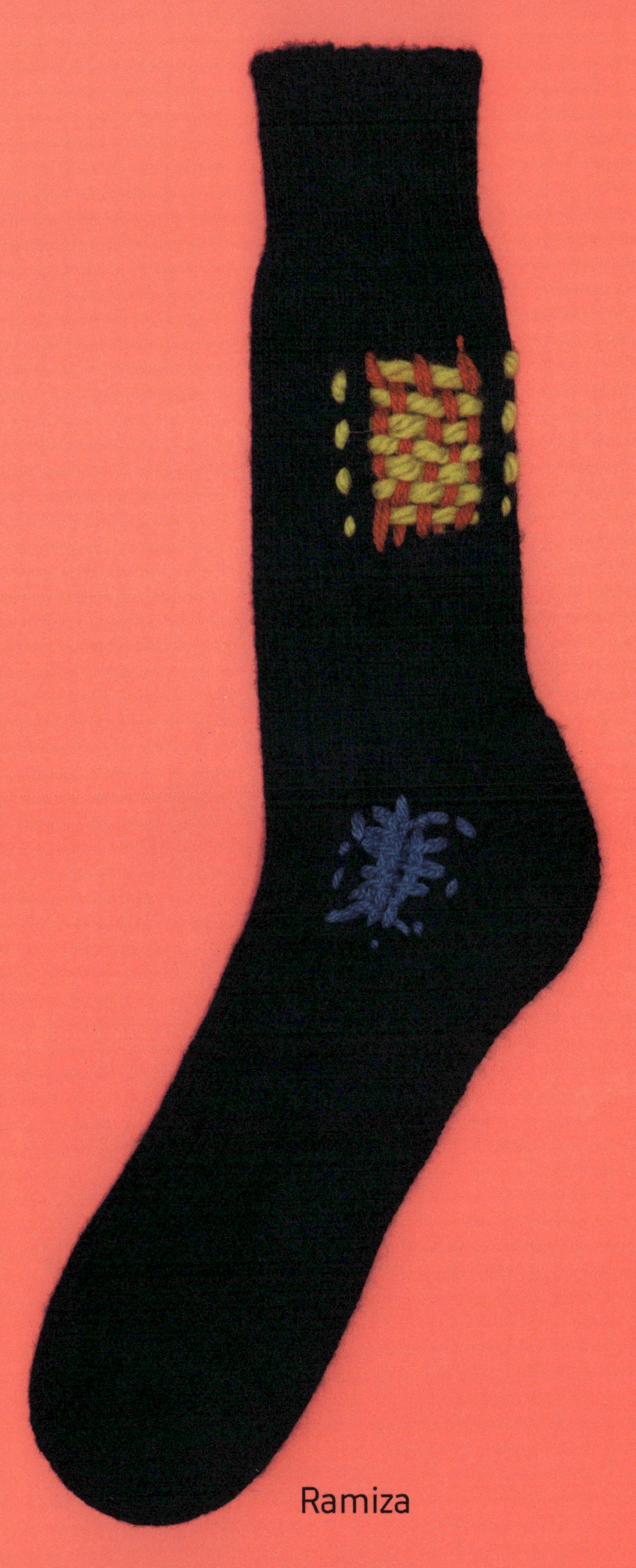

Ramiza

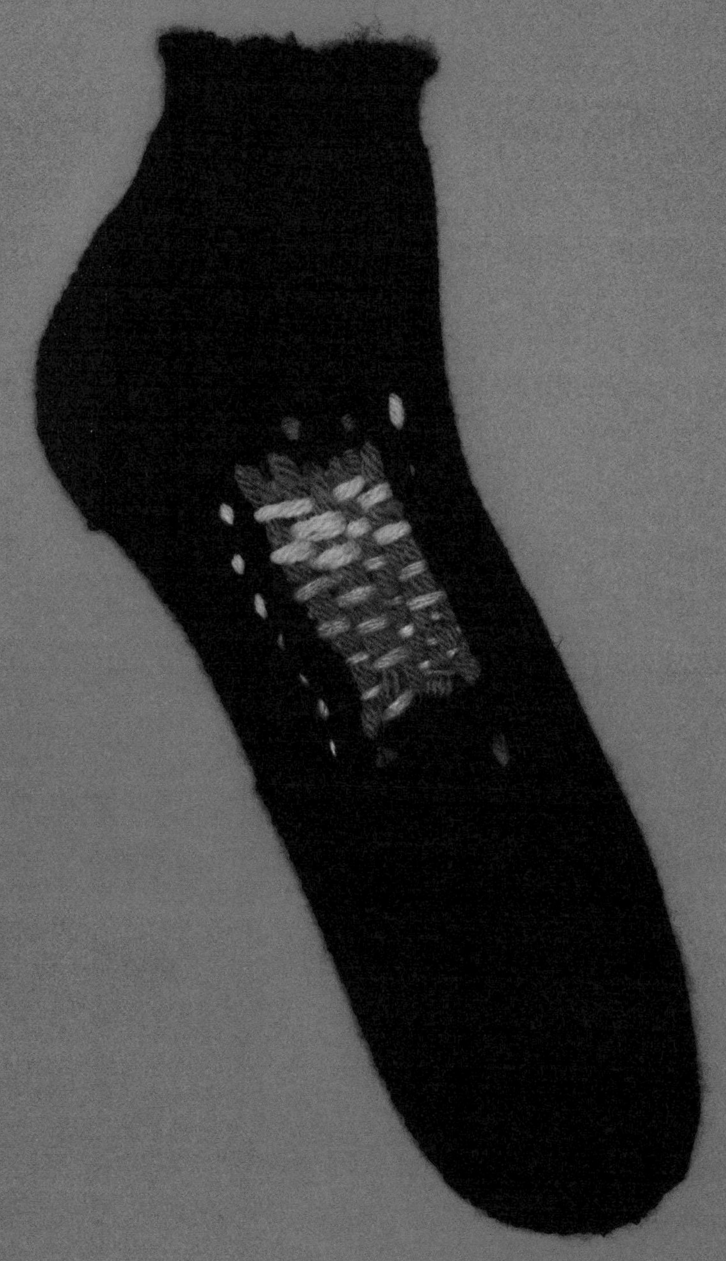

Farid

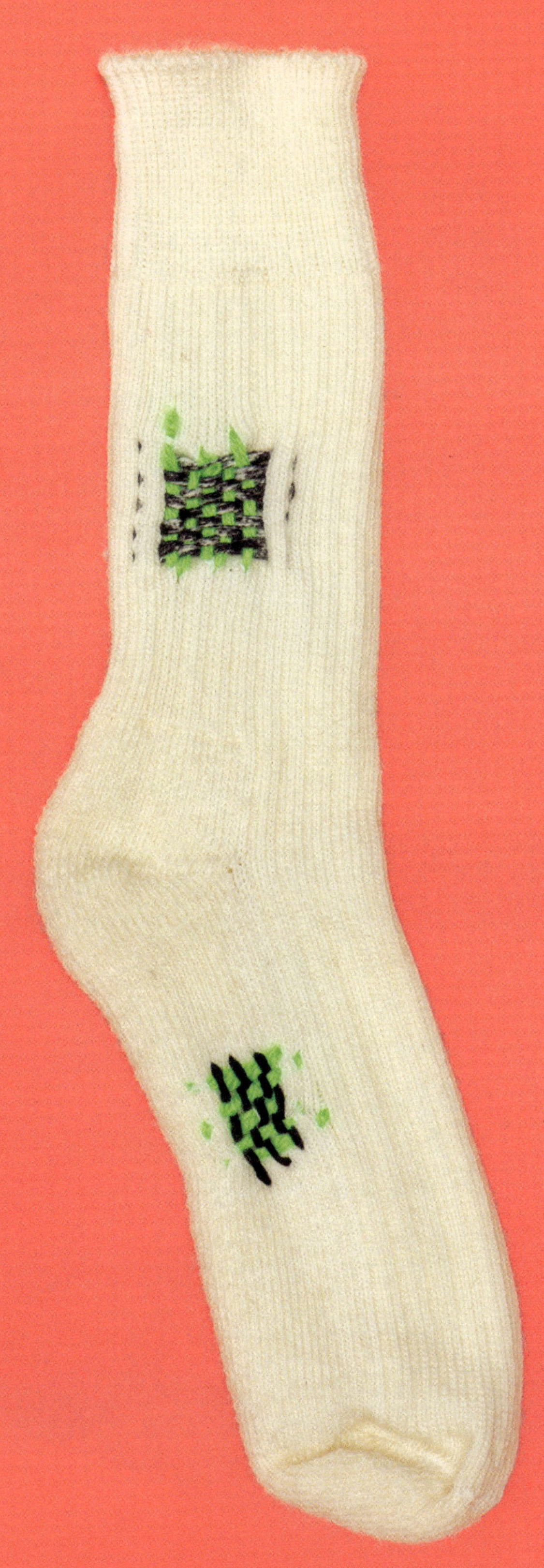

Zach

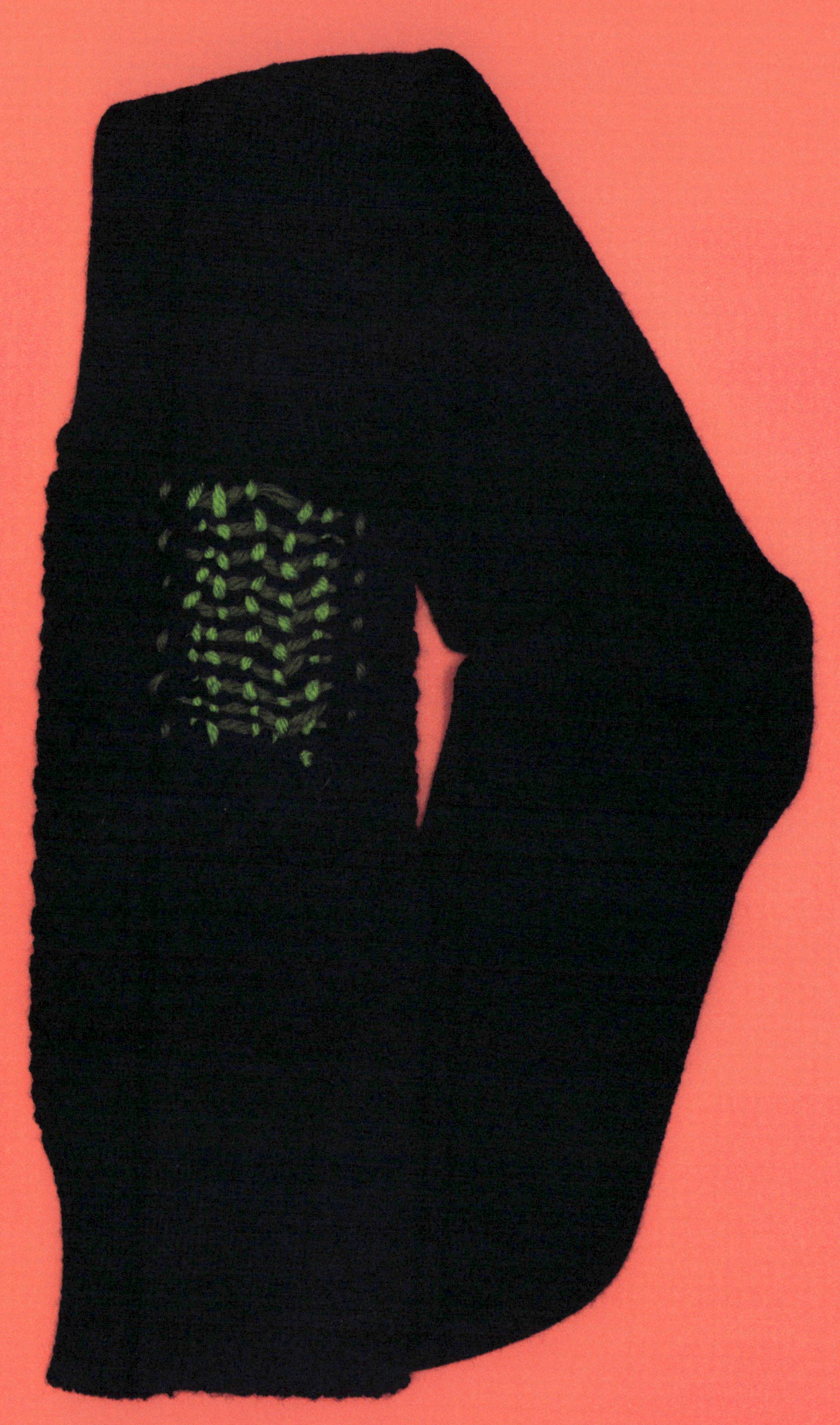

Mariah

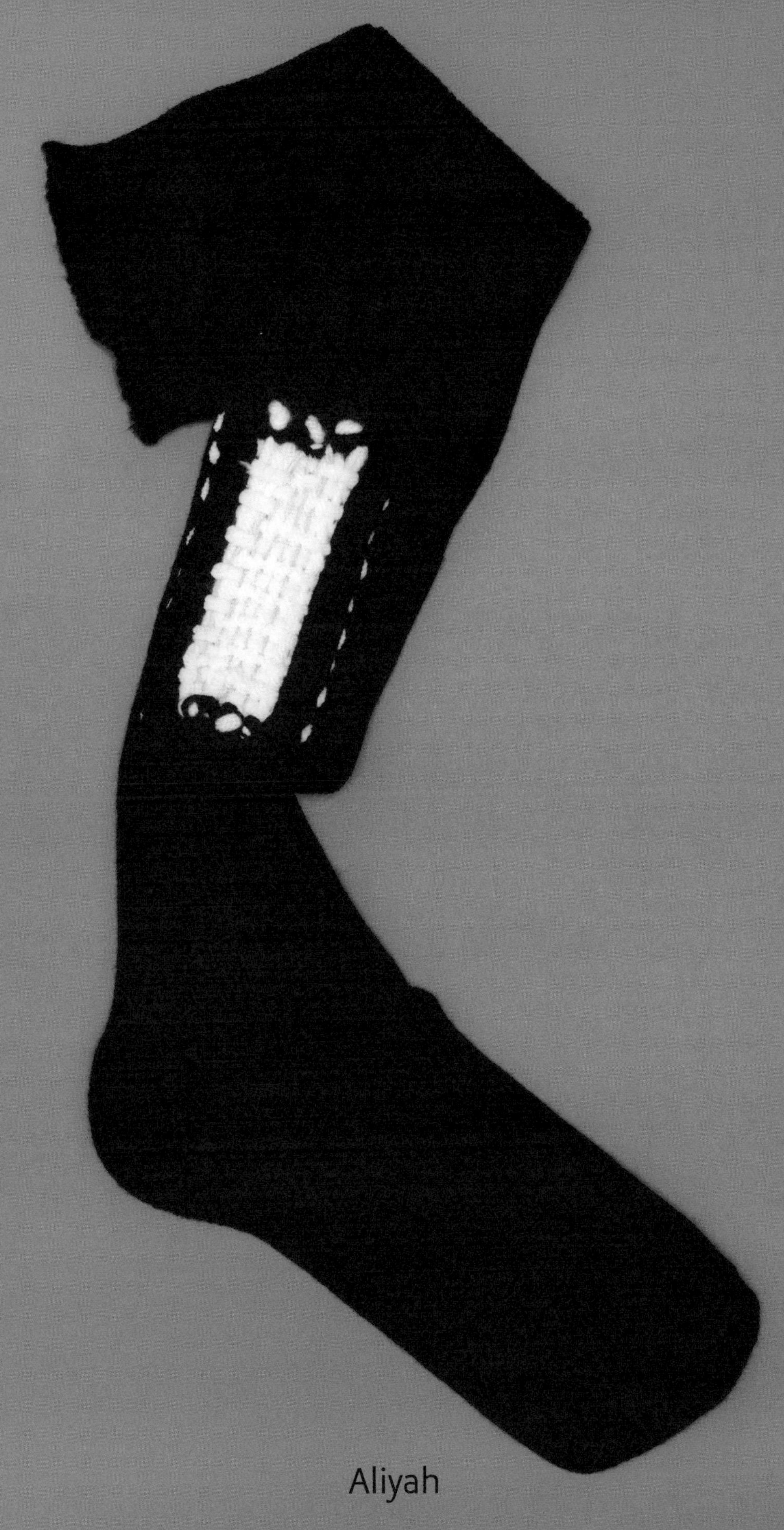

Aliyah

Mac

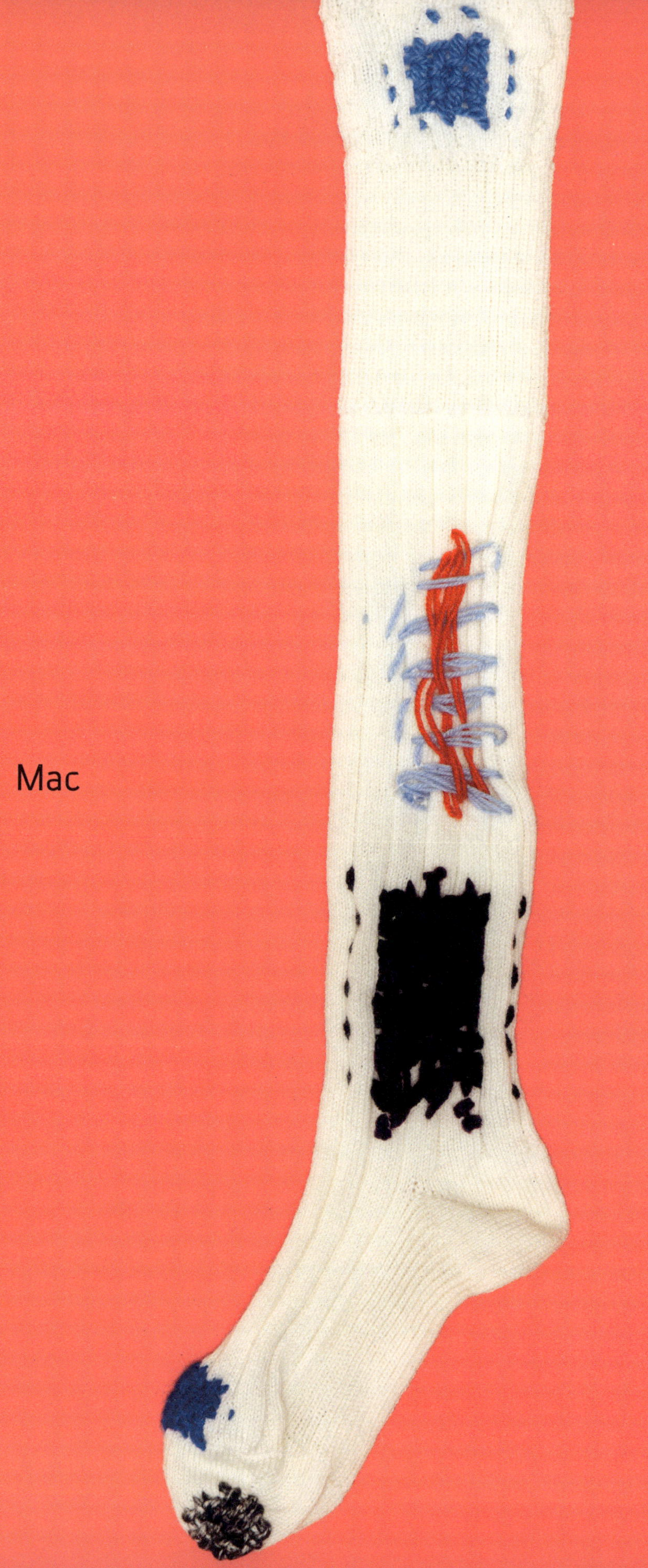

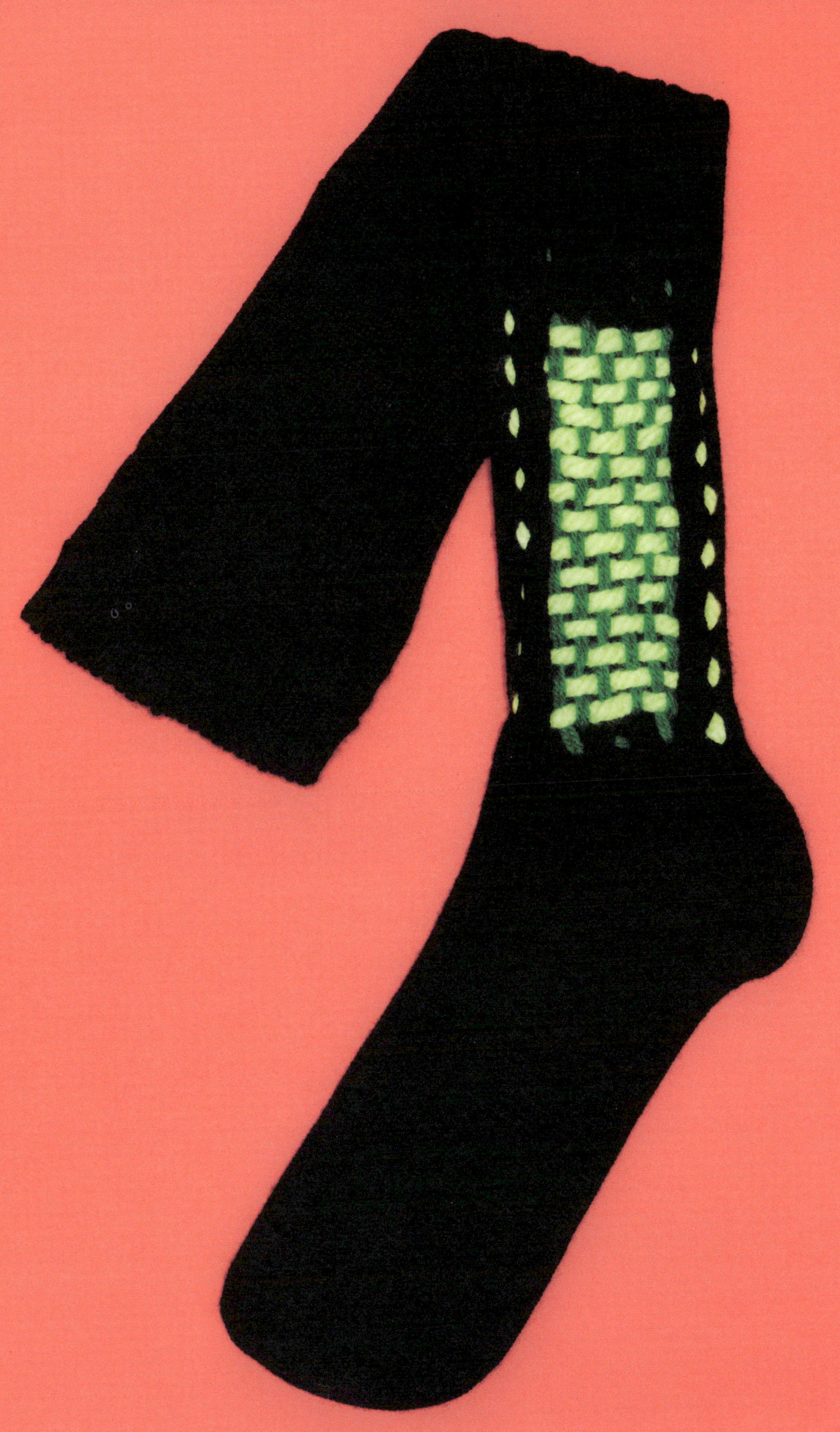

Neyla

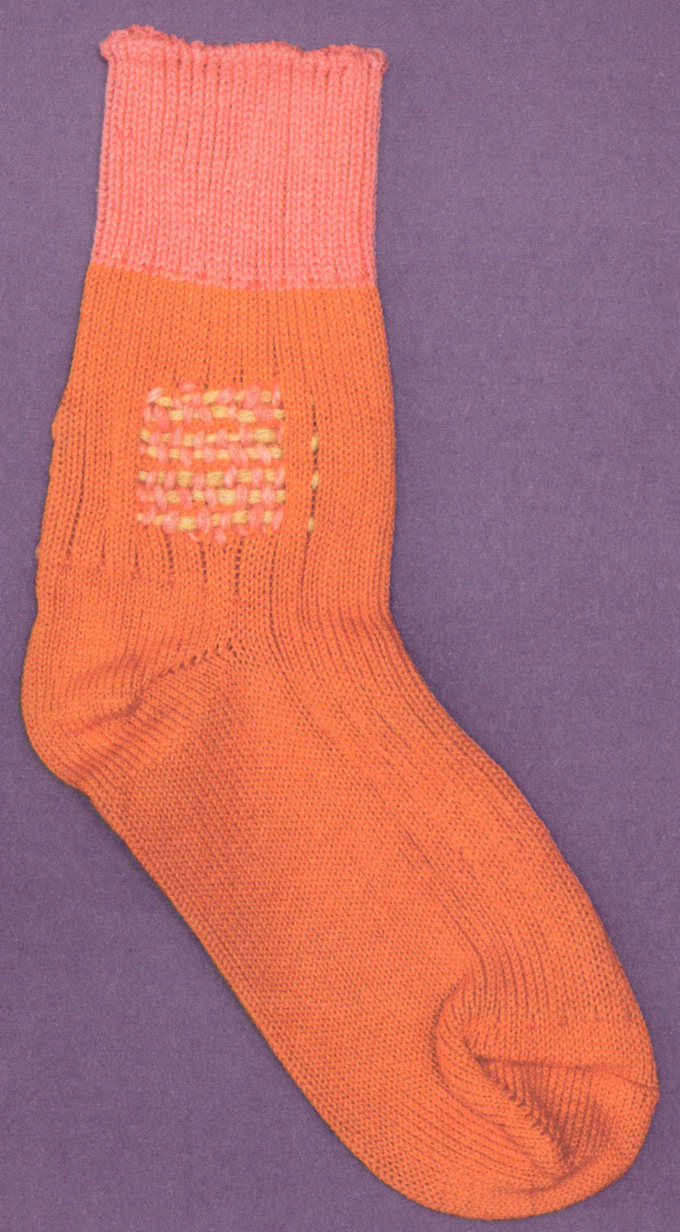

Megan

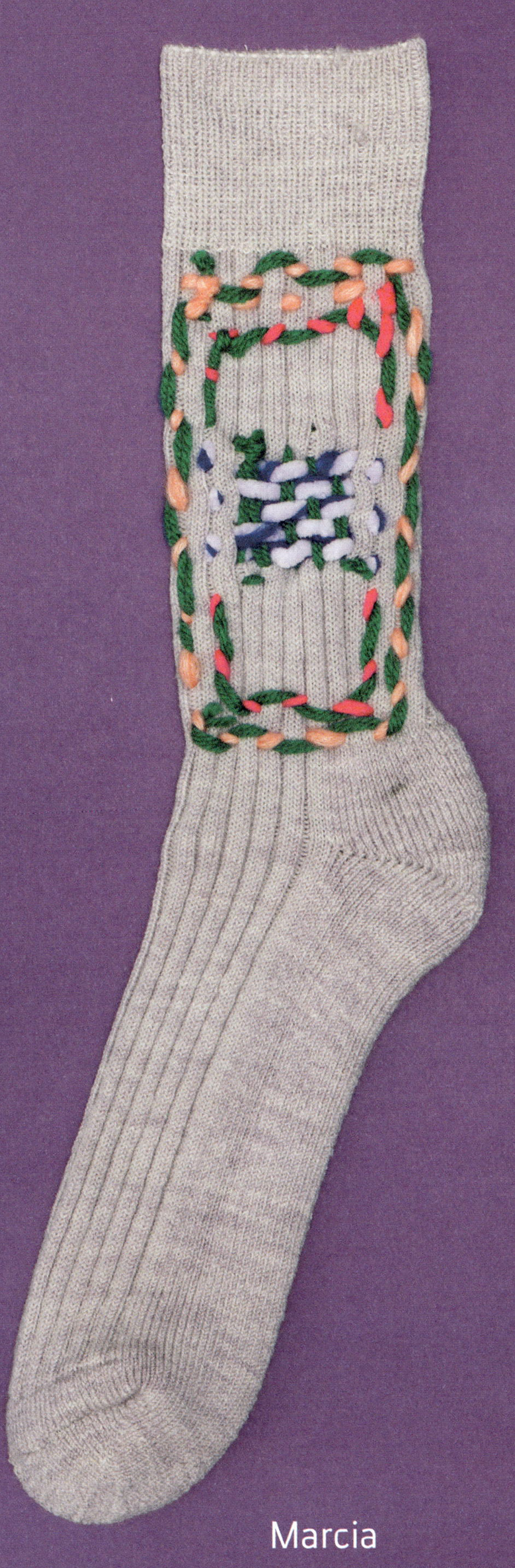

Marcia

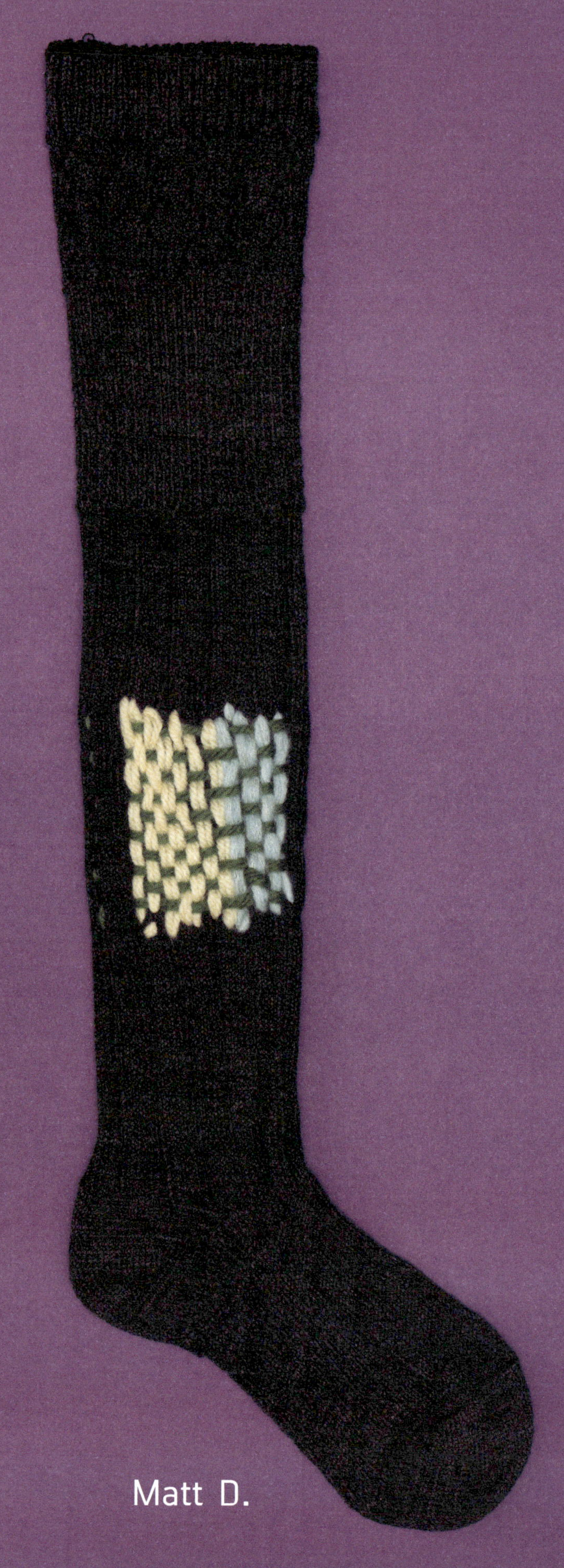

Matt D.

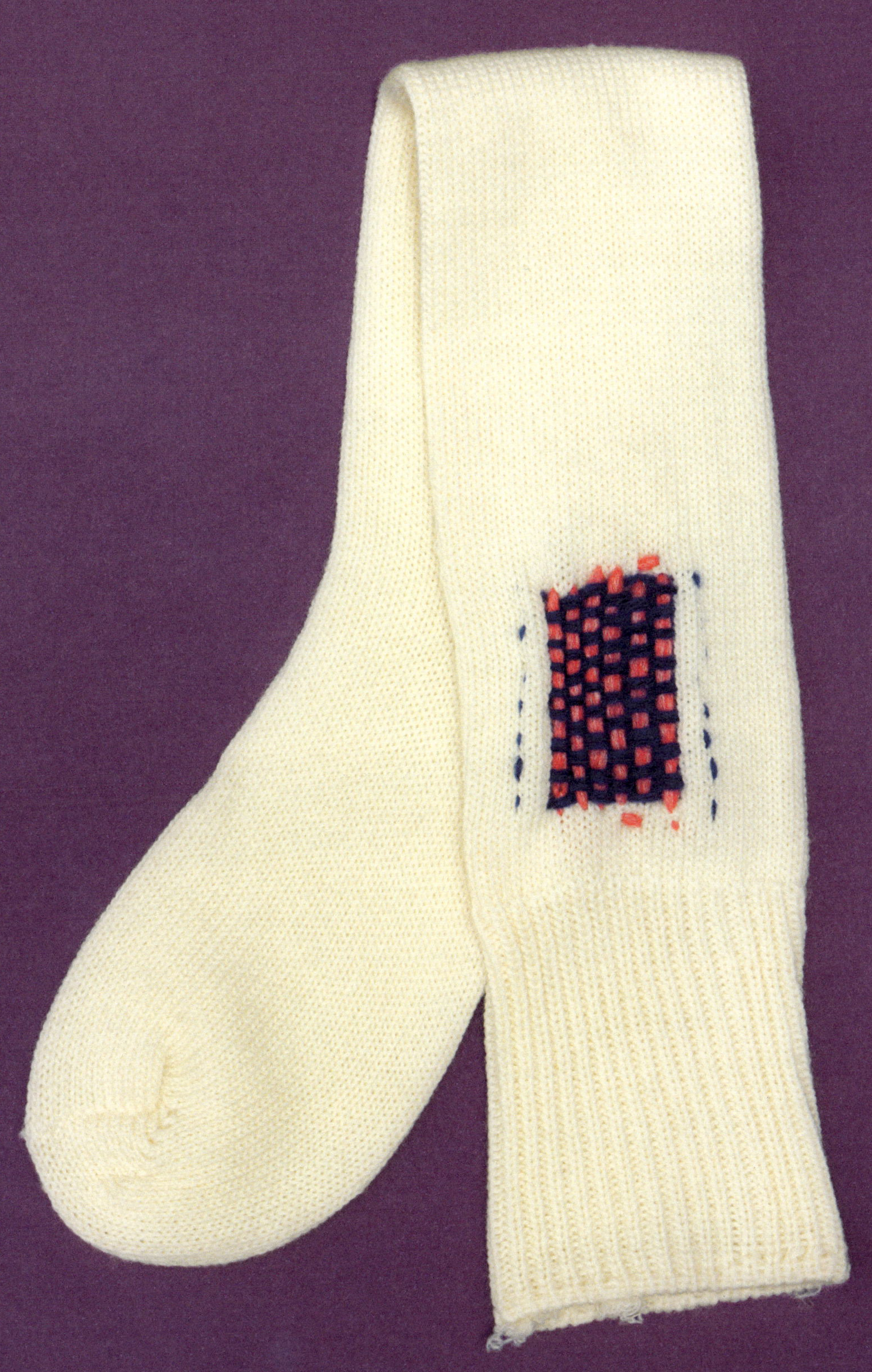

Debbie

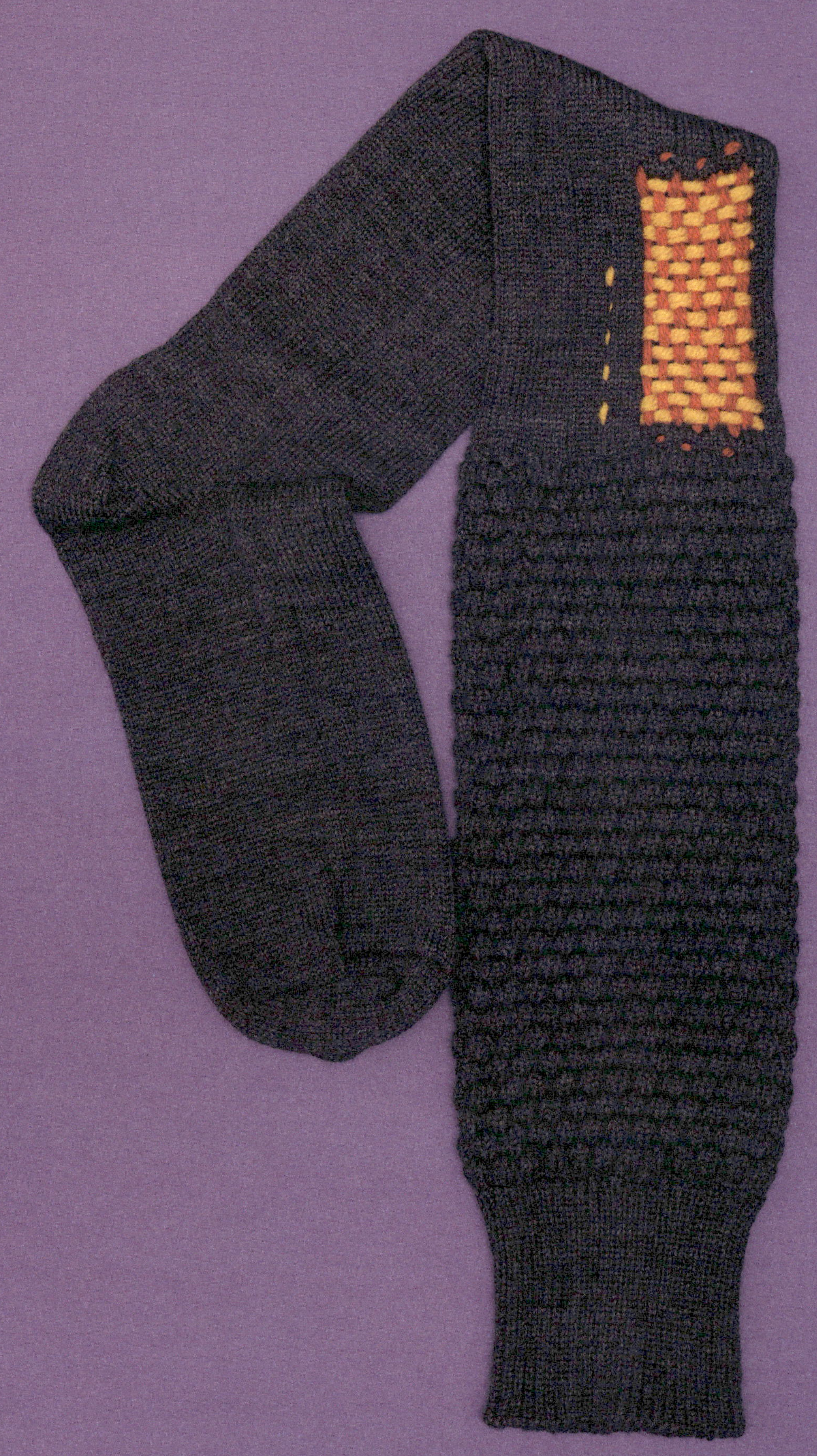

Molly

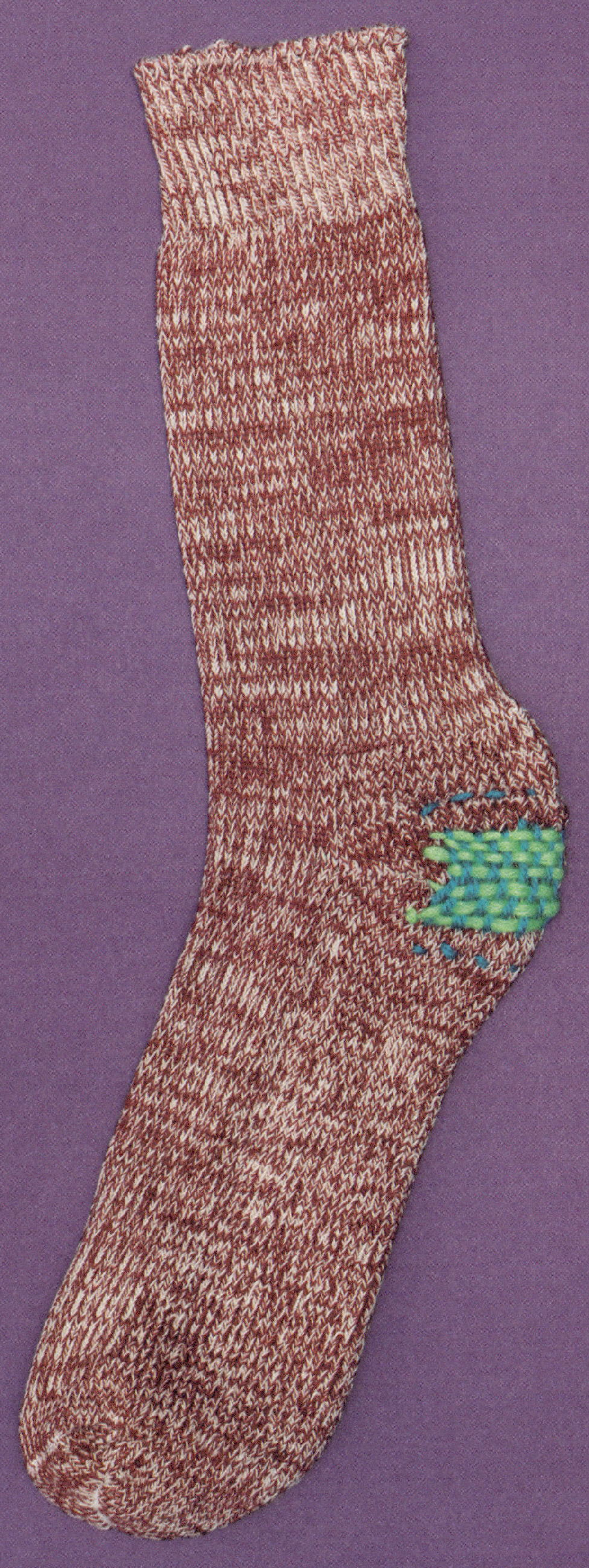

Matt M.

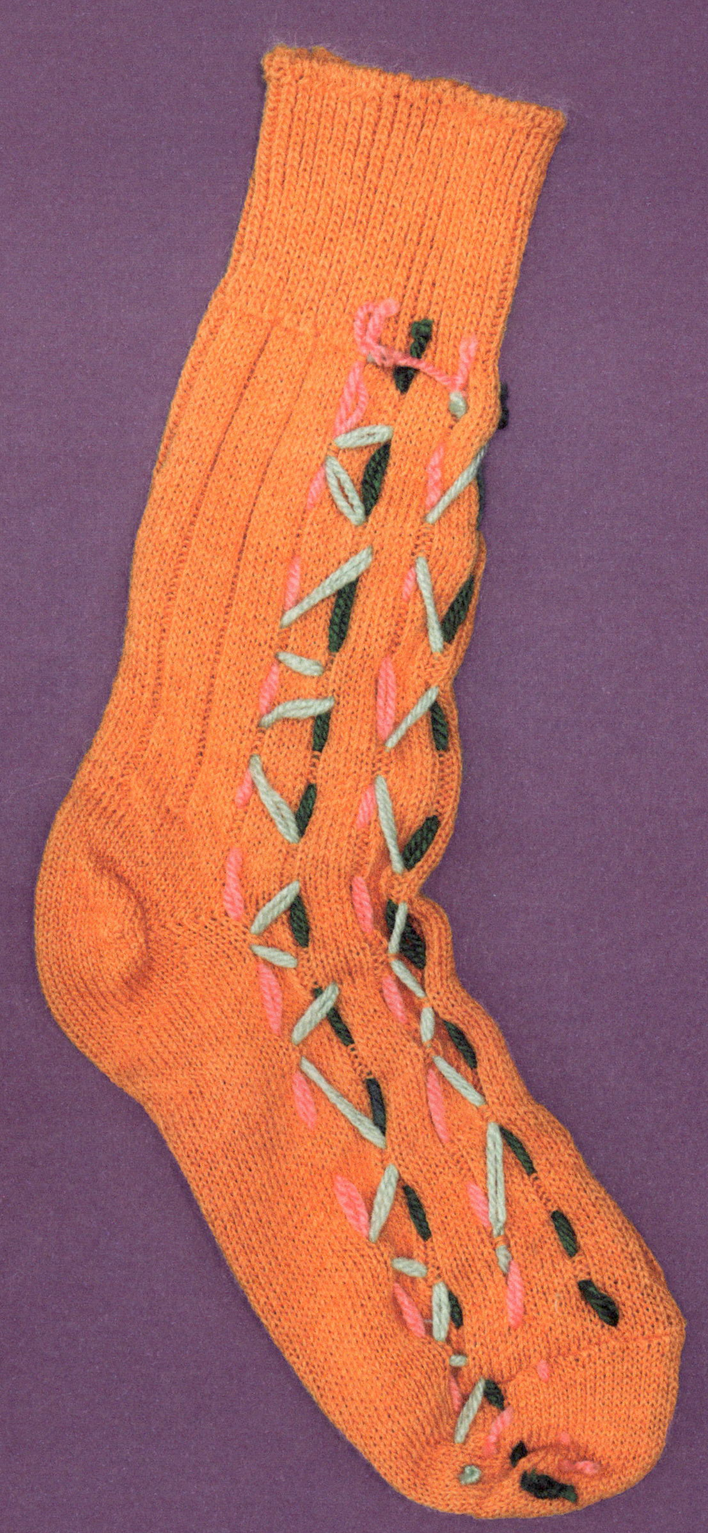

Elizabeth

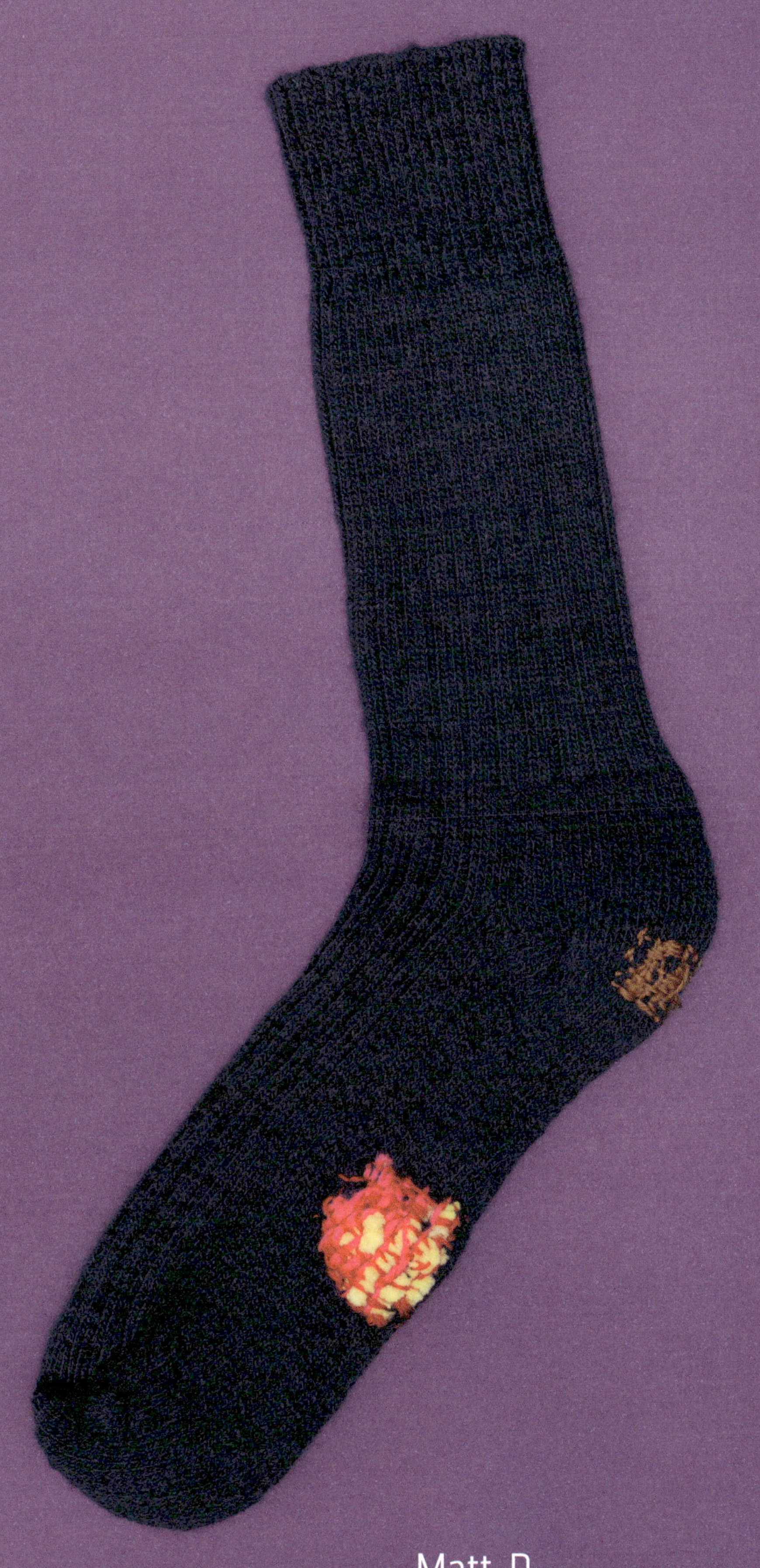

Matt D.

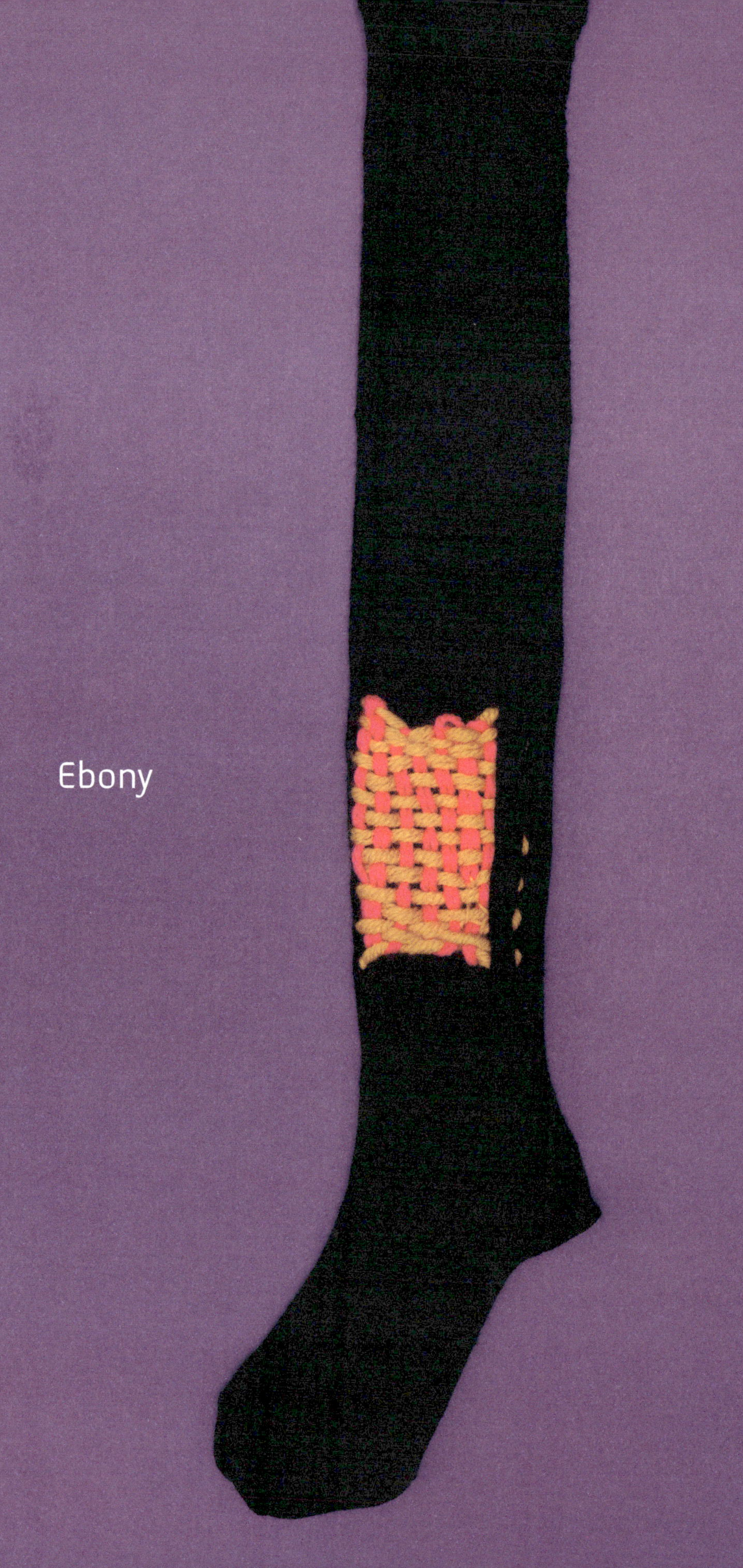

Ebony

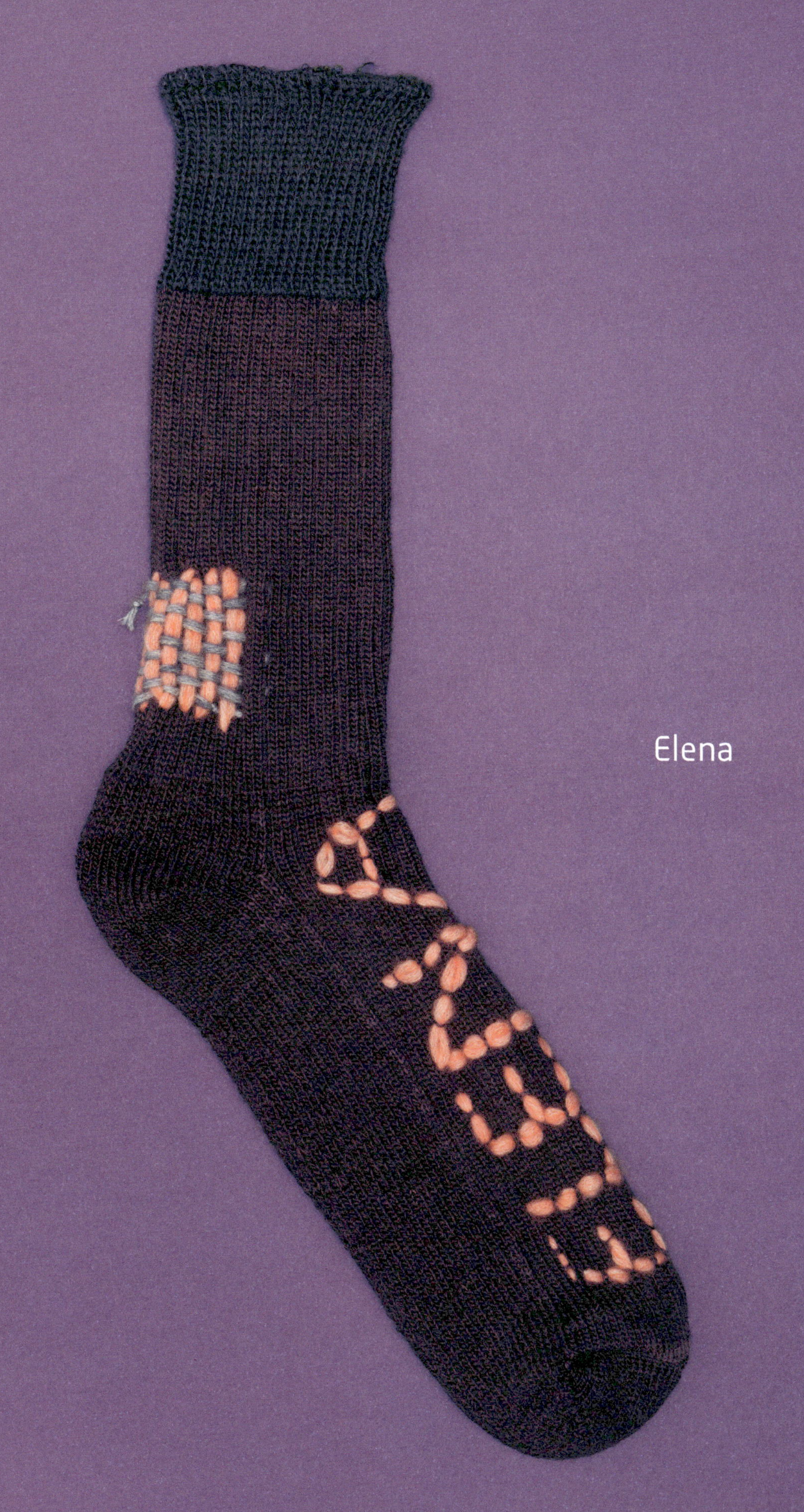

Elena

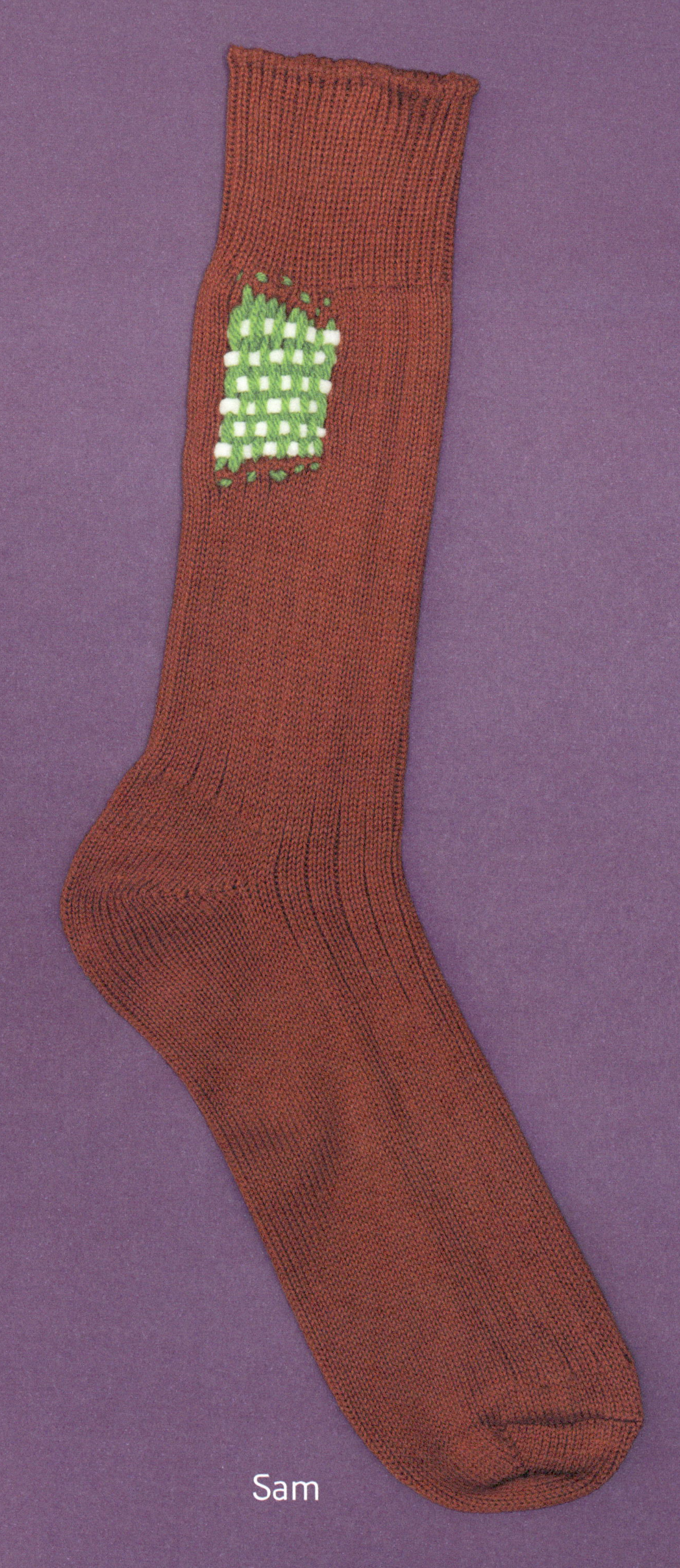

Sam

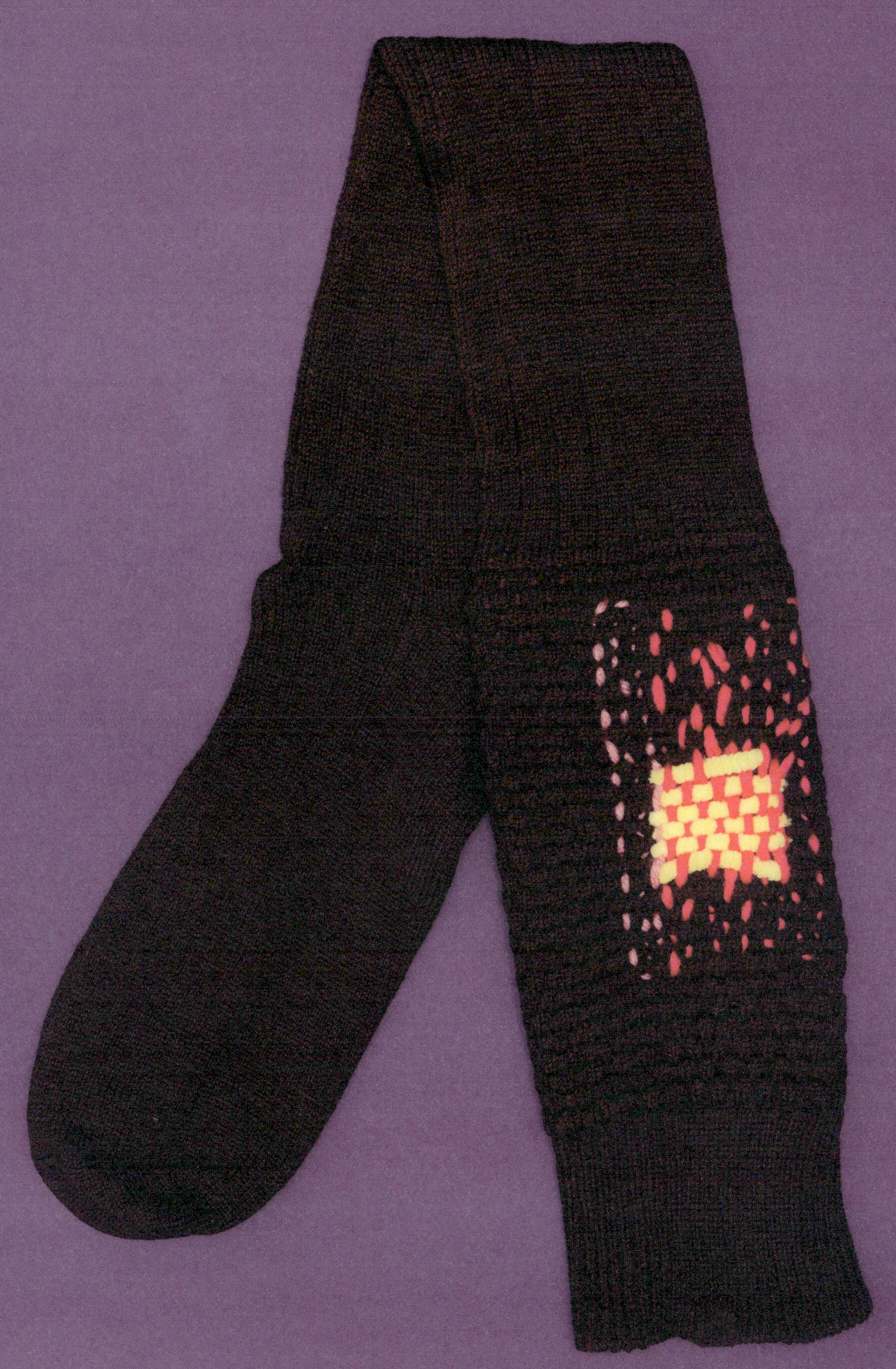

Aruna

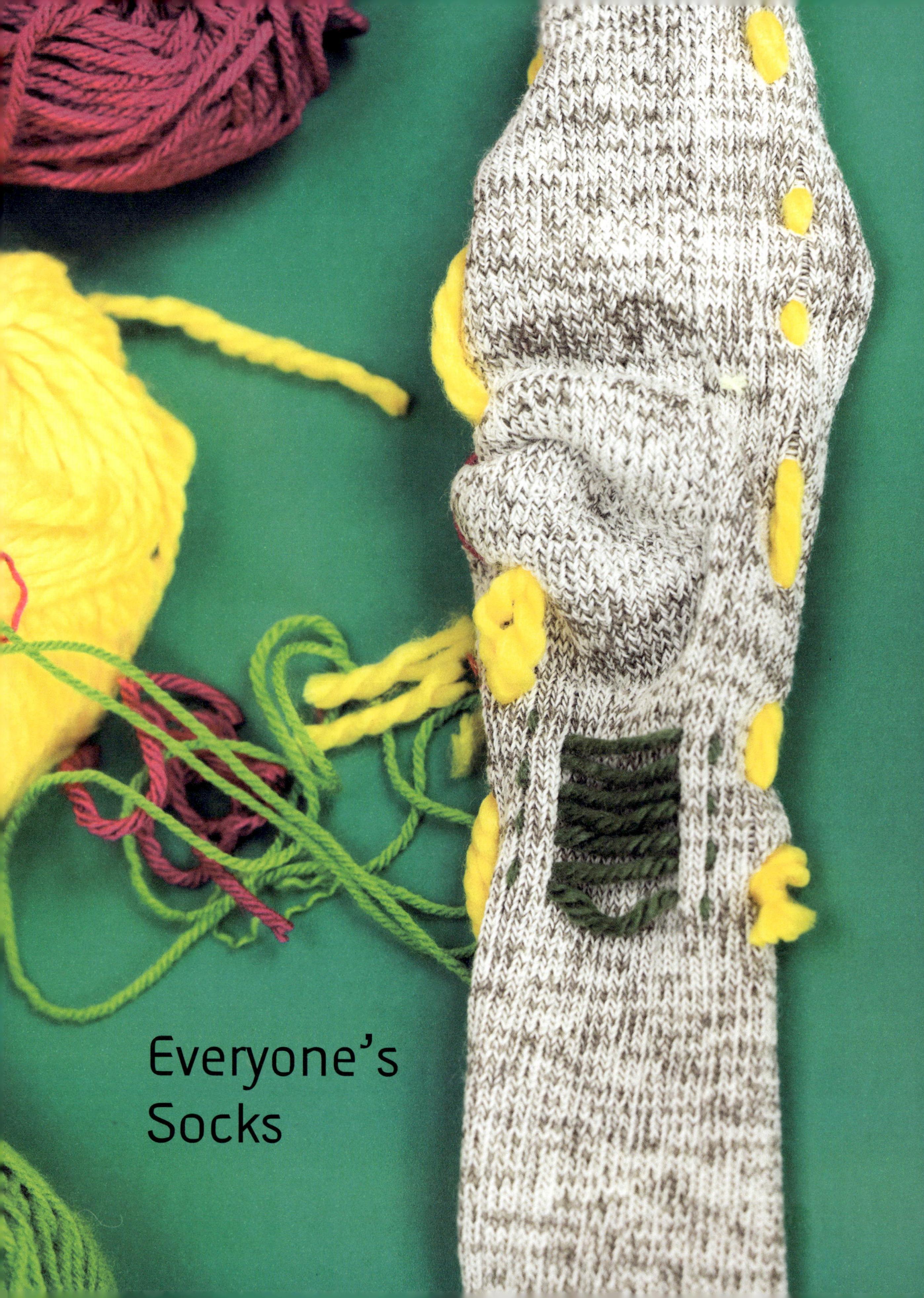

# Everyone's Socks

## Nursery, age 3–4

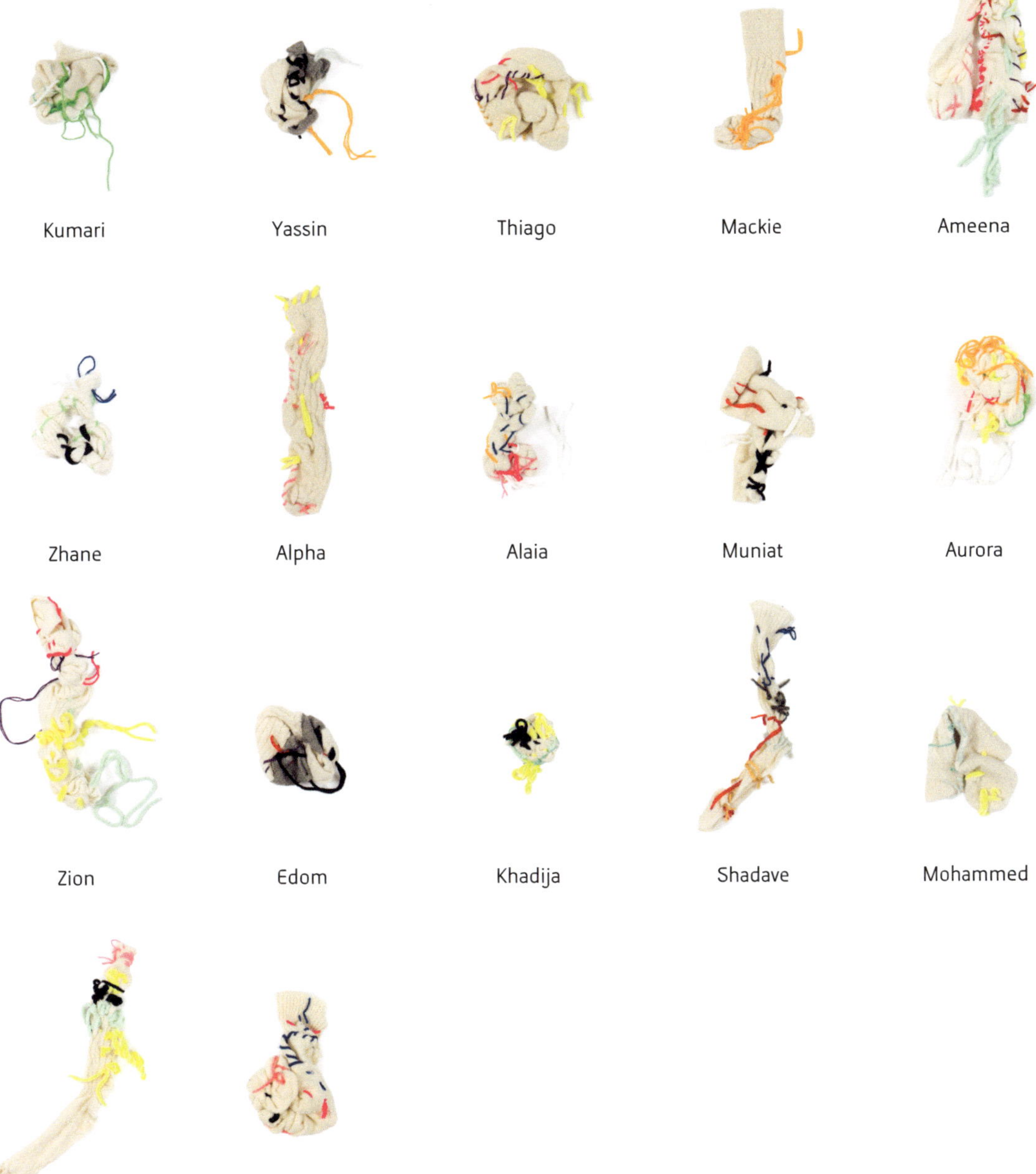
Kumari Yassin Thiago Mackie Ameena

Zhane Alpha Alaia Muniat Aurora

Zion Edom Khadija Shadave Mohammed

Indie Edom

Reception, age 4–5

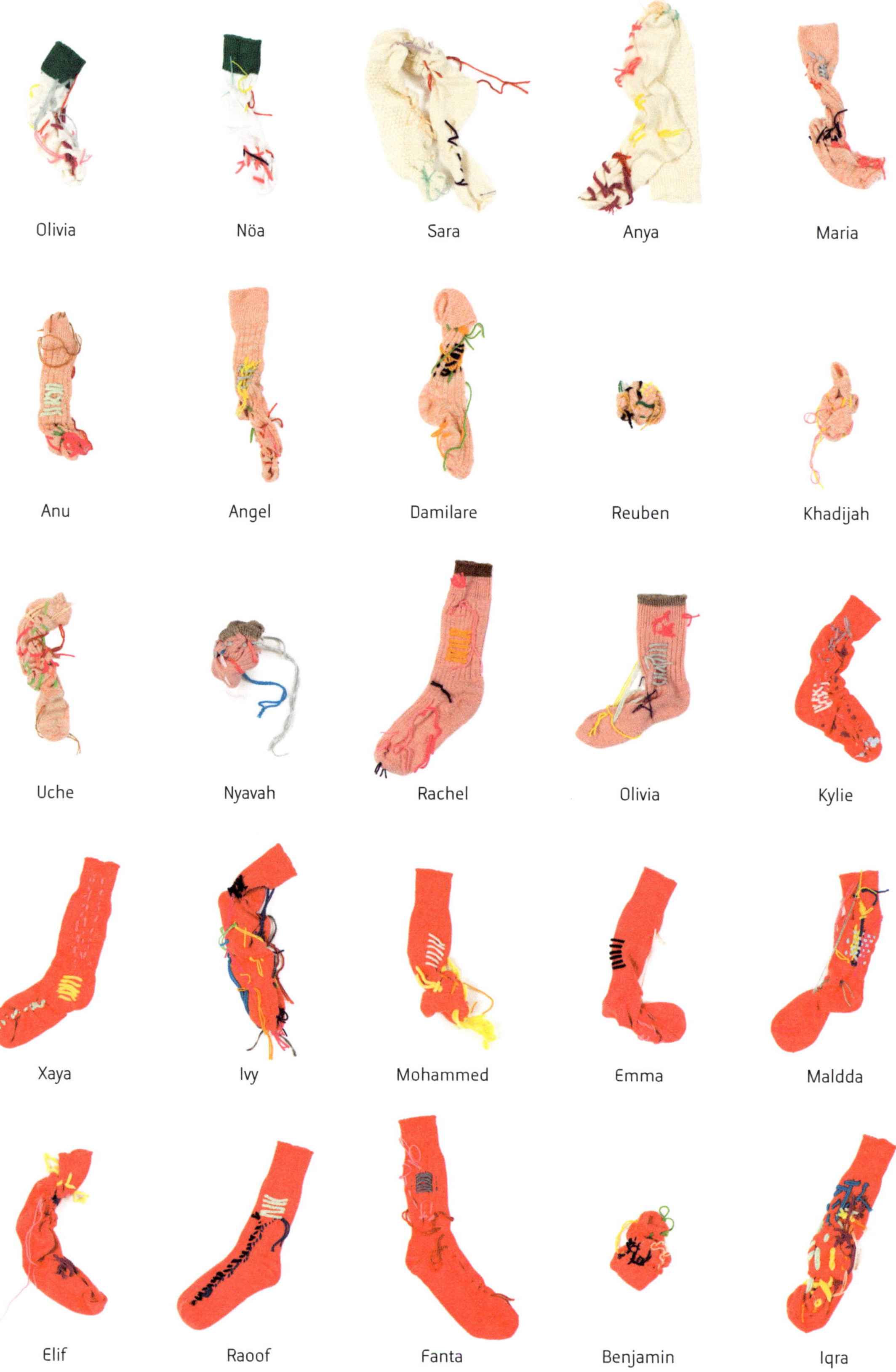

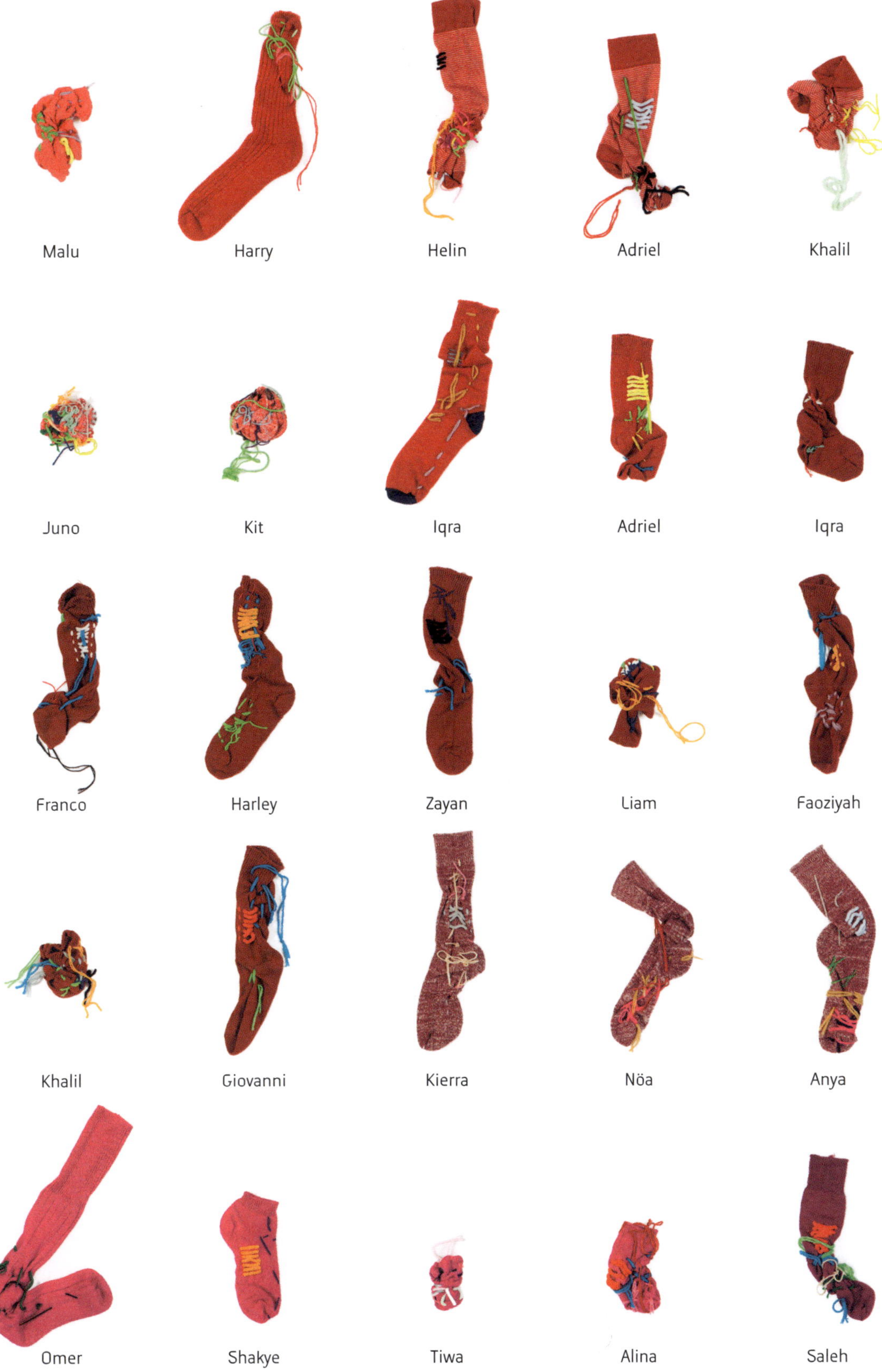
Malu
Harry
Helin
Adriel
Khalil
Juno
Kit
Iqra
Adriel
Iqra
Franco
Harley
Zayan
Liam
Faoziyah
Khalil
Giovanni
Kierra
Nöa
Anya
Omer
Shakye
Tiwa
Alina
Saleh

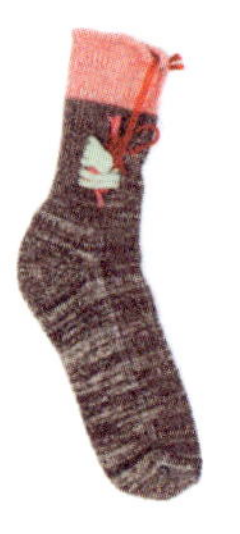
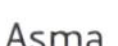

Asma

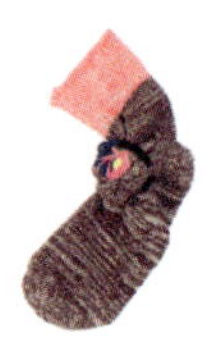

Thiago

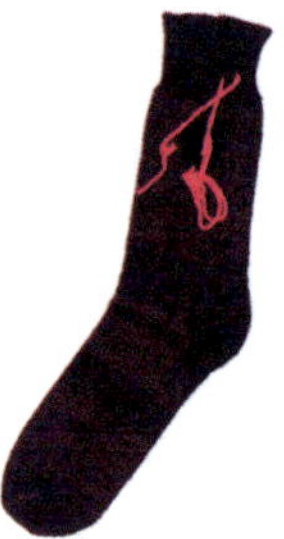

Sanaya

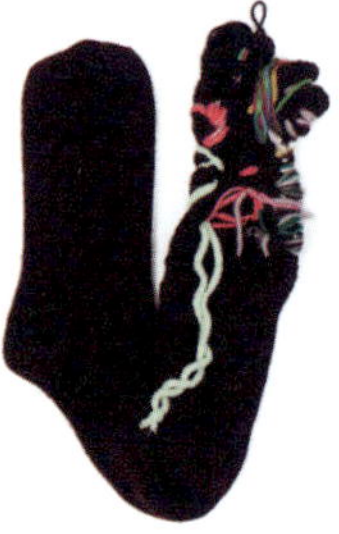

Sara

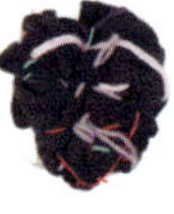

Maldda

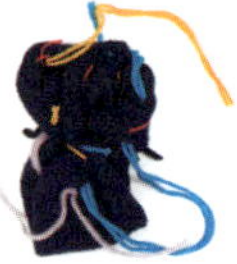

Rachel

## Year 1, age 5–6

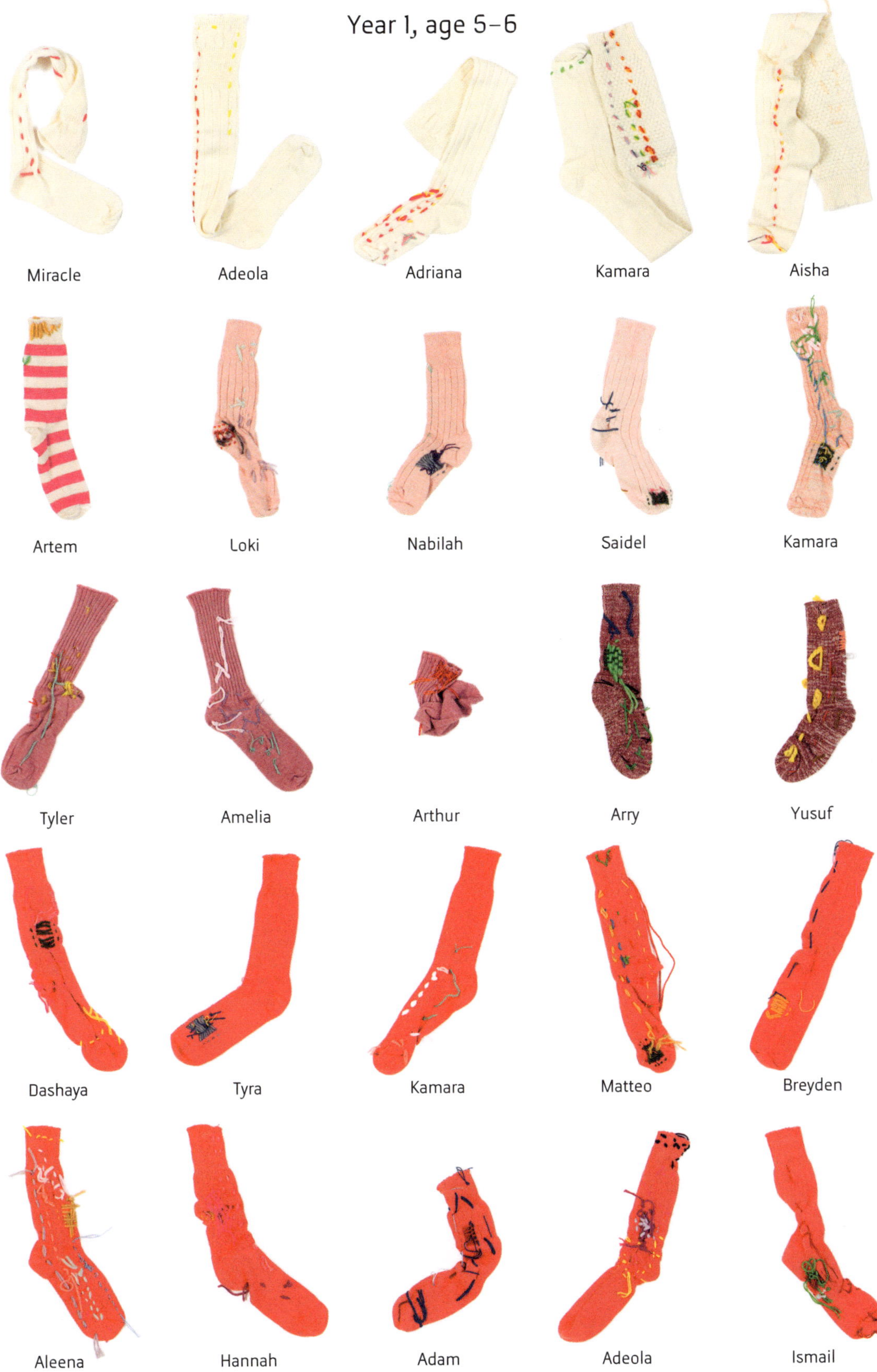

Miracle Adeola Adriana Kamara Aisha

Artem Loki Nabilah Saidel Kamara

Tyler Amelia Arthur Arry Yusuf

Dashaya Tyra Kamara Matteo Breyden

Aleena Hannah Adam Adeola Ismail

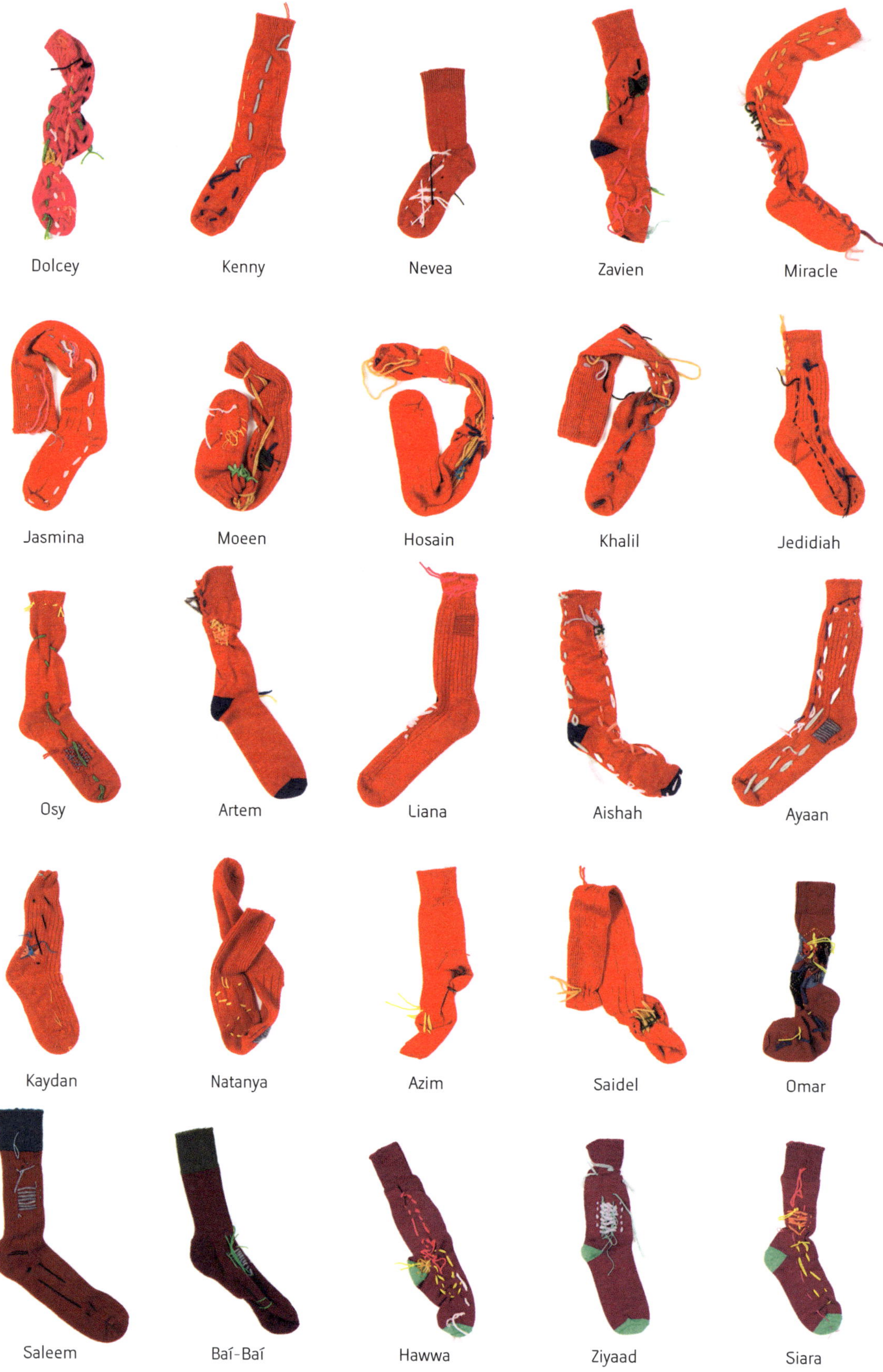
Dolcey
Kenny
Nevea
Zavien
Miracle
Jasmina
Moeen
Hosain
Khalil
Jedidiah
Osy
Artem
Liana
Aishah
Ayaan
Kaydan
Natanya
Azim
Saidel
Omar
Saleem
Baí-Baí
Hawwa
Ziyaad
Siara

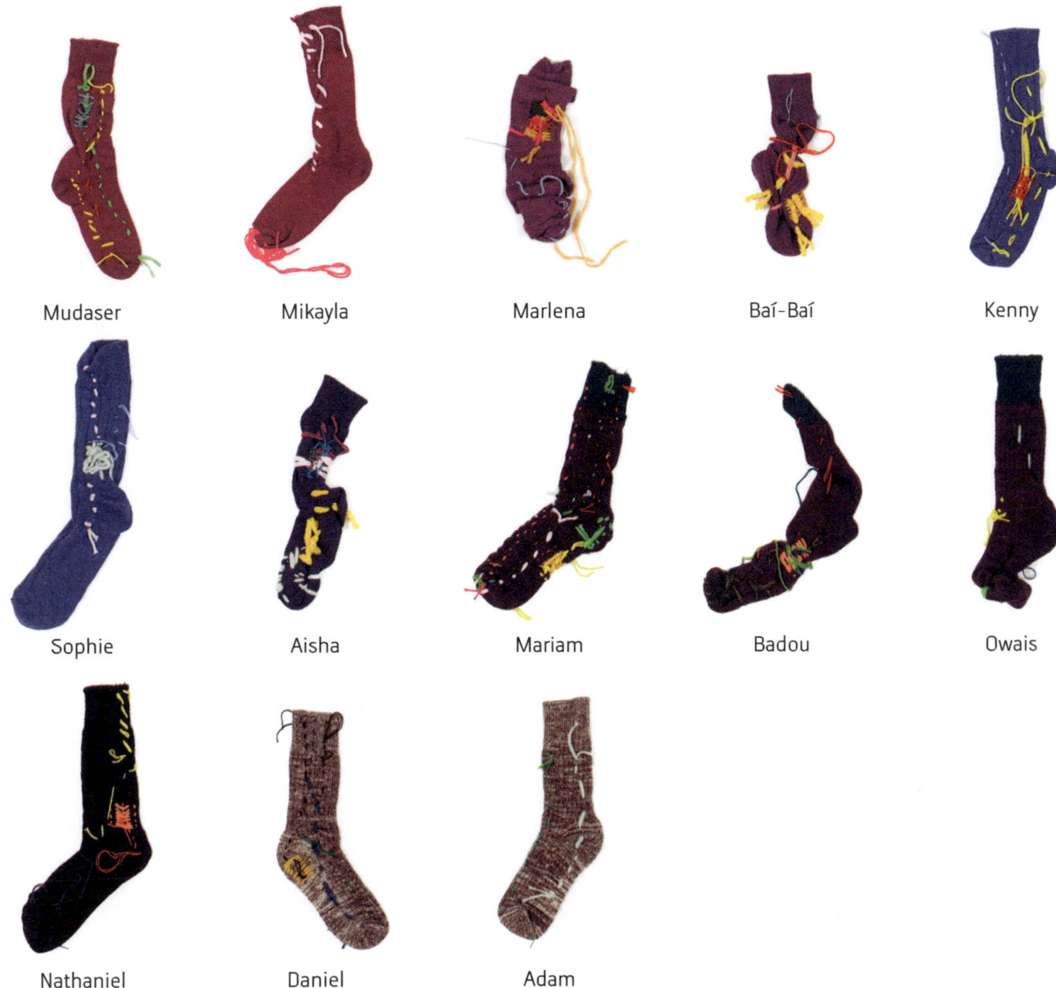
Mudaser
Mikayla
Marlena
Baï-Baï
Kenny
Sophie
Aisha
Mariam
Badou
Owais
Nathaniel
Daniel
Adam

## Year 2, age 6–7

Amirah
Lewis
Azari
Taemoya
Ibrahim
Delkiss
Emily
Kaleb
Anne
Casey
Yassir
Honey
Lamiah
Adriana
Haja
David
Laila
Amber
Scarlett
Clarisse
Makeda
Zamira
Soraya
Maciej
Lamiah

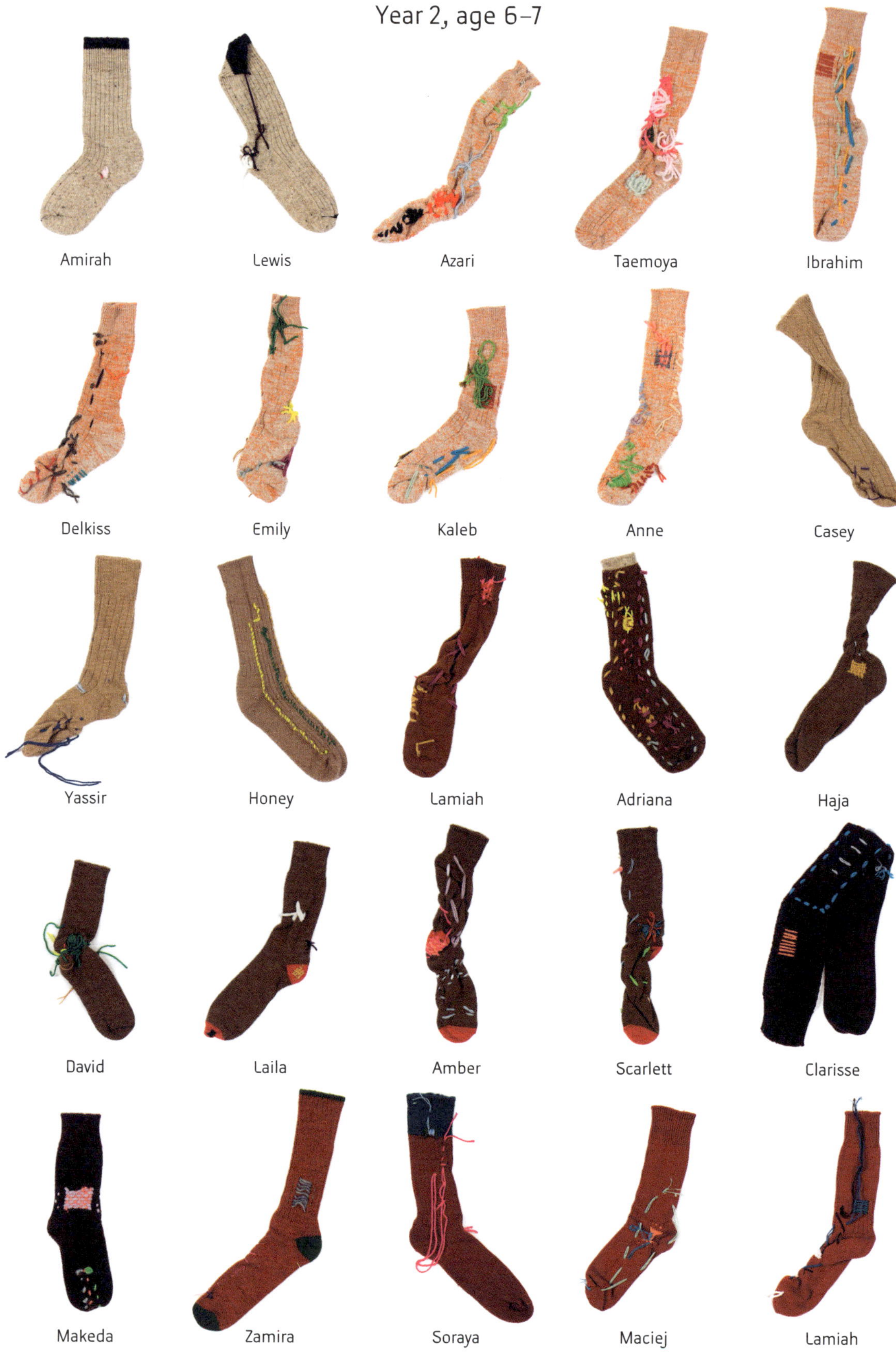

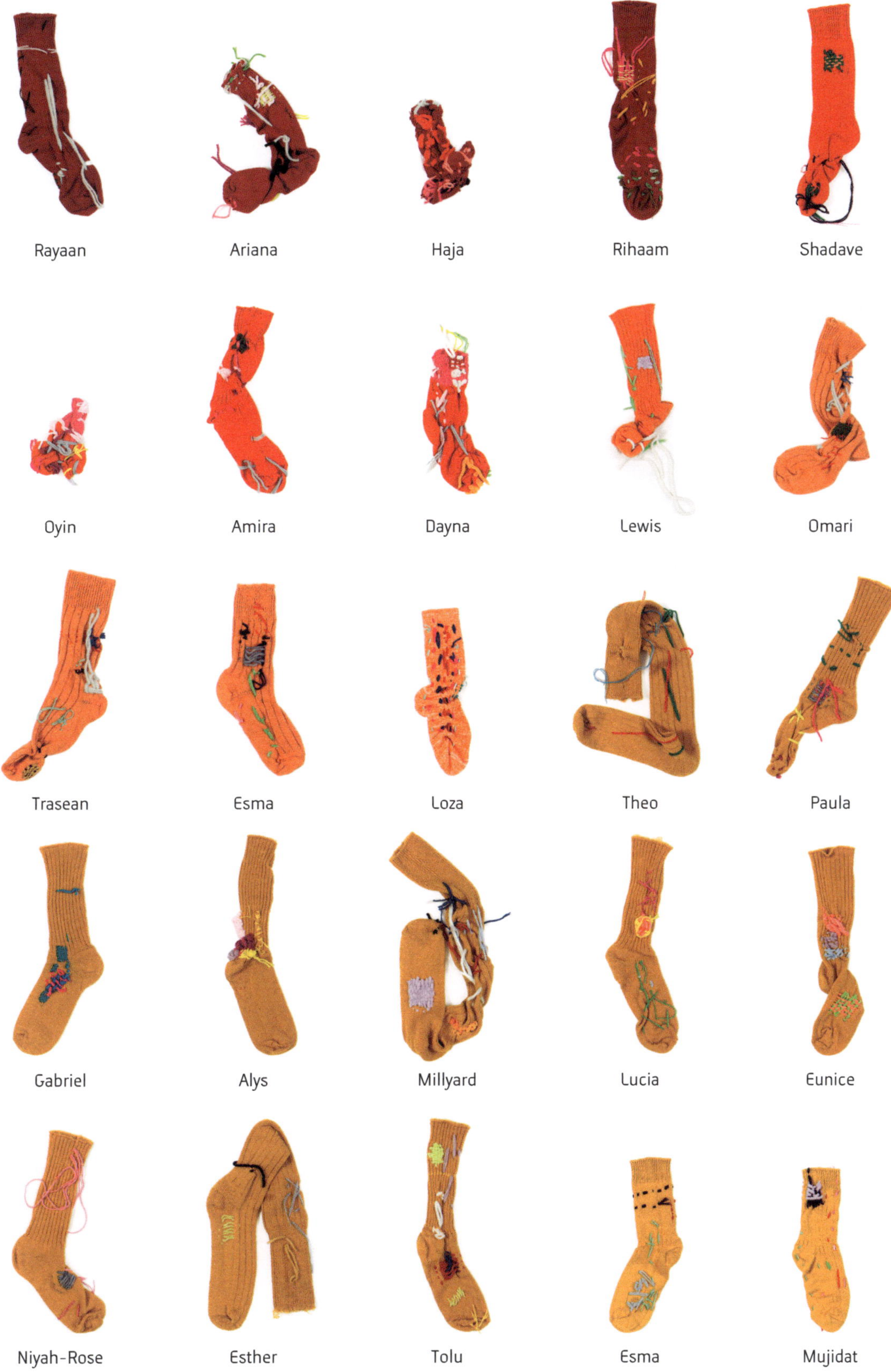
Rayaan
Ariana
Haja
Rihaam
Shadave
Oyin
Amira
Dayna
Lewis
Omari
Trasean
Esma
Loza
Theo
Paula
Gabriel
Alys
Millyard
Lucia
Eunice
Niyah-Rose
Esther
Tolu
Esma
Mujidat

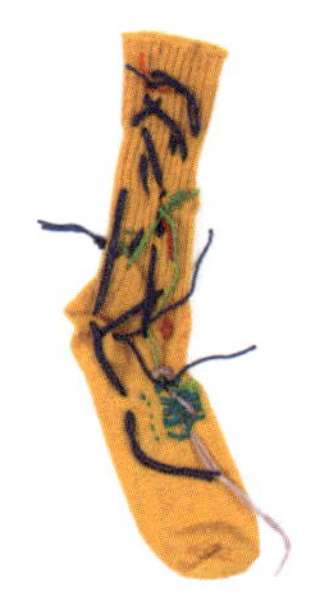

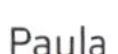

Paula

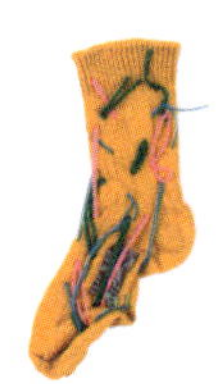

Nabila

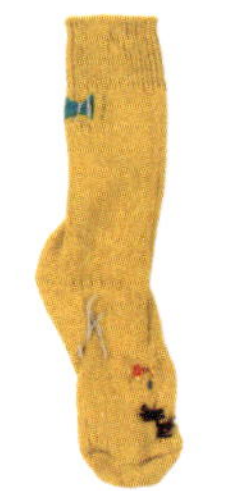

Abdurrahman

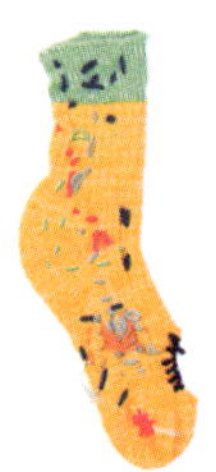

Maryam

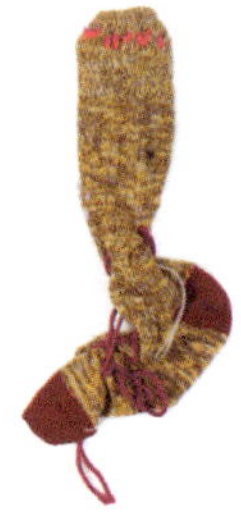

Bertolt

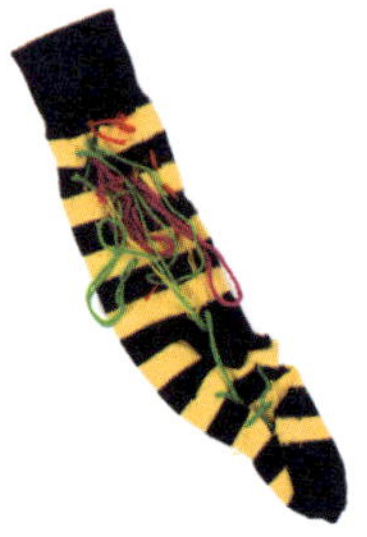

Paula

## Year 3, age 7–8

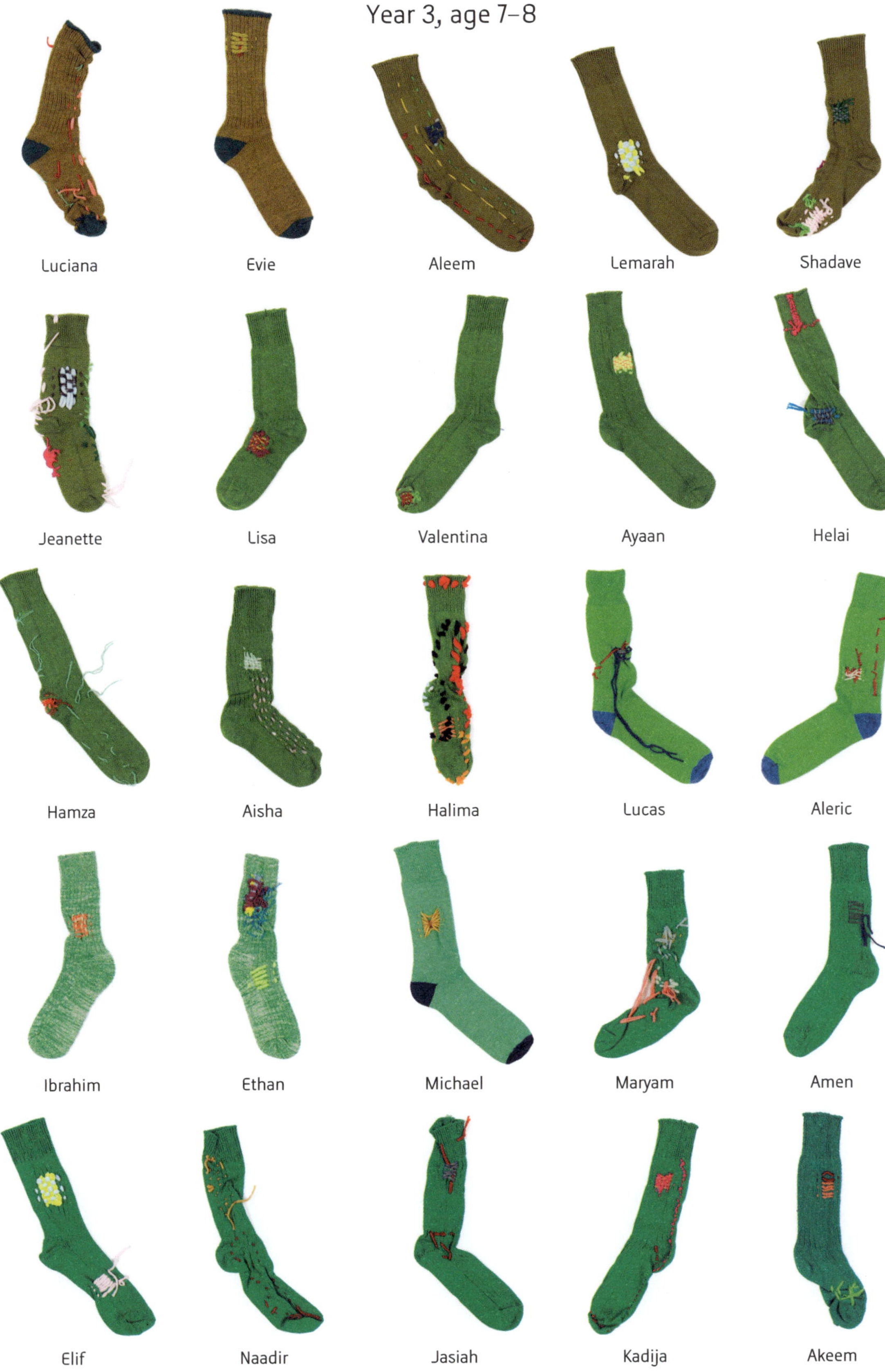

Luciana, Evie, Aleem, Lemarah, Shadave

Jeanette, Lisa, Valentina, Ayaan, Helai

Hamza, Aisha, Halima, Lucas, Aleric

Ibrahim, Ethan, Michael, Maryam, Amen

Elif, Naadir, Jasiah, Kadija, Akeem

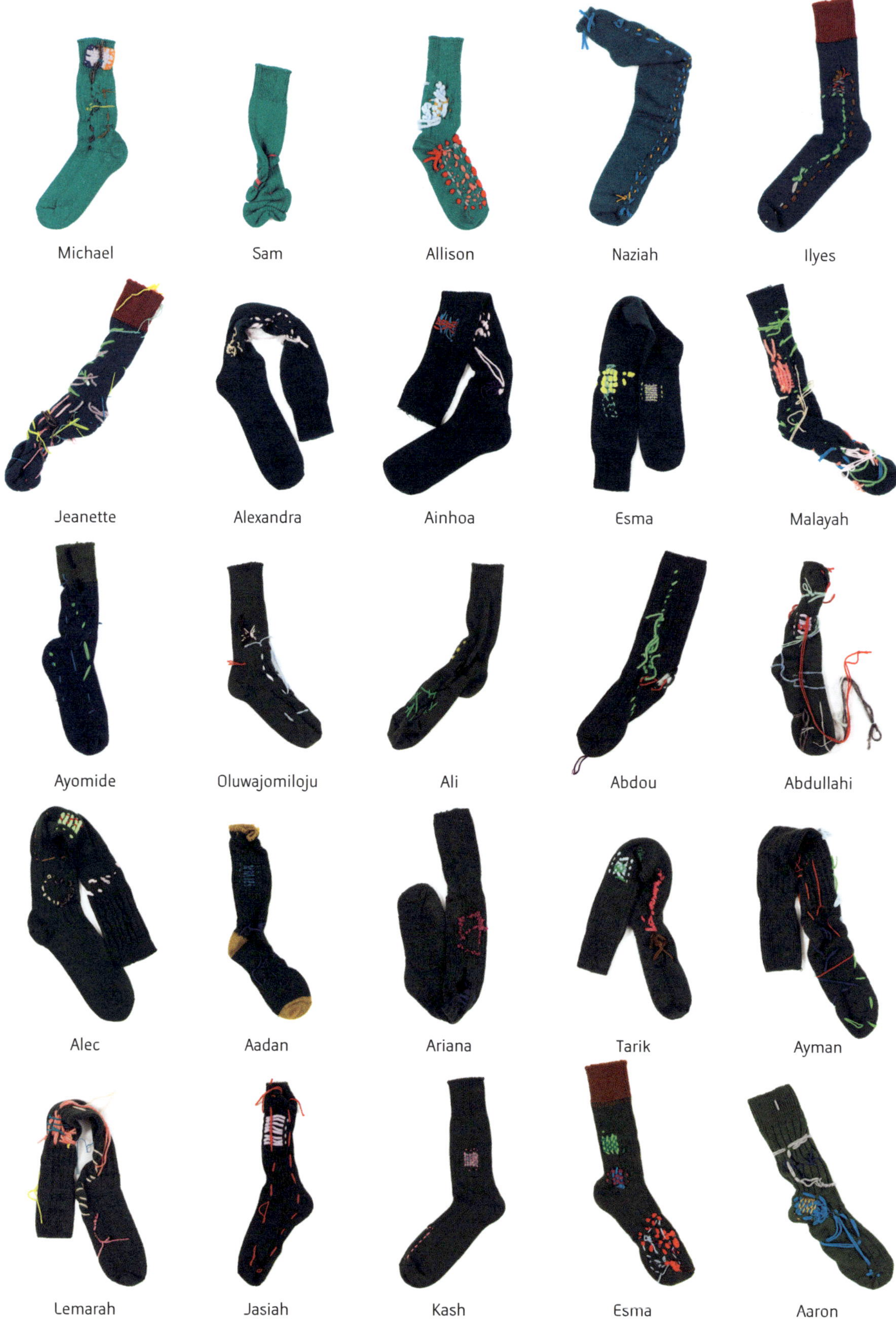
Michael
Sam
Allison
Naziah
Ilyes
Jeanette
Alexandra
Ainhoa
Esma
Malayah
Ayomide
Oluwajomiloju
Ali
Abdou
Abdullahi
Alec
Aadan
Ariana
Tarik
Ayman
Lemarah
Jasiah
Kash
Esma
Aaron

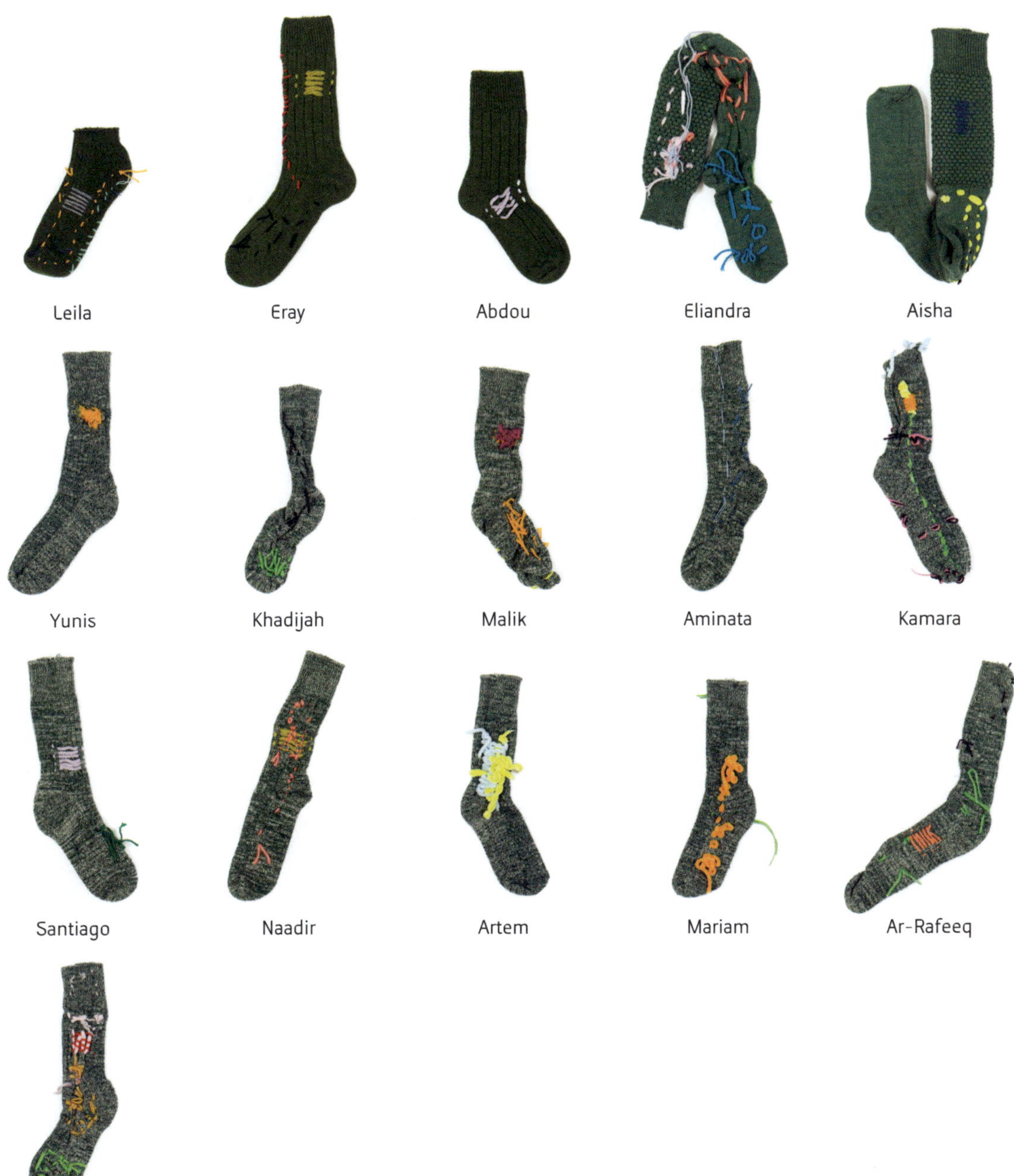

Leila Eray Abdou Eliandra Aisha

Yunis Khadijah Malik Aminata Kamara

Santiago Naadir Artem Mariam Ar-Rafeeq

Elif

## Year 4, age 8–9

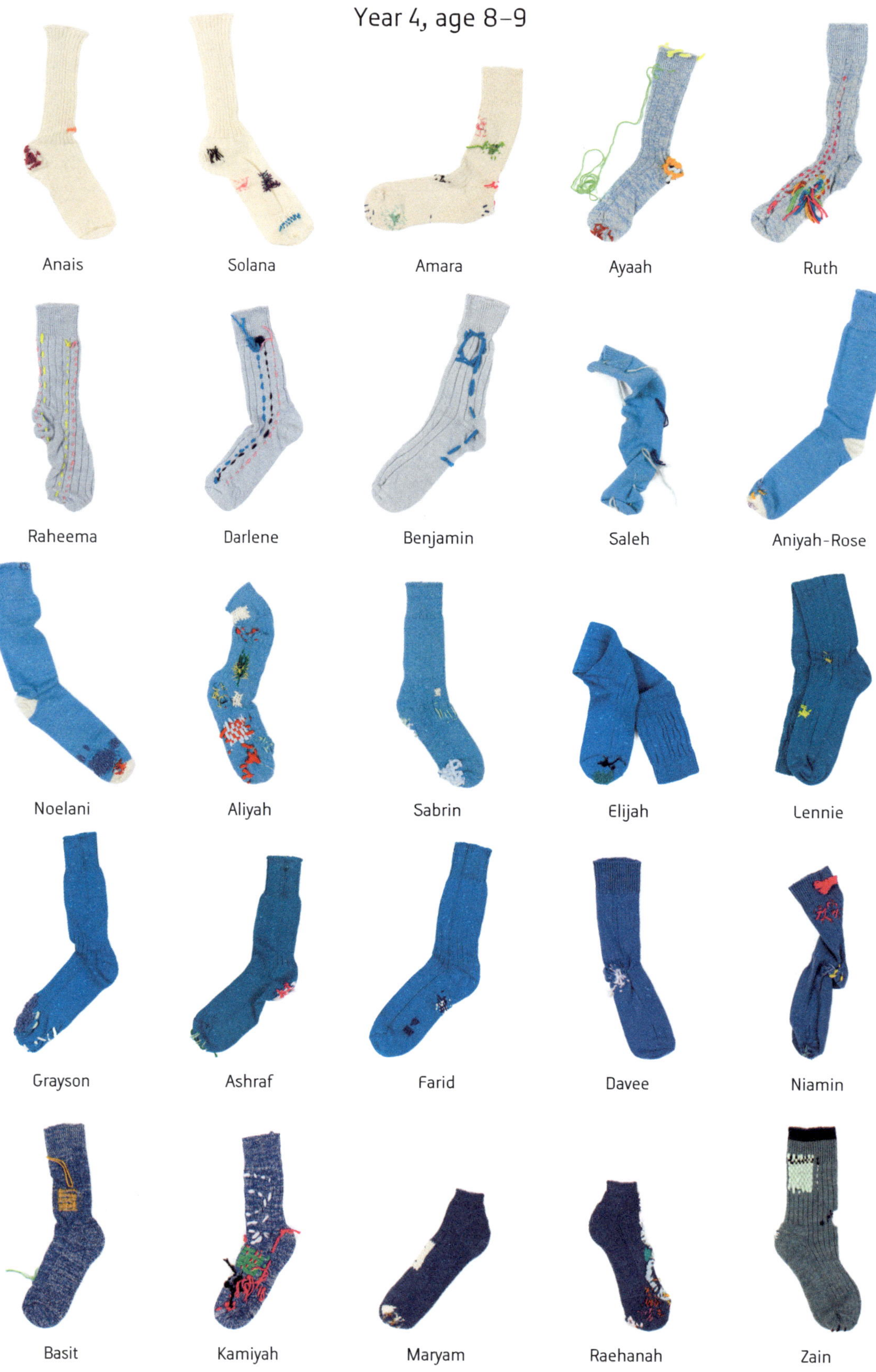

Anais Solana Amara Ayaah Ruth

Raheema Darlene Benjamin Saleh Aniyah-Rose

Noelani Aliyah Sabrin Elijah Lennie

Grayson Ashraf Farid Davee Niamin

Basit Kamiyah Maryam Raehanah Zain

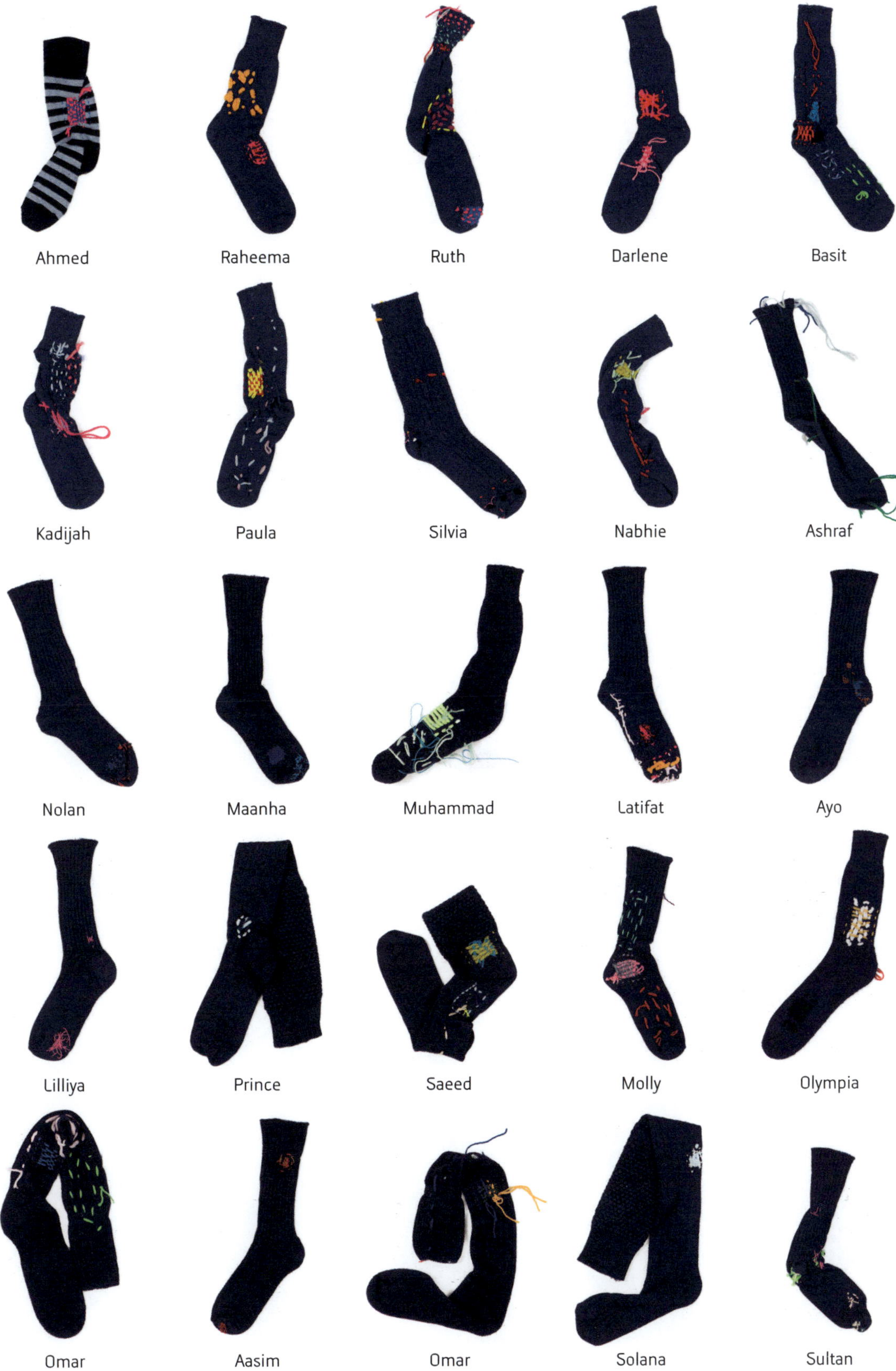

Ahmed Raheema Ruth Darlene Basit

Kadijah Paula Silvia Nabhie Ashraf

Nolan Maanha Muhammad Latifat Ayo

Lilliya Prince Saeed Molly Olympia

Omar Aasim Omar Solana Sultan

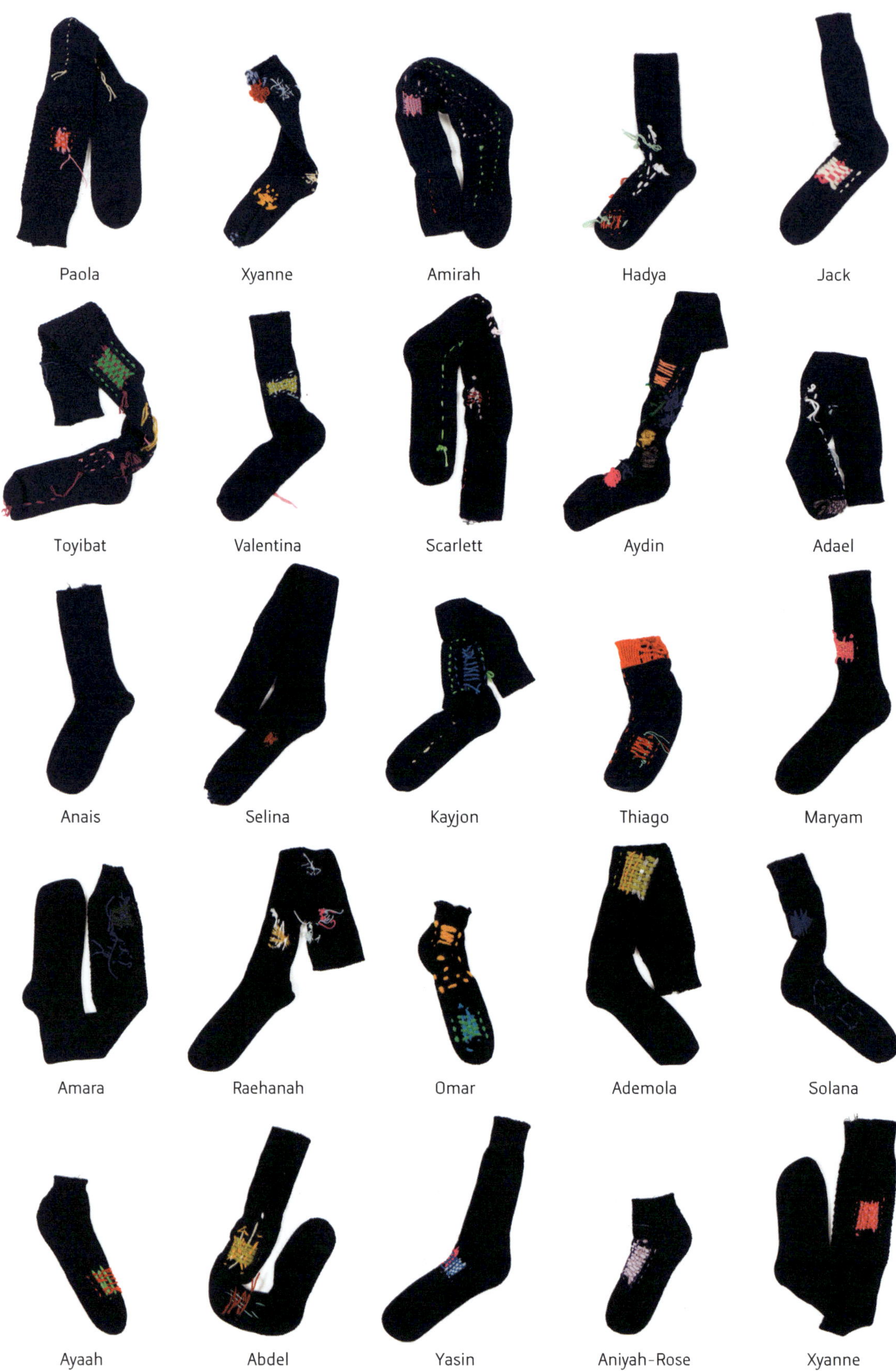

Paola Xyanne Amirah Hadya Jack

Toyibat Valentina Scarlett Aydin Adael

Anais Selina Kayjon Thiago Maryam

Amara Raehanah Omar Ademola Solana

Ayaah Abdel Yasin Aniyah-Rose Xyanne

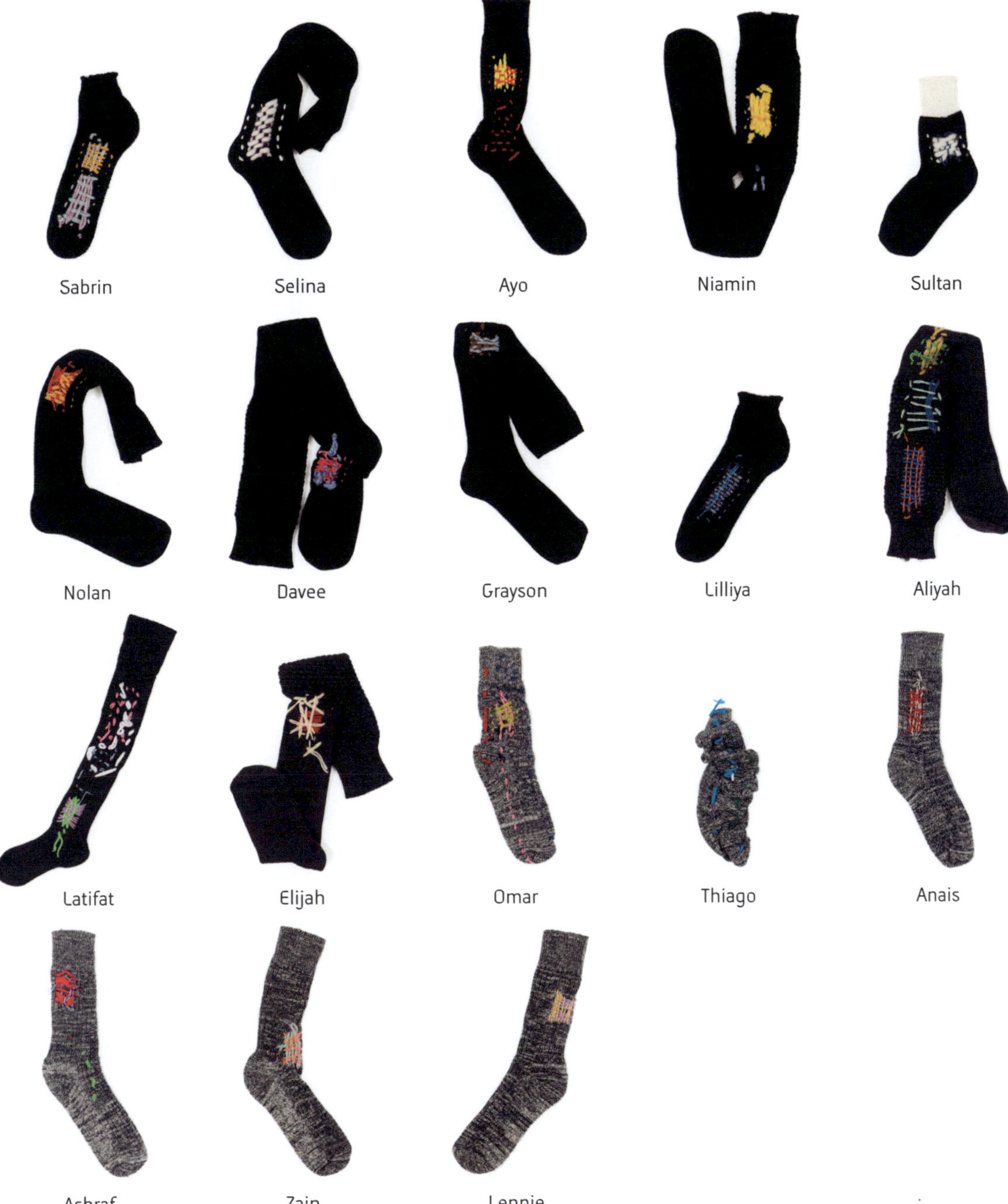
Sabrin
Selina
Ayo
Niamin
Sultan
Nolan
Davee
Grayson
Lilliya
Aliyah
Latifat
Elijah
Omar
Thiago
Anais
Ashraf
Zain
Lennie

## Year 5, age 9–10

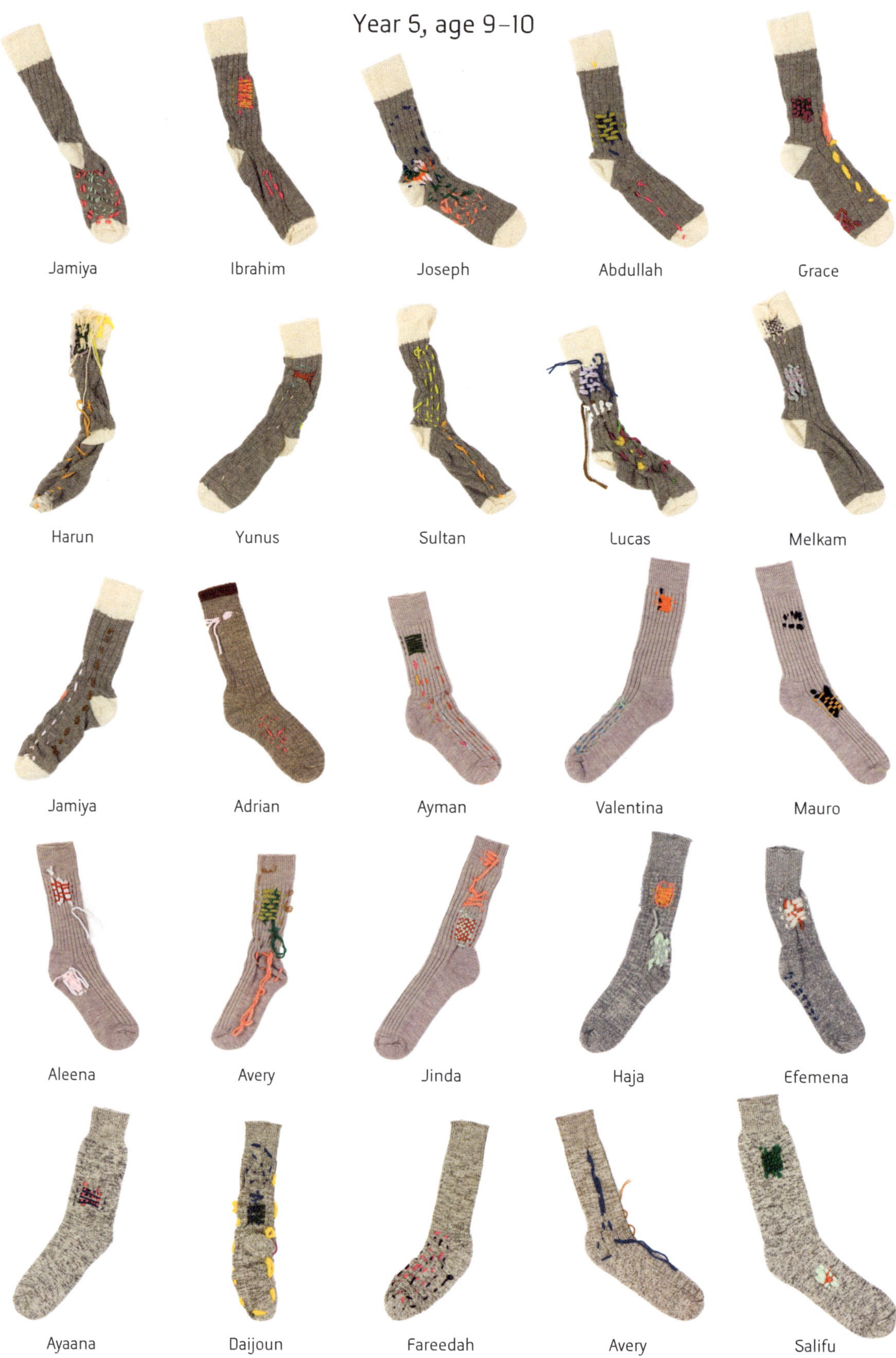

Jamiya  Ibrahim  Joseph  Abdullah  Grace

Harun  Yunus  Sultan  Lucas  Melkam

Jamiya  Adrian  Ayman  Valentina  Mauro

Aleena  Avery  Jinda  Haja  Efemena

Ayaana  Daijoun  Fareedah  Avery  Salifu

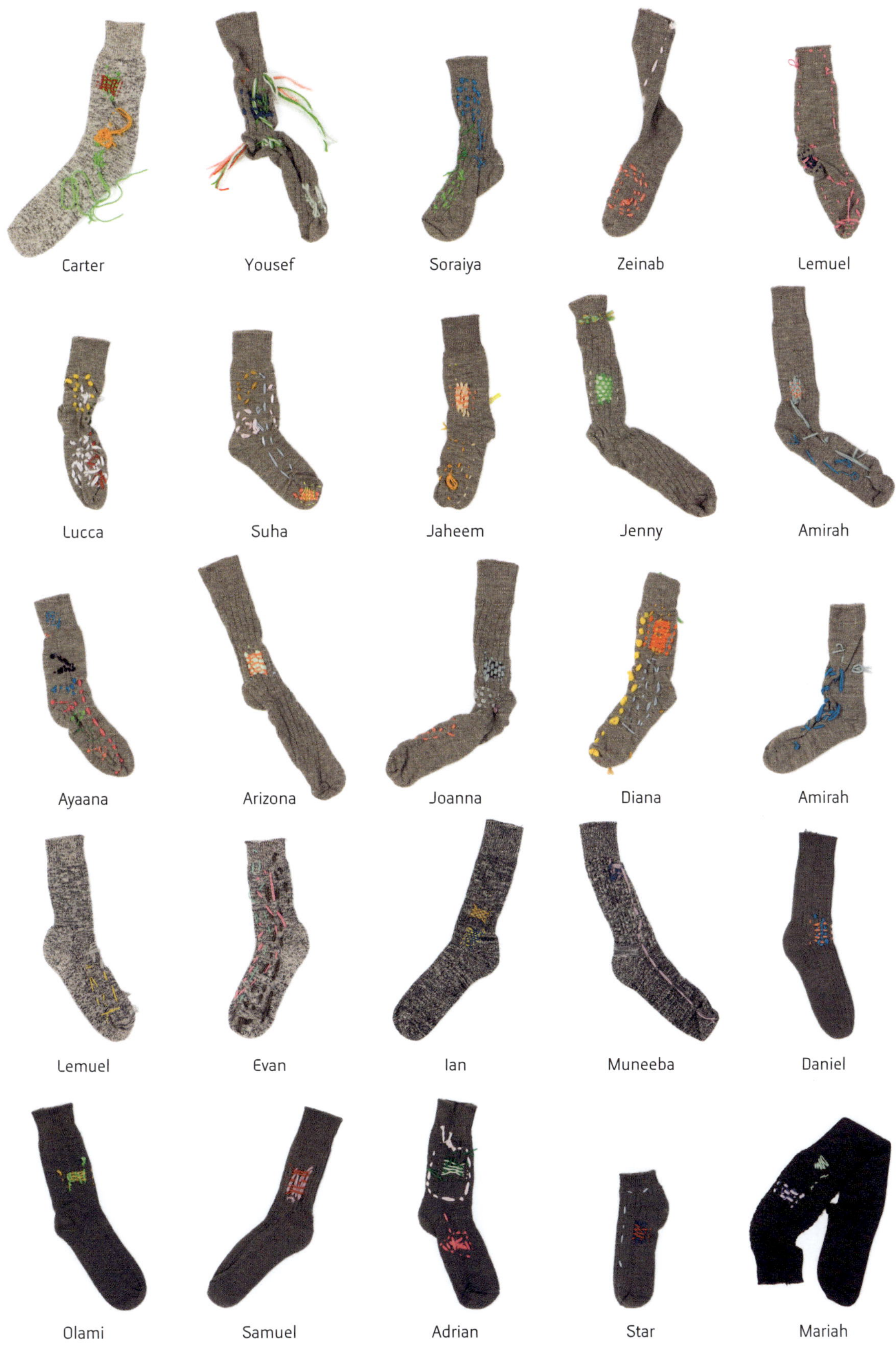

Carter Yousef Soraiya Zeinab Lemuel

Lucca Suha Jaheem Jenny Amirah

Ayaana Arizona Joanna Diana Amirah

Lemuel Evan Ian Muneeba Daniel

Olami Samuel Adrian Star Mariah

## Year 6, age 10–11

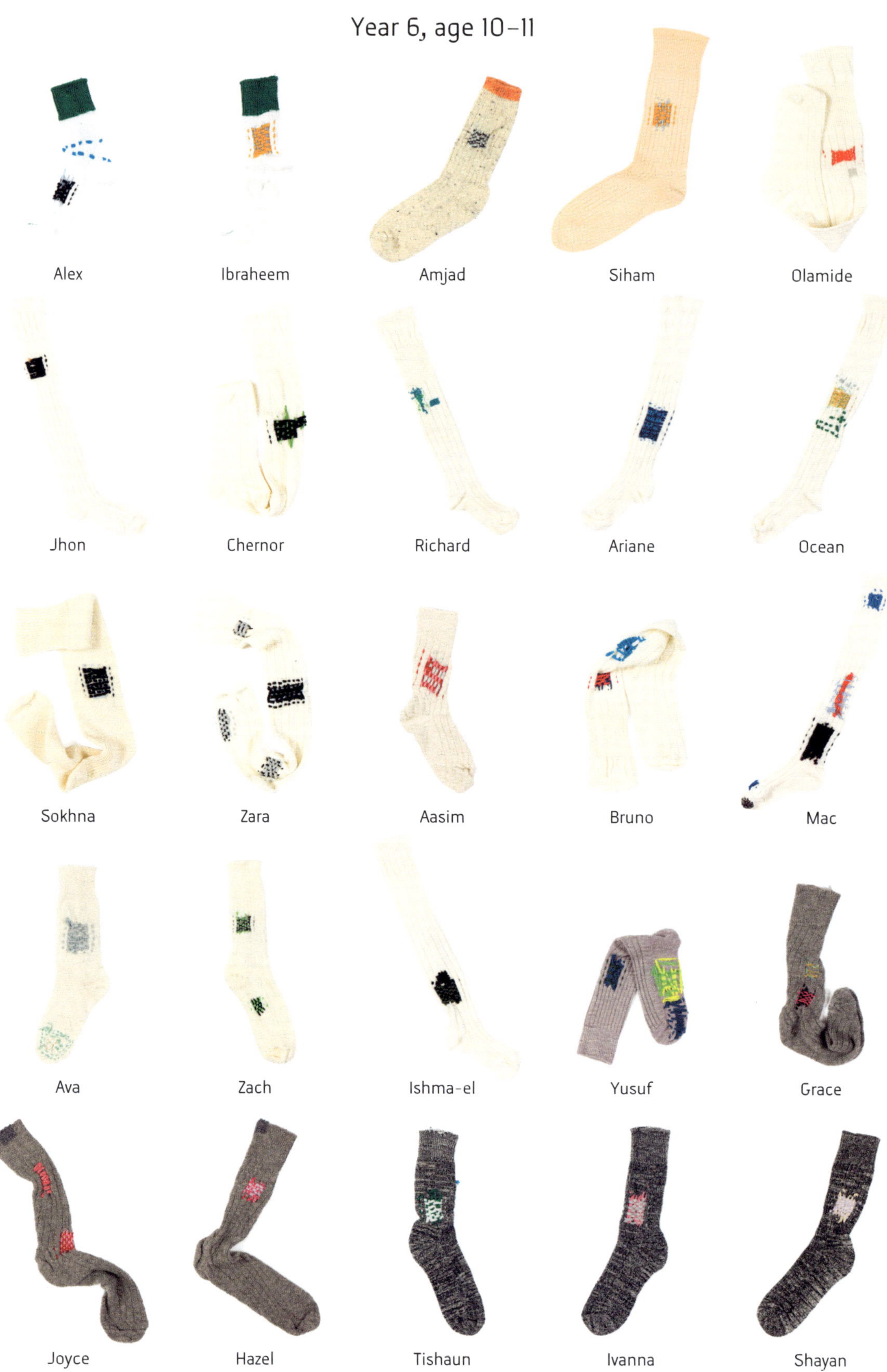

Alex Ibraheem Amjad Siham Olamide

Jhon Chernor Richard Ariane Ocean

Sokhna Zara Aasim Bruno Mac

Ava Zach Ishma-el Yusuf Grace

Joyce Hazel Tishaun Ivanna Shayan

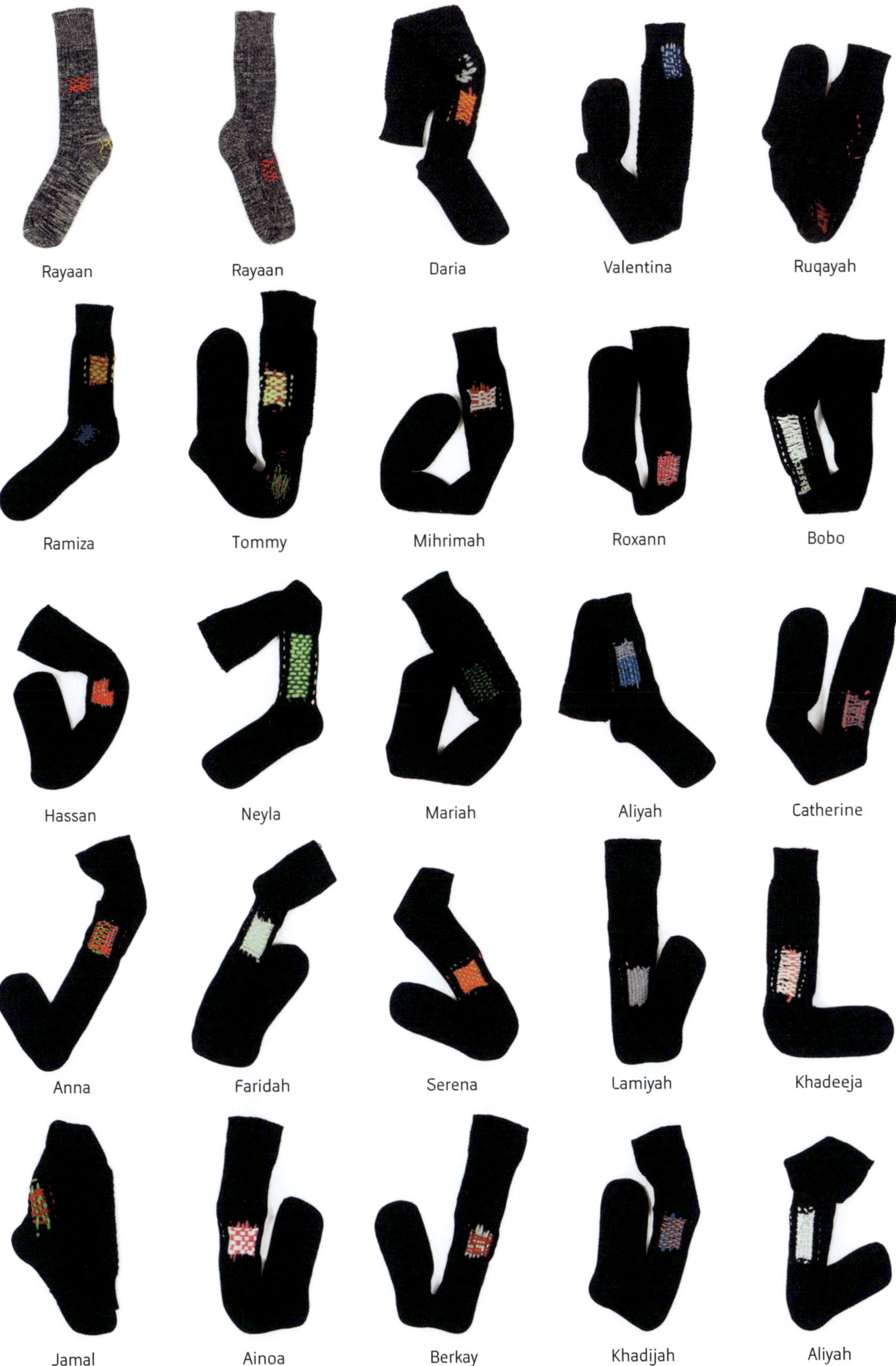
Rayaan
Rayaan
Daria
Valentina
Ruqayah
Ramiza
Tommy
Mihrimah
Roxann
Bobo
Hassan
Neyla
Mariah
Aliyah
Catherine
Anna
Faridah
Serena
Lamiyah
Khadeeja
Jamal
Ainoa
Berkay
Khadijah
Aliyah

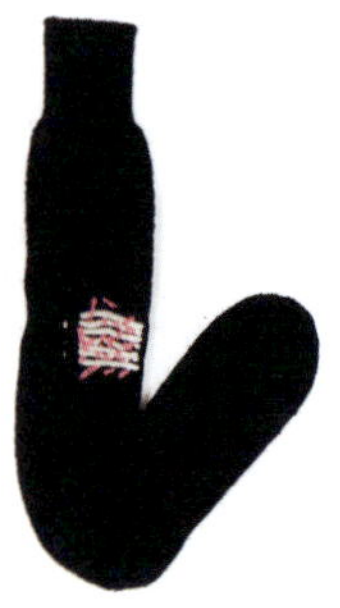

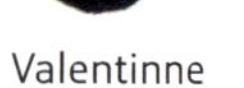

Valentinne

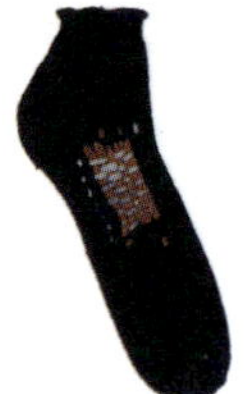

Farid

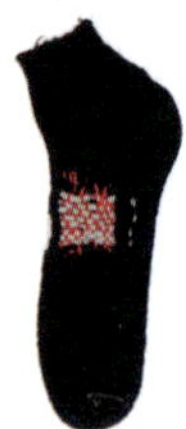

Winston

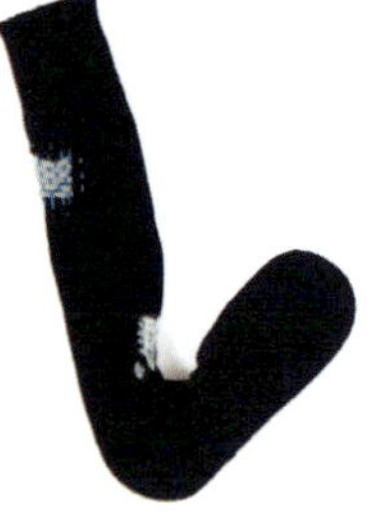

Anne

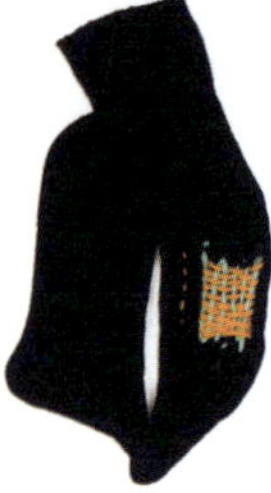

Yamina

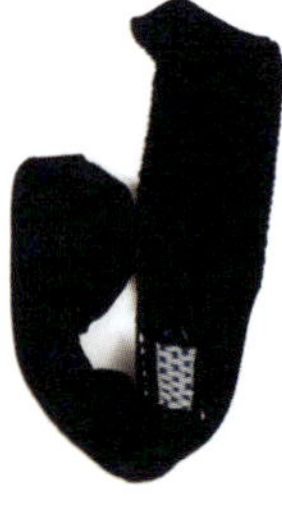

Leyla

## Teachers & Family

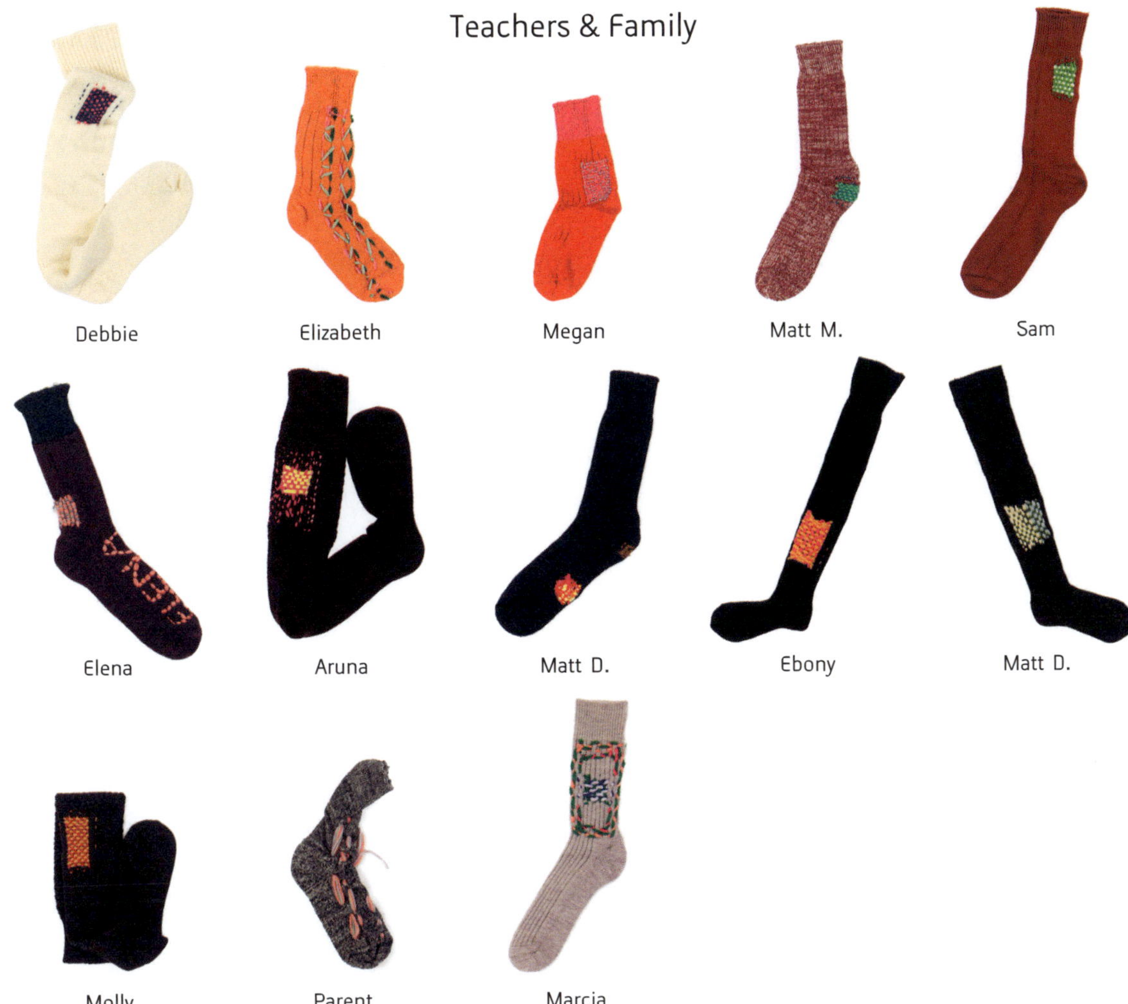

Debbie · Elizabeth · Megan · Matt M. · Sam

Elena · Aruna · Matt D. · Ebony · Matt D.

Molly · Parent · Marcia

## Biography

Celia Pym mends clothes. She remade a threadbare Norwegian sweater which can be seen in the National Museum in Oslo. She saved a gold theatre cape from Monaco and took it on tour in France, Iceland and England. She has repaired the battered rucksacks of London medical students and twice fixed the many moth-holes in her Dad's favourite sweater. Her most recent major project, recorded in this book, was to supervise with Hannah Coulson the darning of more than 500 socks in a London primary school.

Her mending philosophy? To explore the varied evidence of damage and how repair can draw attention to the places where garments and cloth wear down and grow thin. 'Darning consists of small acts of care,' she says, 'and paying close attention.'

Celia Pym has exhibited most recently at the Penland Gallery, North Carolina; the Frauenmuseum, Hittisau, and MAK, Vienna; and at the Cheongju Craft Biennale in South Korea. She is an Associate Lecturer in Textiles at the Royal College of Art, London, and this is her second book.


## Acknowledgments

Celia Pym would like to thank the following individuals for their help and support in the development of this book: Matt Dean, Matt Morden, and the students, staff and families at Surrey Square Primary School; Jasmine Arthur, Jemima Burrill, Kaia Charles, Hannah Coulson, Emma Mathews, John Pym, India Stanbra, Manon Veyssière, Evelien Verkerk; and Neil Swift at J. Alex Swift Ltd.


## Photo Credits

I am grateful to Michele Panzeri who has been photographing my work since 2010, with enthusiasm and sensitivity. All the photographs in this book are Michele's unless otherwise specified:
Celia Pym, 10
Marc Sethi, 11
Charles Emerson, 18–19, 22–23

Mending Diagrams by Ashwin Patel

Published by Quickthorn
Lower Street Atelier, 19a Lower Street
Stroud, Gloucestershire GL5 2HT, UK
info@quickthornbooks.com
www.quickthornbooks.com



Publisher: Katy Bevan
Designer: Fraser Muggeridge studio
Printed by Short Run Press, Exeter

British Library Cataloguing in Publication Data applied for
ISBN 978-1-068321-53-5

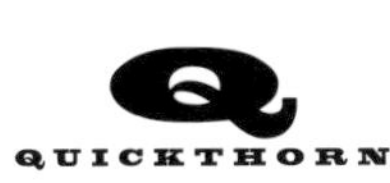


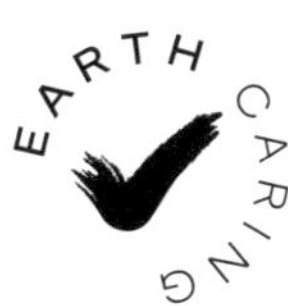


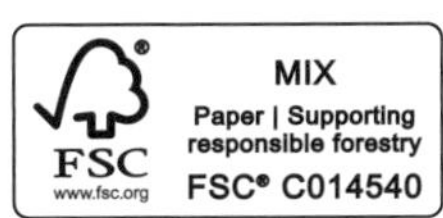

# Start Mending!

A plain, woven darn is ideal for almost every hole. The darn weaves a small new patch that covers and reinforces the hole. Your darn can be made with different colours or weights of yarn. Stitches can be large or small. You can cover your sock with stitches or simply focus on the hole itself. In short, create your own style!

Here are the three steps to a woven darn.

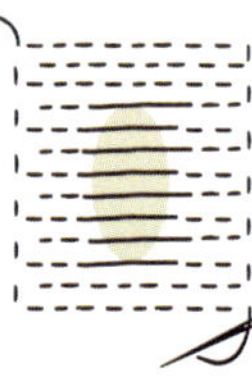

## 1. Setting a warp

Warp threads are those that stretch over the hole and form the structure of the darn. I recommend starting your warp threads a little way from the edge of the hole anchoring them in the strong healthy part of the cloth. You could do a running stitch up to the hole to begin your warp thread or make one stitch to hold the thread in place. You can make a knot at the end of your thread to secure the warp threads, but you can also just leave a tail end of the thread hanging from the back. I prefer leaving the tail, especially if I'm working on clothes, so I can't feel the knot against my skin. But you choose – if you'd like to make a knot – make a knot! The aim of the warp is to give all the warp threads the same tension. They should feel as if they're stretched to the same tightness. Not too tight, not too loose! Sustaining an even tension is the hardest part of darning.

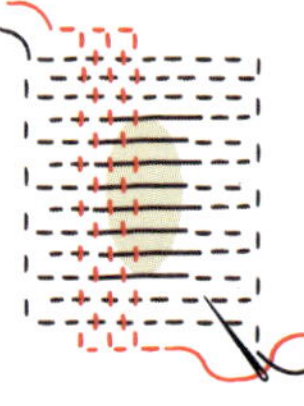

## 2. Weaving the weft

Weft threads are those that weave over and under the warp threads. You can do these in a second colour. Or in any number of colours. It's easier to see what you're doing if you weave the weft in a different colour from the warp. As with the warp, you stitch into the cloth first and then go over and under your warp threads in one direction – and then do the opposite, over and under, when returning in the other direction. For a plain weave you go over one thread and under one thread. With practice, you can make your weaves more complicated – for example, over two then under two.

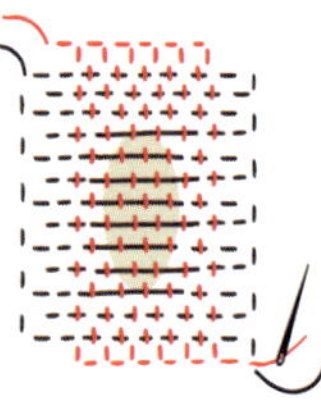

## 3. Sewing in your ends

If you've left an end of thread hanging from the back of your cloth, re-thread the end on the needle and weave it (or tuck it) under the stitches you've made. You can go back and forth or simply in one direction. Pull the needle through and off the thread and it'll be secured neatly underneath your stitches. The stitches will lie smooth against your skin.

The best advice I have for darning and all thread-based craft: keep your fingers loose! As soon as your fingers tighten or you feel them gripping – shake out your hands, take a breath. Then pick up the needle with nimble fingers. There's strength in these gentle fingers and, if you have them, your needle and thread will flow more smoothly.